ENGLISH 900

BOOK FIVE

鄭 憲 鎭
李 東 浩 共譯

prepared by

ENGLISH LANGUAGE SERVICES, INC.

ENGLISH 900 의 三位一体

완전합본

ENGLISH 900 원문

주 해 서

연습, 자습용 WORKBOOK

桂 苑 出 版 社

ENGLISH 900의 三位一体

900원문 + 주해서 + Workbook

ENGLISH 900을 배우고저하는 사람을 위하여 파격적인 제작원가로 봉사하며 이 한권의 책으로 완전히 마스터 할 수 있도록 합본하였다.

완전합본

ENGLISH 900 (영어회화교본)

미국무성 산하 English Language Series 엮음
The Macmillan Co, 발행

全六巻
- English 900 Book 1 + 주해서 + Workbook
- English 900 Book 2 + 주해서 + Workbook
- English 900 Book 3 + 주해서 + Workbook
- English 900 Book 4 + 주해서 + Workbook
- English 900 Book 5 + 주해서 + Workbook
- English 900 Book 6 + 주해서 + Workbook

ENGLISH 900 주해서 (영어회화교본)

1. English 900 원문을 완역.
2. 충실하고 정확한 번역.
3. 문법책을 겸한 충분하고 자세한 문법설명.
4. 간단 명확하고 친절한 diagram식 설명.
5. 새로 나온 낱말과 숙어 풀이.

ENGLISH 900의 Workbook 연습용·자습용·복습용

ENGLISH 900의 원문에서 읽힌 회화를 좀더 습관화 하고 생활화 할 수 있도록 조직적이고 과학적으로 문제를 다루워 놓았으므로 이를 풀이해 본다면 회화에 좋은 반려자가 되리라 믿어 의심치 않는다.

이는 한국 초유의 문제 배열로 ENGLISH 900 1권부터 6권 까지 전 권에 함께 엮어 누구나 쉽게 연습, 자습, 복습 할 수 있도록 하였다.

머 리 말

English 900는 영어를 세계적으로 보급하기 위해서 미국 정부의 위촉을 받아 English Language Services Inc. 가 교재의 연구개발을 담당하고, The McMillan Co. 가 발행을, 그리고 Collier-McMillan이 보급을 맡은 영어회화 교재입니다.

English 900는 영어를 외국어로 하는 사람들이 기초부터 중급에 이르기까지 공부할 수 있도록 엮은 교재로서 전부 6권으로 되어 있읍니다. English 900란 제목은 총 6권의 text에 나오는 기본문형의 수가 900개란 데서 연유한 것으로서 900개의 기본문형에는 영어의 기본적인 문장구조와 어휘가 모두 들어 있읍니다. 900개의 기본문형은 각 과의 첫머리에 15개씩 수록되어 있고, 또한 한개의 기본문형마다 대개 4개의 변형문이 수록되어 있으므로 문장의 개수는 전부 3, 600개라 할수 있을 것입니다.

매과의 구성요소를 살펴 보면, 15개의 기본문형이 나오고, 뒷페이지에 Intonation 연습, 이어 기본문형으로 연습해보게 되어 있는 Questions and Answers 나 Verb Study, 그 다음에는 활용연습을 위한 Substitution Drills, 그 다음에는 독해력 향상을 위한 Reading, 마지막으로 앞에서 익힌 대화를 실제로 응용해 볼 수 있는 Conversation으로 되어 있읍니다. 특히 매 과에 Exercise 가 붙어 있어서, 그것 마저 스스로 해 보면 영어적 습관이 입술에 붙게되지 않을까 생각됩니다.

원래는 각과와 병용할 수 있는 Workbook도 각각 마련되어 있으나 우리나라에서는 Workbook이 있다는 사실조차 모를 뿐 아니라 Workbook의 구입도 쉽지 않으므로 본 해설서에는 독자를 위해서 매권 권말에 Workbook을 특히 같이 달아 놓았읍니다. English 900의 Workbook은 교실에서의 학습내용을 기초로 하여 학생들의 실력을 테스트하는 한편, 미처 익히지 못한 중요사항을 복습하기 위한 것입니다.

English 900는 예문 하나 하나가 모두 일상 회화체의 문장으로서 영어가 모국어가 아닌 외국인을 상대로 한 책이기 때문에 내용이 비교적 쉽고 노력만 하면 누구나 영어 회화를 할 수 있겠금 펴낸 책입니다. 게다가 이 주해서만 가지면 문법 책을 따로 볼 필요 없이 정확한 회화를 배울 수 있으리라 확신합니다.

English 900는 Edwin T. Cornelius, Jr. 와 Joyce R. Manes의 지도로 제작된 것임을 밝혀 둡니다.

Intonation (抑揚)에 관하여

다른 사람에게 다음 두 문장을 읽게 하고 두 문장이 어떻게 다른가를 비교하여 보면

그 분이 오셨어요. (서술문)

그 분이 오셨어요? (의문문)

모음이나 자음에는 아무 차이도 없으나 음성의 고저에는 차이가 있다는 것을 알수 있다. 이와 같이 말할 때의 음조를 Intonation이라 한다. 언어학자들은 이 억양을 선이나, 숫자, 또는 음악의 악곡표시 같은 것으로 나타내지만 본서는 어디까지나 900의 해설서이므로 900에서 취급하고 있는 방법, 즉 선에 의해서 설명하고자 한다.

2 I want a cup of [3] coffee. 1

4 선 : 아주 높음(extra high)

3 선 : 높음(high)

2 선 : 보통(normal)

1 선 : 낮음(low)

위의 맨밑의 선 1은 가장 낮은 소리, 2는 보통 소리, 3은 높은 소리를 나타낸다.

높이는 부분이 문장끝에 온 단음절의 낱말이면 소리를 점차로, 낮추어 선을 곡선으로 나타낸다.

2 What do you [3] want? 1

i) **끝을 내려가게 읽는 것(Falling Intonation)**

다음 경우에는 보통 문장 끝을 내려 읽는다.

2 It doesn't [3] matter to me. 1 ……평서문

2 Please give me a piece of [3] pie. 1 ……명령문

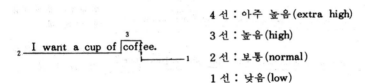

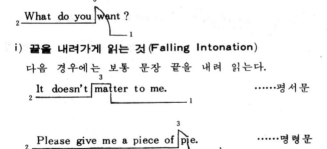

What beautiful trees those are! ……감탄문

What would you like to eat? ……의문사로 시작되는 의문문

ii) **끝을 올려서 읽는 것 (Rising Intonation)**

다음 경우에는 보통 문장 끝을 올려 읽는다.

Do you speak English ……보통 의문문

I have juice, cereal, toast, and coffee for breakfast…… 같은 품사를 나열 때

Mrs. Jones, this is Mr. John Smith. ……사람을 부를때

If you want a towel, look in the linen closet.…… 부사절이 문장머리에 나올 때

Which one would you like—this one or that one? … or가 섞인 의문문의 or의 앞

iii) 특수한 예

부가 의문문의 경우에는 Intonation이 Rising이냐 Falling이냐에 따라 뜻이 달라진다.

He likes ice-cream, doesn't he? ……상대방의 동의를 구할 때

He likes ice-cream, doesn't he? ……의문의 뜻이 강할 때

특히 4선은 감탄문의 경우 있을 수 있으나 보통의 경우에는 쓰이는 일이 드물다.

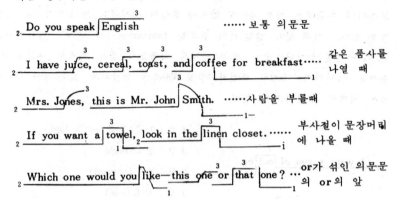

액센트에 관하여

두 음절 이상의 단어에 있어서 영어에서는 습관적으로 한 음절은 강하게, 다른 한 음절은 약하게 발음하는 것이 보통이다. 이 때 강하게 발음되는 음절을 **액센트가 있는 음절**(accented syllable) 이라고 한다.

액센트의 위치를 표시하는 방법에는 다음의 세 가지가 있다.

(a) 액센트가 있는 음절 앞에 표식을 한다. 〔보기〕 **ˊdictionary**

(b) 액센트가 있는 음절의 모음 위에 표식을 한다. 〔보기〕 **díctionary**

(c) 액센트가 있는 음절 뒤에 표식을 한다. 〔보기〕 **dicˊtionary**

이상 세 가지 중에서 만국표음기호로 발음을 표시할 때에는 (a)의 형식을 쓰고, 철자(綴字)에다 직접 액센트의 표식을 할때에는 (c)의 형식을 사용하는 것이 보통이지만, (b)의 형식이 아주 확실하고 잘못 볼 염려가 없으므로 우리나라 사전에서는 거의 이 형식을 채택하고 있다.

때로는, 특히 다음절(多音節)인 단어에서는 리듬 관계로 두 개 이상의 액센트를 붙이는 수가 있다. 이 때 두 액센트가 똑 같이 강하면 둘다 (ˊ) 표로 표시하고, 강약의 차가 있을 때에는 강한 쪽의 액센트는 (ˊ)로 표시하고, 약한 쪽은 (ˋ)로 표시한다.

〔보기〕 **thirteent**〔θə́:tí:n〕 **afternoon** 〔ɑ́:ftənú:n〕 **cigarette** 〔sìgərét〕 **independent** 〔ìndipéndənt〕 (독립한) **characteristic** 〔kæ̀riktərístik〕 (특징있는)

액센트의 형

영어의 액센트의 형에는 다음과 같이 여러 가지 종류가 있다.

(1) 이음절어(二音節語)

a) — ⌣

〔보기〕 **father** 〔fɑ́:ðə〕 **mother** 〔mʌ́ðə〕

visit 〔vízit〕 **pretty** 〔príti〕

limit 〔límit〕 (제한하다)

b) ⌣ —́

〔보기〕 **away** 〔əwéi〕 **about** 〔əbáut〕

address 〔ədrés〕 **prepare** 〔pripέə〕

permit 〔pəmít〕

c) ˗́ ˗́

〔보기〕 **thirteen** 〔θə́:tí:n〕 **fourteen** 〔fɔ́:tí:n〕 *etc.*

이 형태에 속하는 것이 다른 단어 뒤에 올 때에는 리듬관계로 a) 또는 b)의 형태로 되는 수가 있다.

예를 들면

She is júst thirtéen. (ˊ) ‿ ˗́

She is thírteen yéars of age. ˗́ ‿ (ˊ)

(2) **삼음절어**(三音節語)

a) ˗́ ‿ ‿

〔보기〕 honesty 〔ɔ́nisti〕 (정직)

beautiful 〔bjú:tiful〕

Englishman 〔íŋgliʃmən〕

b) ‿ ˗́ ‿

〔보기〕 tomato 〔təmá:tou〕

potato 〔pətéitou〕

banana 〔bəná:nə〕

attention 〔əténʃ(e)n〕 (주의)

c) ˗̀ ‿ ˗́

〔보기〕 cigarette 〔sìgərét〕 (담배)

chandelier 〔ʃændilíə〕 (샨데리아)

engineer 〔èndʒiníə〕 (기사〔技師〕)

(3) **다음절어**(多音節語)

음절의 수가 많아짐에 따라 액센트의 형도 복잡해지는데, 중요한 것은 주요한 액센트의 위치를 정확하게 배우고 필요한 때는 리듬에 따라 제 2 의 액센트를 붙여야 한다는 것이다.

PREFACE

ENGLIST 900®, a course for students of English as a second language, contains material from beginning through intermediate levels of study. The whole series consists of textbooks, workbooks, and tape recordings, with a teacher's handbook.

ENGLISH 900® is one of the basic instructional courses in the Collier-Macmillan English Program. Included in the Program is a series of graded readers in which six are keyed to the vocabulary and structure of each study unit in the basic texts of ENGLISH 900®.

The series takes its name from the 900 base sentences presented in the six textbooks. The sentences cover the basic structures and a basic vocabulary of the English language. They are introduced at the rate of fifteen in each study unit, or a hundred and fifty in each book, and are numbered consecutively from Base Sentence 1 in the first unit of Book One through Base Sentence 900 in the last unit of Book Six. These structures provide "building blocks" for all of the material studied in the series, e.g., there are approximately four variation sentences for each base sentence. As a part of his mastery of English, therefore, the student practices and learns approximately 3,600 variation sentences in addition to the basic 900 patterns.

There are ten study units in each textbook in the series. Each study unit contains a group of fifteen base sentences related to a meaningful situation. In Book One of the series, the typical study unit begins with the presentation of the fifteen *Base Sentences* together with *Intonation* patterns. *Questions and Answers* follow and give the student practice in pairing and matching the base sentences into conversational form. *Substitution Drills* introduce the variation sentences, using vocabulary and grammatical substitution techniques. These early sections of the unit provide the pronunciation practice and drill material needed for the mastery of language forms. The *Conversation* section consists of short dialogues giving the student the opportunity to practice the new lesson material in informal conversation in the classroom. *Exercises* in each unit can be used as oral and written drills for all of the materials introduced in the unit.

Units in the succeeding books in the series (Books Two to Six) contain Base Sentences, Intonation practice, Substitution Drills, Conversation, and Exercises, and, in addition, certain new features. Beginning with Book Two, a *Reading Practice* section is added to each unit, and, beginning with Book Three, a *Verb Study* section. Books Four, Five, and Six include *Participation Drills* for classroom use, and Books Five and Six present *Grammar Study* materials and *review exercises*.

Each textbook includes a *Key* to the exercises and a *Word Index* which lists in alphabetical order every word introduced in the book, and cites the sentence and unit number in which the new word first occurred. There are special *Review Units* in Books One through Four.

A companion Workbook is available for each of the six textbooks, and a series of 180 pre-recorded tapes has been prepared for language laboratory use. ENGLISH 900® Workbooks are unique in that they have been programmed for use by the student as home study material to reinforce classroom work. The Workbooks "test" the student on the textbook materials, and review the important points in each unit that he may not have mastered in class.

For classes that meet for three to five hours a week, each textbook in the series provides material for approximately three months of study. Suggestions for teaching the course, as well as detailed descriptions of all of the materials in ENGLISH 900®, have been given in the Teacher's Manual which accompanies the series.

A wide range of material has been created for the Collier-Macmillan English Program by the Materials Development Staff of English Language Services, Inc., under the co-direction of Edwin T. Cornelius, Jr. and Willard D. Sheeler. ENGLISH 900® was prepared under the direction of Edwin T. Cornelius, Jr., with Joyce R. Manes as Project Editor.

CONTENTS

UNIT		Page
	안 내 서	1
	머 리 말	2
	INTONATION	3
	액 센 트	5
	PREFACE	9
1	TELLING ABOUT PAST EXPERIENCES *(601-615)*	13
2	ASKING ABOUT FURNITURE AND PLACES TO LIVE *(616-630)*	31
3	TALKING ABOUT THINGS TO WEAR *(631-645)*	49
4	DISCUSSING DIFFERENT POINTS OF VIEW *(646-660)*	67
5	THINKING ABOUT POSSIBLE FUTURE ACTIVITIES *(661-675)*	85
6	TALKING ABOUT PAST POSSIBILITIES *(676-690)*	103
7	ASKING ABOUT LIKES AND DISLIKES *(691-705)*	121
8	GIVING ADVICE AND ASKING OPINIONS *(706-720)*	141

9 ASKING FAVORS OF OTHER PEOPLE *(721-735)* 159

10 MAKING PREPARATIONS TO TRAVEL *(736-750)* 177

WORD INDEX 195

KEY to Exercises 211

The numbers of the Base Sentences in each unit follow the unit titles.

ENGLISH 900 WORKBOOK 223

INTRODUCTION

머 리 말

본 문

UNIT 1 TELLING ABOUT PAST EXPERIENCES

601 **A strange thing happened to me this morning.**
602 **I was crossing the street and was almost hit by a car.**
603 **Fortunately, I jumped back in time to avoid being hit.**
604 **It was a terrible experience, and I won't forget it.**
605 **Yesterday was such a beautiful day we decided to go for a drive.**
606 **We prepared a picnic lunch and drove down by the river.**
607 **After a while, we found a shady place under some poplar trees.**
608 **On the way back home, we had a flat tire.**
609 **It was after dark when we got back, and we were all tired.**
610 **I wish you would give me a more detailed description of your trip.**
611 **Speaking of trips, did I ever tell you about the experience I had?**
612 **We used to have a lot of fun when we were that age.**
613 **I can't recall the exact circumstances.**
614 **I never realized that someday I would be living in New York**
615 **We never imagined that John would become a doctor.**

601. 오늘 아침 나에게 이상한 일이 생겼읍니다.

602. 나는 거리를 건너 가다가 차에 거의 치일 뻔 했읍니다.

603. 다행히, 나는 늦지않게 뒤로 홀쩍 뛰어 차에 치이는 것을 피할 수 있었읍니다.

604. 그것은 소름끼치는 경험이었고, 그래서 나는 그것을 잊지 못할 것 입니다.

605. 어제는 너무나 아름다운 날이었으므로, 우리는 드라이브 나가기로 결정했읍니다.

606. 우리는 피크닉용 점심을 준비하여 강가를 따라 차를 몰았읍니다.

607. 잠시 후 우리는 포푸라 나무 밑의 그늘 곳을 발견했읍니다.

608. 집으로 귀가하는 도중, 차가 빵꾸가 났읍니다.

609. 우리가 돌아왔을 때는, 어두어진 뒤었고, 그래서 우리 모두 기진맥진해 졌읍니다.

610. 나는, 당신이 당신의 여행에 대해서 좀 더 자세히 설명해 주시길 바랍니다.

611. 여행에 대해서 말한다면, 이미 나의 경험에 대해서 말씀드리지 않았읍니까?

612. 우리가 그 나이였을 때는 무척 재미있게 지냈읍니다.

613. 나는 그 경우를 정확히 다시 생각해낼 수는 없읍니다.

614. 내가 언젠가는 뉴욕에 살고 있게 되리라고는 생각도 안 했읍니다.

615. 죤이 의사가 되리라고는 결코 생각도 못했읍니다.

＊ 새로 나온 단어와 어귀 ＊

strange「이상한」 **cross**「횡단하다」 **was almost hit**「거의 치일뻔 했다」 **fortunately**「다행히」 **jump back**「뛰어 물러나다」 **in time to～**「～하기에 늦지 않게」 **avoid～**「～을 피하다」 **terrible**「소름끼치는」 **experience**「경험」 **after a while**「한참 후」 **shady**「응달진, 그늘진」 **poplar**「포푸라」 **on the way back home**「집으로 돌아오는 도중」 **flat tire**「빵꾸」 **after dark**「어두워진 후」 **get back**「돌아오다」 **detailed**「자세한, 상세한」 **description**「설명」 **give a description**「설명하다」 **speaking of～**「～에 관해서 말하자면」 **fun**「즐거움」 **have fun**「재미있게 지내다」 **recall**「상기하다, 생각하다」 **imagine**「상상하다, 생각하다」

문 법

603. ~I jumped back in time to avoid being hit. : 글자 그대로의 뜻은 「차에 치이는 것을 피하기에 늦지 않게 뒤로 뛰어 물러섰다」의 뜻.

I realized the danger *in time to* avoid being hit.
(늦지 않게 위험을 알아차려서 치이지 않았다)
I reacted *in time to* avoid being hit.
(늦지 않게 행동하여 치이지 않았다)
I got out of the way *in time to* avoid being hit
(늦지 않게 길을 비켜서 치이지 않았다)

605. Yesterday was such a beautiful day we decided to go ~ : 이것은 원래 such~ that··· 구문으로서 「너무나 ~해서 ···하다」로 번역한다. 본문에서는 such a beautiful day 다음에 that가 생략된 것 이다.

Yesterday was *such a magnificent day*(that) we decided to go for a drive.
(어제는 너무나 좋은 날이어서 우리는 드라이브 가기로 결정했다)
Yesterday was *such a glorious day*(that) we decided to go for a drive.
(어제는 너무나 유쾌한 날이었으므로 우리는드라이브 가기로 결정 했다)
Yesterday was *such a perfect day*(that) we decided to go for a drive.
(어제는 너무나 완벽한 날이었으므로 우리는 드라이브 가기로결정했다)

a~day와 같은 「명사」일 경우 such~that 구문을 쓰고, day와 같은 명사가 없고 beautiful, magnificent, glorious와 같은 형용사나 부사뿐일 경우 so~that구문을 쓴다. 뜻은 같다.

Yesterday was *so beautiful*(that) we decided to go for a drive.
(어제는 너무나 아름다웠으므로 우리는 드라이브 가기로 결정했다)

608. On the way back home, we had a flat tire. : On the way back home은 「집으로 가는 도중에」, 이와 같은 표현으로 On my way to school 「내가 학교로 가는 도중에」 on his way to school 「그가 학교로 가는 도중에」 등의 표현이 있다.

610. ~ you would give me a more detailed description of your trip : give a description of ~ 「~을 설명하다」, 이 이외에 give an account of ~, give a report of ~, give a story of ~등도 같은 뜻이다.

611. Speaking of trips~ : Talking about ~, On the subject of ~도 같은 뜻이다.

615. We never imagined that John would become a doctor. : John would become~은 원래 John will become~이었으나 앞의 we never imagined~가 「과거시제」이므로 「시제의 일치」에 좇아 will이 would가 된 것이다. 따라서 John will become~이나 John would become~이나 해석은 꼭 같다.

I *think* he *will* be a doctor someday.
(그가 언젠가는 의사가 되리라 생각한다)
I *thought* he *would* be a doctor someday.
(그가 언젠가는 의사가 되리라 생각했다)

INTONATION

601 A strange thing happened to me this morning.

602 I was crossing the street and was almost hit by a car.

603 Fortunately, I jumped back in time to avoid being hit.

604 It was a terrible experience, and I won't forget it.

605 Yesterday was such a beautiful day we decided to go for a drive.

606 We prepared a picnic lunch and drove down by the river.

607 After a while, we found a shady place under some poplar trees.

608 On the way back home, we had a flat tire.

609 It was after dark when we got back, and we were all tired.

610 I wish you would give me a more detailed description of your trip.

611 Speaking of trips, did I ever tell you about the experience I had?

612 We used to have a lot of fun when we were that age.

613 I can't recall the exact circumstances.

614 I never realized that someday I would be living in New York.

615 We never imagined that John would become a doctor.

VERB STUDY

1. avoid, jump back

a. I jumped back in time to avoid being hit by a car.
b. I avoided an accident by jumping back.
c. He always avoids driving on busy streets.
d. Mr. Cooper is avoiding me these days.

2. become

a. We never imagined that John would become a doctor.
b. Did you know that Ralph became a doctor?
c. The meeting is becoming interesting.
d. Whatever became of Mr. and Mrs. Cooper?

3. cross

a. I was crossing the street and was almost hit by a car.
b. Please don't cross the street here. Cross at the corner.
c. I crossed the street and went into the restaurant.
d. It's important to cross busy streets at the corner.

4. live

a. I'm now living in New York.
b. I've lived here for more than 20 years.
c. My sister lives in California.
d. We live in a big white house on Washington Street.

5. prepare

a. We prepared a picnic lunch and drove down by the river.
b. We're preparing the lunch now.
c. My mother prepares wonderful food.
d. Be prepared for engine trouble if you take my car.

6. realize

a. I never realized that someday I would be living in California.
b. She realizes that it costs too much, but she wants it anyway.
c. I'm just realizing how hard it is to speak another language.
d. Do you realize that you were almost hit by a car?

7. wish

a. I wish you would give me a more detailed description of your trip.
b. She wishes she could go with us to Africa.
c. Have you ever wished you could travel around the world?
d. Do you wish you could have a new car?

VERB STUDY

1. **avoid, jump back** (피하다, 뒤로 뛰어 물러서다)
   a. 늦지않게 뒤로 뛰어 물러나서 차에 치이는 것을 피했다.
   b. 나는 뒤로 뛰어 물러나므로서 사고를 피하였다.
   c. 그는 항상 복잡한 거리에서 차를 모는것을 피한다.
   d. 쿠우퍼 씨는 요새 나를 피하고 있다.
2. **become** (~이 되다)
   a. 우리는 죤이 의사가 되리라고는 결코 생각도 하지 않았다.
   b. 당신은 랠프가 의사가 된 것을 알고 있었읍니까?
   c. 그 회합은 재미있어져 가고 있다.
   d. 쿠우퍼 씨 부부는 어떻게 되었을까요?
3. **cross** (건너다)
   a. 나는 거리를 건너 가고 있었는데 차에 거의 치일뻔 했다.
   b. 여기서 길을 건너가지 마십시요. 저 모퉁이에서 건너 가세요.
   c. 나는 거리를 건너 그 식당으로 들어갔다.
   d. 그 모퉁이에서 혼잡한 거리를 건너 가는 것이 중요하다.
4. **live** (살다, 거주하다)
   a. 나는 지금 뉴욕에 살고 있는 중입니다.
   b. 나는 여기에 20년이상이나 살고 있읍니다.
   c. 나의 누나는 캘리포니아에 살고 있읍니다.
   d. 우리는 와싱톤 스트리트에 있는 큰 흰 집에 살고있읍니다.
5. **prepare** (준비하다)
   a. 우리는 피크닉용 점심을 준비해 가지고 강을 따라 드라이브를 했다.
   b. 우리는 지금 점심을 준비하고 있는 중이다.
   c. 나의 어머니는 훌륭한 음식을 준비한다.
   d. 만약 당신이 나의 차를 타시면 엔진 고장에 대해 준비하십시오.
6. **realize** (깨닫다, 인식하다)
   a. 나는 결코 내가 캘리포니아에 살게 되리라는 것을 인식하지 못했다.
   b. 그녀는 그것이 값이 몹시 비싸다는 것을 알지만, 어쨌든 그것을 원한다.
   c. 나는 다른 언어를 말한다는 것이 얼마나 힘든다는 것을 인제 깨달아 가고 있다.
   d. 당신은 차에 거의 치일뻔 한 사실을 알고 있읍니까?
7. **wish** (원하다)
   a. 나는 네가 너의 여행에 대해서 더 자세히 설명해 주기를 바란다.
   b. 그녀는 우리들과 함께 아프리카에 갈수 있으면 하고, 바란다.
   c. 당신은 당신이 세계를 여행하고 싶어한 적이 있읍니까?
   d. 당신은 새 차를 갖고 싶다고 원하느냐?

＊ 새로 나온 단어와 어귀 ＊

these days「요새」 **What becomes of～?**「～는 어떻게 되는가?」
it costs too much「그것은 값이 너무 비싸다」
travel around the world「세계일주 여행을 하다」

SUBSTITUTION DRILLS

1. | A strange | thing happened to me this morning.

 A strange
 An odd
 An interesting
 A funny
 A peculiar
 An amazing

2. I was crossing the street and was almost hit by

 a car
 an ambulance
 a fire engine
 a truck
 a motorcycle
 a sports car

3. Fortunately, I

 jumped back
 realized the danger
 reacted
 got out of the way

 in time to avoid being hit.

4. It was a terrible

 experience
 shock
 feeling
 situation

 , and I won't forget it.

5. Yesterday was such a

 beautiful
 magnificent
 glorious
 perfect

 day we decided to go for a drive.

6. We prepared a picnic lunch and brove down by the

river
creek
brook
lake
canal

7. After a while, we found a shady place

under some poplar
beneath some oak
near some elm
by some redwood

trees.

8. On the way back home,we had

a flat tire
some engine trouble
a blowout
motor trouble
an accident
a breakdown

.

9. It was after dark when we got back and we were all

tired
exhausted
worn-out

.

10. I wish you would give me a more detailed

description
account
report
story

of your trip.

11.

Speaking of
Talking about
On the subject of

trips, did I ever tell you about my experience?

12. We used to

have a lot of fun
get into a lot of trouble
behave strangely
tell a lot of jokes

when we were that age.

13.	I can't	recall remember reconstruct report	the exact circumstances.

14.	I never realized that someday I would be	living in New York married to a genius flying a plane learning a foreign language	.

15.	We never	imagined suspected dreamed realized	that John would become a doctor.

16.	Please I wish you would I'd like you to	tell me about your trip.

17.	Let me tell you	the exact circumstances all the details the whole story	.

18.	Are you sure Do you think	he'll be	a doctor someday?
	Did you think Did you realize Did you ever dream	he would be	

SUBSTITUTION DRILLS

1.
이상한
괴상한
흥미있는
재미있는
독특한
놀랄만한

2.
자동차
구급차
소방차
화물차
오토바이
경기용차

3.
뒤로 뛰었다
위험을 인식했다
반사적으로 움직였다
비켜났다

4.
경험
충격
느낌
처지

5.
아름다운
훌륭한
영광된
완전한

6.
강
샛강
개울
호수
수로

7.
포푸라 나무아래
오우크 나무밑에
느릅나무 근처
삼나무 옆에

8.
타이어가 터지다
엔진 고장
빵구나다
모터 고장
사고가 있었다
고장났다

9.
피곤한
지친
기진한

10.
설명
이야기
보고
이야기

11.
여행에 대해서
여행에 관해서
여행을 주제로

12.
재미가 많았다
많은 곤란이 있었다
이상한 행동을 했다
농담을 많이하다

13.
회상
기억
재건
보고

14.
뉴욕에 살리라고
수재와 결혼하리라고
비행기를 조정하리라고
외국어를 배우리라고

15.
상상했다
기대했다
꿈꾸었다
인식했다

16.
제발
당신이 그렇기를
당신이 그렇게 하기를

17.
정확한 경우
모든 내용
전체의 이야기

18.

당신은	확신합니까
당신은	생각합니까
당신은	생각했었읍니까
당신은	실감했었읍니까
당신은	꿈을 꾸어본일이 있읍니까

READING

Telling About Past Experiences

An odd thing happened to me last Sunday. It was such a beautiful day that I decided to go for a leisurely drive in the country.

On the way back home, my motor stopped. I was out of gasoline on a lonely road far from a town. I decided to walk until I found someone who could sell me a gallon or two of gasoline.

I had walked almost a mile before I finally found a big house near the road. I was glad to see it because it was starting to get dark.

I knocked on the door and a little old lady with long white hair answered. She said, "I've been waiting for you for a long time. Come in. Tea is almost ready."

"But I only came for some gasoline," I answered. I couldn't imagine what she was talking about.

"Oh, Alfred! Gasoline? You used to prefer tea."

I quickly explained that my car was out of gasoline, but she didn't seem to hear me. She just kept calling me Alfred and talking about how long it had been since she had seen me. She was behaving very strangely and I was anxious to leave. As soon as she went to get the tea I went out of the house as fast as I could.

Fortunately, there was another house down the road, and I was able to buy several gallons of gasoline. When I told the man about my experience, he said, "Oh, that's Miss Emily. She lives by herself in that big house. She's peculiar, but she wouldn't hurt anyone. She's still waiting for the man she was supposed to marry thirty years ago. The day before their wedding he went away and never came back."

Questions

1. Why did the man in the story decide to go for a drive?
2. Where was he when his motor stopped?
3. What was wrong with his car?
4. What did he decide to do?
5. What did the old lady say to him?
6. Why did he run out of the house?
7. What did the man tell him about Miss Emily?

READING PRACTICE

(과거 경험에 관한 대화)

지난 일요일 이상한 사건이 나에게 일어났읍니다. 그 날은 너무나 아름다운 날씨였으므로 나는 시골로 한가롭게 드라이브나 하기로 결정했읍니다.

집으로 돌아오는 길에, 자동차의 모터가 섰읍니다. 나는 마을로부터 멀리 떨어진 외따른 길 위에서 개솔린이 떨어진 것입니다. 나는 한 두 갈론의 개솔린을 팔 사람을 만날때 까지 걸어가기로 결정했읍니다.

나는 거의 일마일을 걷고 나서야 비로서 길가에 있는 커다란 집을 하나 발견하게 되었읍니다. 나는 그 집을 보자 기뻤읍니다. 왜냐하면 어둠이 깔리고 있는 중이었기 때문이었읍니다.

문에 노크를 하자 기다란 백발머리를 한 작은 노 부인이 나왔읍니다. 그녀는 "나는 오랫동안 당신을 기다리고 있었어요. 들어 오세요. 차가 거의 준비됐어요." 라고 말하는 것이었읍니다.

"허지만 전 개솔린을 구하려고 온겁니다"라고 나는 대답했읍니다. 나는 그녀가 무슨 말을 하고 있는지 상상조차 할 수가 없었던겁니다.

"아니, 앨프레드! 개솔린이라니요? 당신은 전에는 차를 더 좋아 했었는데."

나는 재빨리 나의 차가 개솔린이 떨어졌다고 설명했지만, 그녀는 내말을 듣는 것 같지 않았읍니다. 그녀는 계속 나를 앨프레드라고 부르면서, 나를 본지 무척 오래 되었다는 말만 하는 것이었읍니다. 그녀의 행동은 매우 이상했읍니다. 나는 그 자리를 떠나고 싶었읍니다. 그래서 그녀가 차를 가지러 가자마자 나는 한껏 빨리 집 밖으로 나왔읍니다.

다행히 길 아래쪽으로 또 하나의 집이 있었읍니다. 그래서 나는 몇 갈론의 개솔린을 살 수가 있었읍니다. 내가 나의 경험에 대해 그 남자에게 말하자, 그는 이렇게 말했읍니다. "아, 그것은 미쓰 에밀리 말이군요. 그 여자는 그 큰 집에 혼자 살고 있답니다. 이상한 여자지요. 허지만 누구에게도 해는 끼치지 않읍니다. 그 여자는 30년 전에 결혼하기로 되어 있던 남자를 아직도 기다리고 있는 겁니다. 결혼식 전날 남자가 떠나버리고 나서는 다시는 돌아오지 않았죠."

＊ 새로 나온 단어와 어귀 ＊

leisurely「한가한」 **in the country**「시골로」 **be out of～**「～이 떨어지다」 **lonely**「외따른」 **～before…**「～하고 나서야 비로서 …하다」 **knock on～**「～에 노크를하다」 **keep～ing**「계속 ～하다」 **behave**「처신하다, 행동하다」 **by herself**「그 여자 혼자」 **peculiar**「이상한」돌았다는 뜻 **hurt**「해치다」 **be supposed to～**「～하기로 되어 있다」

CONVERSATION

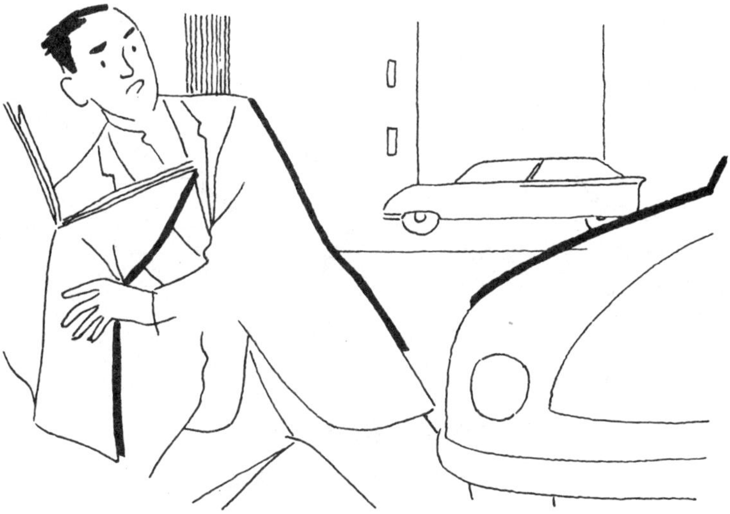

Telling About Past Experiences

JIM: Harry! What's the matter? You look pale. Are you sick?

HARRY: I just had a terrible experience.

JIM: Sit down. Let me get you a glass of water.

HARRY: No thanks, Jim. I'll be fine in a minute.

JIM: Did you have an accident?

HARRY: Not quite, but almost. I was crossing the street just now and was almost hit by a car. Fortunately, I jumped back in time.

JIM: How awful! I hope you got the license number of the car so you can report this man to the police department.

HARRY: Before I realized what had happened, the car was gone.

JIM: Drivers like that should have their licenses taken away from them.

HARRY: I agree. I won't forget this for a long time.

JIM: I'm sure you won't.

HARRY: Yes, from now on I won't cross the street in the middle of the block reading my newspaper. I'll have to watch where I'm going, since there are dangerous drivers like that one on road.

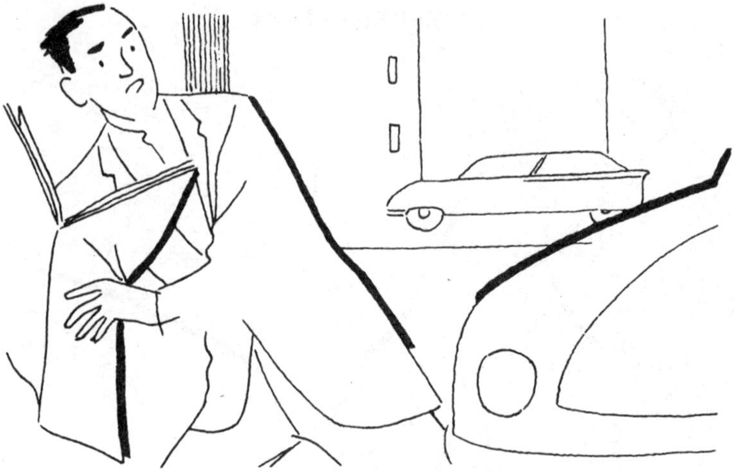

CONVERSATION

(과거의 경험에 관한 대화)

Jim : 해리! 무슨일이야? 창백한 것 같구나, 병이 났니?

Harry : 방금 무시무시한 것을 겪었어.

Jim : 앉어라. 물 한 컵을 갖다 줄께.

Harry : 아냐 고마워 짐. 곧 회복될거야.

Jim : 사고라도 있었니?

Harry : 그렇지는 않지만, 거의 그럴번 했어. 방금 거리를 건너 오다가 차에 거의 치일뻔 했어. 다행히 제때에 뒤로 뛰어 물러섰지.

Jim : 어마나! 그 차의 번호판을 알아 두었으면 좋았을 걸. 그랬더라면 경찰서에 그 사람을 고발할 수도 있을텐데.

Harry : 무슨일이 일어났다는 것을 깨닫기도 전에, 그 차는 떠나 버렸어.

Jim : 그런 운전사는 면허를 빼앗아야 해.

Harry : 내 생각도 그래. 나는 이것을 오랫동안 잊지 못할거야.

Jim : 그럴거야.

Harry : 그래. 앞으로는 신문을 읽으면서 블록의 중간에서 거리를 건너가지는 않을테야. 살피면서 건너가야 되겠어. 그와 같은 위험한 운전사들이 차도에 있으니까 말야.

*** 새로 나온 단어와 어귀 ***

let me get you~ 「너에게 ~을 갖다 줄께」 **license number** 「번호 판」 **police department** 「경찰서」 **have~taken away from them** 「~을 빼앗기다」 **from now on** 「지금으로 부터는」

PARTICIPATION DRILLS

Drill 1

STUDENT A	STUDENT B
Did you have *some engine trouble?*	Yes, we did. We had *some engine trouble.*

some engine trouble
a flat tire
a blowout
motor trouble
an accident
a breakdown
a terrible experience
a lot of trouble

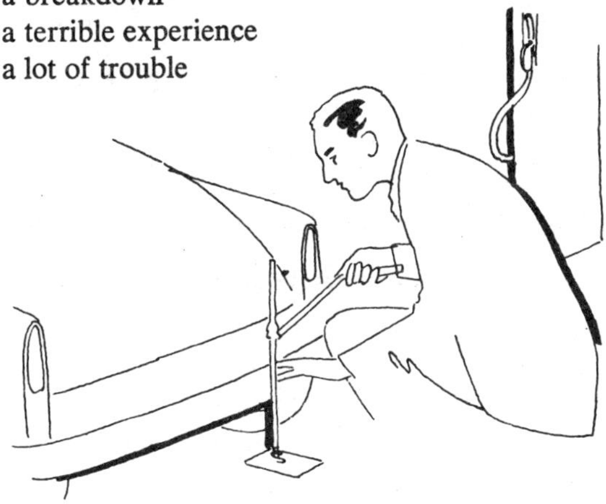

Drill 2

STUDENT A	STUDENT B
Did you *realize the danger?*	Yes, I did. I *realized the danger.*

realize the danger
react in time
get out of the way
have a picnic
jump back
go for a drive
cross the street

EXERCISES

The Subject of the Sentence

1. Complete the sentences below by selecting the appropriate **subject** from the following list of nouns and pronouns:

I	peculiar thing	blowout
yesterday	we	accident
lunch	shady place	

a. ______ was a beautiful day and my friend and I decided to have a picnic.

b. A picnic ______ on a summer day can be a wonderful experience.

c. A ______ happened to us on the way to the picnic.

d. ______ was driving to the picnic when I had trouble with my tire.

e. A ______ on a busy road can be a terrible experience.

f. Fortunately, we didn't have an ______.

g. ______ were worn-out after changing the tire.

h. A ______ would have been wonderful, but we couldn't find one near the road.

2. Complete the sentences below by selecting the correct **substitute noun** and inserting it in the space provided.

a. Some people are very careful when they drive. ______ are dangerous and have accidents. (*Others, Another, Other*)

b. The children were having a good time. ______ were watching TV. (*This, Several, Another*)

c. This account of the President's trip was complete. That ______ was not very detailed. (*one, three, another*)

d. One of my friends was always telling jokes, but ______ was more serious. (*several, a few, another*)

e. We had a good time in New York City. ______ was a wonderful place to visit. (*That, Others, Another*) *f*. John would like to become a doctor. ______ is an excellent profession. (*One, That, Other*)

g. The poplar trees over here gave us some shade, but ______ over there were too small. (*these, that, those*)

h. Those tires in the back of the car are new, but ______ in front are worn out. (*these, that, this*)

3. In the following questions, verb forms are used in subject position. Give a complete answer to each question to practice using this sentence pattern.

Example: Was learning a foreign language difficult?
Yes, *learning a foreign language was difficult.*

a. Could reacting quickly to a blowout avoid an accident?
Yes, ______.

b. Was having an automobile accident a terrible experience?
Yes, ______.

c. Is flying a plane difficult? Yes, ______.

d. Was having a picnic near the river a wonderful experience?
Yes, ______.

e. Was exchanging stories about foreign countries interesting?
Yes, ______.

f. Was crossing the street against the light a good joke? No, ______.

4. Select a subject from Column A and complete the sentence by selecting an appropriate ending from Column B.

A	B
a. A beautiful morning and a picnic lunch	*u*. is a small stream of water.
b. An ambulance and a police car	*v*. were all we needed for a perfect holiday.
c. A flat tire or engine trouble	*w*. are beautiful shade trees.
d. An oak and an elm	*x*. went down the street to the accident.
e. My friends and I	*y*. were exhausted after driving all day.
f. A brook or a creek	*z*. is a terrible problem.

5. The function words "there" and "it" are often used in **subject** position in sentences.

Change each of the following sentences so that the subject is "there" or "it".

Examples: Getting a job is not difficult. *It is not difficult to get a job.* Many students are in the class. *There are many students in the class.*

a. Taking a trip is expensive.
b. Remembering the exact circumstances of an accident is important.
c. Picnicking near a lake is wonderful.
d. Telling jokes is a lot of fun.
e. Forgetting a terrible experience is not easy.
f. A big oak tree was near the canal.
g. Several accounts of the accident were given to the police.

WORD LIST

account	danger	fire engine	oak	shock
amazing	description	flat	odd	someday
ambulance	detail	fortunately	peculiar	sports car
beneath	detailed	genius	picnic	strangely
blowout	elm	glorious	poplar	such
breakdown	engine	lake	redwood	tire
brook	ever	magnificent	report	under
canal	exhausted	motor	river	whole
circumstance	experience	motorcycle	shady	worn-out
creek	feeling			

Verb Forms

avoid	happen
become, became (*p.*), become (*p. part.*)	hit, hit (*p. and p. part.*)
behave	jump back
cross	react
dream	realize
get back	reconstruct
	report
	suspect

Expressions

get into trouble
get out of the way
have fun
in time
on the way back
tell jokes

Supplementary Word List
(Conversation and Reading Practice)

driver	hair	knock	license

UNIT 2 ASKING ABOUT FURNITURE AND PLACES TO LIVE

616 **We're looking for a house to rent for the summer.**
617 **Are you trying to find a furnished house?**
618 **This split-level house is for rent. It's a bargain.**
619 **That house is for sale. It has central heating.**
620 **We have a few kitchen things and a dining room set.**
621 **This is an interesting floor plan. Please show me the basement.**
622 **The roof has leaks in it, and the front steps need to be fixed.**
623 **We've got to get a bed and a dresser for the bedroom.**
624 **Does the back door have a lock on it?**
625 **They've already turned on the electricity. The house is ready.**
626 **I'm worried about the appearance of the floor. I need to wax it.**
627 **If you want a towel, look in the linen closet.**
628 **What style furniture do you have? Is it traditional?**
629 **We have drapes for the living room, but we need kitchen curtains.**
630 **The house needs painting. It's in bad condition.**

UNIT 2 ASKING ABOUT FURNITURE AND PLACES TO LIVE

616. 우리는 여름 동안 세 들 집을 찾고있는 중 입니다.

617. 가구가 비치된 집을 구하려고 하십니까?

618. 이 세칸으로 된 집은 세를 놓는 집입니다. 그것은 월등 싼 건물입니다.

619. 저 집은 팔 집입니다. 그 집은 중앙식 난방 시설이 되어 있읍니다.

620. 우리는 몇개의 부엌 기구와 거실의 장식기구를 가지고 있읍니다.

621. 이것은 흥미있는 평면도입니다. 저에게 지하실을 보여 주십시요.

622. 그 지붕에는 새는데가 있읍니다. 그리고 정면의 계단은 손질할 필요가 있읍니다.

623. 우리는 침실용으로 침대와 경대를 구입 하여야만 합니다.

624. 그 뒷문은 자물쇠가 있읍니까?

625. 그들은 이미 전류 공급을 했읍니다. 그 집은 준비가 돼 있읍니다.

626. 나는 그 마루의 겉모습에 대해 걱정을 하고 있읍니다. 왁스칠을 할 필요가 있읍니다.

627. 만약 수건을 원한다면, 린네르벽장을 들여다 보세요.

628. 어떤 스타일의 가구를 가지고 있읍니까? 그것은 고풍의 것입니까?

629. 우리는 거실에다 휘장을 치고 있읍니다. 그러나, 우리는 부엌에 커튼이 필요합니다.

630. 그 집은 페인트 칠이 필요합니다. 그것은 손질이 안 되있읍니다.

* 새로 나온 단어와 어귀 *

rent「세내고 빌리다, 세 놓다」 **a house to rent** 셋집. **furnished hous**[illegible]가 딸린 집」 **split-level house**「1,2층과 중간 2층의 세층으로 되어있는 2층집」 **for rent**「세놓기 위한 집」 **bargain**「거래, 월등 싼 물건」 **for sale**「팔기 위한 집」 **central heating**「중앙식 난방법」 **set**「(도구)한 벌」 **floor plan**「평면도」 **basement**「지하실」 **roof**「지붕」 **leak**「새는 데」 **front**「정면의」 **step**「계단」 **need～**「～필요가 있다」 **fix**「고치다」 **have got to**=have to「～하여야 한다」 **dresser**「경대」 **lock**「자물쇠」 **electricity**「전기」 **be worried about～**「～에 대해서 걱정하다」 **appearance**「외관, 겉 모습」 **wax**「왁스 칠을 하다」 **towel**「수건」 **linen**「린네르」 **furniture**「가구」 **traditional**「고풍의, 구식의」 **drape**「휘장(커튼 비슷한)」 **curtain**「커튼」 **in bad condition**「(물건이) 보존상태가 좋지 않은」

문 법

616. **We're looking for a house to rent～** : a house to rent「셋집」의 뜻. to rent가 앞의 house라는 명사를 설명해 주고 있다.

an apartment to rent「세놓는 아파아트」 a cottage to rent「세놓는 농가」
a room to rent「셋방」 a cabin to rent「세놓는 오두막」

617. **～a furnished house?** : a furnished house「가구가 딸린 집」의 뜻. an unfurnished house「가구가 딸리지 않은 집」, a 3-bedroom house「침실이 3개인 집」, an inexpensive house「비싸지 않은 집」

618. **This split-level house is for rent.** : for rent「세놓기 위한 것」. 619번의 for sale「팔기 위한 것」의 뜻.

622. **～and the front steps need to be fixed.** : need to be fixed는 need fixing이라 표현할 수도 있다.

The house *needs to be painted.* =The house *needs painting.*
The grass *needs to be cut.* =The grass *needs cutting.*
The side door *needs to be repaired.* =
The side door *needs repairing.*

623. **We've got to get a bed and a dresser～.** : have got to～에는 must와 마찬가지로「～하지 않으면 안된다」의 뜻이 있다.

I'*ve got to* do with him.
(나는 그와 할 것이 있다)
I'*ve got to* help him.
(나는 그를 도와야 한다)
I'*ve got to* buy a car.
(나는 차를 사야 한다)

626. **I'm worried about the appearance of the floor.** : be worried about ～는「～이 걱정스럽다, 염려된다」의 뜻.

I'*m worried about* the looks of the woodwork.
(나무세공의 모양이 염려된다)
I'*m worried about* the condition of the steps.
(계단의 상태가 염려스럽다)

628. **What style furniture do you have?** : What style furniture～? (어떤 스타일의 가구～?)는 다음과 같이 여러가지로 표현 할 수도 있다.

What style of furniture～?
What type furniture～?
What type of furniture～?
What kind of furniture～?
What sort of furniture～?

INTONATION

616 We're looking for a house to rent for the summer.

617 Are you trying to find a furnished house?

618 This split-level house is for rent. It's a bargain.

619 That house is for sale. It has central heating.

620 We have a few kitchen things and a dining room set.

621 This is an interesting floor plan. Please show me the basement.

622 The roof has leaks in it, and the front steps need to be fixed.

623 We've got to get a bed and a dresser for the bedroom.

624 Does the back door have a lock on it?

625 They've already turned on the electricity. The house is ready.

626 I'm worried about the appearance of the floor. I need to wax it.

627 If you want a towel, look in the linen closet.

628 What style furniture do you have? Is it traditional?

629 We have drapes for the living room, but we need kitchen curtains.

630 The house needs painting. It's in bad condition.

VERB STUDY

1. worry (about), be worried (about)

a. I'm worried about the appearance of the floor.
b. Aren't you worried about the roof? It has leaks in it.
c. I'm worrying about my new job.
d. There's nothing to worry about.
e. Mr. Cooper worries about his health.
f. Did you worry about me while I was away?
g. I'm worried about our front steps. They need to be fixed.
h. I've never known anybody who worried as much as you do.

2. rent

a. We're looking for a house to rent for the summer.
b. Who rented the house next door to you?
c. We're renting this house for the summer.
d. Would you rather rent the house than buy it?
e. Who's renting your house in Florida this winter?
f. Did you rent this house just for the summer?
g. She rents two houses: one for the summer, and one for the winter.
h. I'm sorry. We've already rented the house to somebody else.

3. show

a. This is an interesting floor plan. Please show me the basement.
b. The usher will show you to your seats.
c. The salesman showed me a new car yesterday afternoon.
d. She's sick, but she doesn't show it.
e. The waiter is showing them to a table.
f. Mr. Cooper is going to show me his new house at 2 o'clock.
g. Why didn't you show me the front steps? They need to be fixed.
h. May I show you to the door?

4. wax

a. I need to wax the floor.
b. Did you wax your car yesterday as you planned to?
c. I couldn't wax the car because it rained all day.
d. My car looked new after I finished waxing it.
e. My wife waxed the dining room table because we were having guests.
f. John waxes his car once a month.
g. This floor needs waxing. Look at its appearance!
h. When was the last time you waxed the kitchen floor?

VERB STUDY

1. **worry(about), be worried(about)** (…에 대해) 걱정하다)
   a. 마루의 결 모양이 걱정 됩니다.
   b. 당신은 지붕이 걱정되지 않습니까? 지붕에는 새는데가 있읍니다.
   c. 나는 새 일자리 때문에 걱정하고 있읍니다.
   d. 근심할 것은 전혀 없읍니다.
   e. 쿠우퍼 씨는 그의 건강에 대해 걱정을 합니다.
   f. 당신은 내가 없는 동안 나에 대해서 걱정을 했읍니까?
   g. 나는 우리의 정면의 계단이 걱정됩니다. 층계를 고칠 필요가 있읍니다.
   h. 나는 당신처럼 걱정이 많은 사람을 보지 못했읍니다.

2. **rent** (세 놓고 빌리다, 세 놓다)
   a. 우리는 여름동안 세들 집을 구하고 있는 중입니다.
   b. 당신네 옆 집에는 누가 세들었읍니까?
   c. 우리는 여름동안 이 집에 세들고 있읍니다.
   d. 당신은 사시기 보다는 세를 들렵니까?
   e. 올 겨울에는 플로리다에 있는 당신의 집에 누가 세를 들고 있읍니까?
   f. 당신은 여름동안 이 집에 세들었읍니까?
   g. 그녀는 두 채의 집을 빌리고 있읍니다. 한 채는 여름동안, 그리고 한 채 채는 겨울 동안에.
   h. 죄송합니다. 우리는 벌써 그 집을 딴 사람에게 세 주었읍니다.

3. **show** (보여주다, 안내하다)
   a. 이것은 흥미있는 평면도입니다. 나에게 지하실을 안내해 주세요.
   b. 안내원은 당신을 당신 좌석으로 안내해 줄 겁니다.
   c. 판매원은 어제 오후 나에게 새차를 보여주었읍니다.
   d. 그녀는 아픕니다. 그러나 그녀는 내색을 하지 않읍니다.
   e. 웨이터가 그들을 테이블로 안내하고 있읍니다.
   f. 쿠우퍼 씨는 두시에 나를 그의 새 집에 안내할 예정입니다.
   g. 왜 내게 앞 계단을 보여주지 않았죠? 계단은 수리할 필요가 있읍니다.
   h. 내가 문까지 안내해 드릴까요?

4. **wax** (왁스를 칠하다)
   a. 나는 마루에 왁스를 칠해야 합니다.
   b. 당신은 당신이 계획 했던 대로 당신 차에 왁스를 칠 했나요?
   c. 차에 왁스를 칠할 수 없었읍니다. 종일 비가 내렸기 때문입니다.
   d. 내 차는 내가 왁스를 칠한 뒤에 새 것 처럼 보였읍니다.
   e. 아내는 손님을 초대했기 때문에 식당 테이블에 왁스를 칠했읍니다.
   f. 죤은 한 달에 한 번씩 그의 차에 왁스를 칠합니다.
   g. 이 마루는 왁스를 칠해야만 합니다. 이 마루의 꼴을 좀 보세요.
   h. 당신이 부엌 마루에 왁스를 마지막으로 칠한 때는 언제입니까?

SUBSTITUTION DRILLS

1. We're looking for | a house / an apartment / a cottage / a cabin / a room | to rent for the summer.

2. Are you trying to find | a furnished / an unfurnished / a 3-bedroom / an inexpensive | house?

3. This | split-level house / colonial style house / efficiency apartment / duplex apartment / third -floor room | is for rent. It's a bargain.

4. That house is for sale. It has | central heating / air conditioning / a nice fireplace / a big back yard / all the modern conveniences / a double garage | .

5. We have a few kitchen things and | a dining room set / a few pieces of furniture / some antiques / an automatic washing machine | .

6. This is an interesting floor plan.

Please show me the		
	basement attic hallway laundry room den stairway	.

7. The roof has leaks in it, and the		
	front steps need to be fixed house needs to be painted grass needs cutting flower beds have to be weeded side door ought to be repaired	.

8. We've got to get a		for the		
	bed and a dresser sofa and a chair lamp and a desk mirror and a rug sink and a stove telephone stand refrigerator		bedroom living room den bathroom kitchen hallway kitchen	.

9. Does the		have a		on it?
	back door mailbox front porch garage wall		lock number street number sliding door picture	

10. They've already		
	turned on the electricity installed the telephone carpeted the floors put in the plumbing completed the interior	. The house is ready.

11. I'm worried about

the	appearance	of the	floor	. I need te	wax it	
	looks		woodwork		scrub it	
	condition		step		repair them	

12.	If you want	a towel	, look	in the linen closet	.
		some sheets		down in the laundry room	
		a trunk		up in the attic	
		scissors		over on the table	
		your shoes		down under the bed	
		a paper clip		inside the drawer of the desk	
		a wastebasket		beside the desk	

13.	What style furniture do you have? Is it	traditional	?
		modern	
		period furniture	
		rattan	

14.	We have drapes, but we need	kitchen curtains	.
		pictures to hang on the walls	
		paint to paint the house with	
		carpets for the floors	

15.	The house needs	painting	. It's in bad condition.
		repairing	
		remodeling	

16.	What	style	furniture will you buy?
		style of	
		type	
		type of	
		kind of	
		sort of	

SUBSTITUTION DRILLS

1.
- 집
- 아파아트
- 초가
- 오두막집
- 방

2.
- 가구가 비치된
- 가구가 비치되지 않은
- 침실이 셋 있는
- 값이 싼

3.
- 2 층형의집
- 구식 식민지 풍의집
- 효율적인 아파트
- 고급아파트
- 3 층방

4.
- 중앙난방시설
- 에어콘디시설
- 벽난로
- 큰 후원
- 모든 현대적인 편리한 설비
- 차 두대가 들어갈수 있는 차고

5.
- 식당 셋트
- 몇개의 가구
- 약간의 골동품
- 자동 세탁기

6.
- 지하실
- 고미다락
- 현관
- 세탁실
- 사실
- 계단

7.
- 앞 계단은 고쳐야 한다
- 집은 페인트를 칠해야 한다
- 잔디는 깍어야 합니다
- 화단은 잡초를 뽑아주어야 합니다.
- 옆문은 수리를 하지않으면 안됩니다

8.

침대와 화장대	침실
소파와 의자	거실
램프와 책상	서재
거울과 깔개	목욕실
설겆이통과 스토브	부엌
전화스탠드	현관
냉장고	부엌

9.

뒷문	자물쇠
우편함	번지수
현관	가 번호
차고	미닫이
벽	그림

10.
- 전기를 들였다
- 전화를 가설했다
- 마루에 카펫트를 깔았다
- 수도관을 설치했다
- 내부장치를 완료했다

11.

외모	마 루	왁스칠을 하다
모양	목공물	걸래질을 하다
상태	층 계	수리를 하다

12.

수건	수건장속에
몇장의 시이트	세탁실 아래
트렁크	고미다락위
가위	테이블 위
당신의 구두	침대아래
종이 집게	책상서랍안
휴지통	책상옆

13.
- 구식
- 현대식
- 어느시대의 일시적인
- 등나무

14.
- 부엌커텐
- 벽에 걸 그림
- 집에 칠할 페인트
- 마루에 깔 카페트

15.
- 칠
- 수리
- 개조

16.
- 스타일의
- 스타일의
- 의의
- 종류의

READING

Asking About Furniture and Places To Live

There are many things to consider when you are looking for a house, whether you intend to buy or only rent. After all, it is going to be your home, perhaps for quite a long time, and you want to be happy with it. You have to decide exactly what kind of house you want, how much you can afford to pay, and the type of neighborhood you wish to live in.

Last week my wife and I arranged to see a house that was for sale.

The agent said it might need a few repairs, but he thought we should look at it anyway. He told us it was a bargain. Some bargain! The roof leaked and the plumbing didn't work. The front steps were broken and the back door had no lock on it. It needed to be painted both inside and outside. It was in terrible condition.

"What do you think?" the agent asked.

"It isn't exactly what we want," we told him.

"You're very difficult to please," he said. "Perhaps you'd better have your house custom built."

Questions

1. What should you consider before buying a house?
2. What did the agent tell my wife and me about the house that was for sale?
3. What was wrong with the house?
4. Do you think this house was a good "bargain"?
5. What did the agent say when we told him we didn't want this house?

READING
(가구와 주택 구입)

당신이 사려고 하든 그저 세를 들려고 하든 간에, 집을 구할 때는 염두에 두어야 할게 많이 있읍니다. 결국, 그 집은 꽤 오랫동안 당신의 집이 될 것이고, 당신은 그 집에서 행복하기를 바랄 겁니다. 당신이 어떤 집을 원하는지며, 당신이 돈을 얼마나 지불할 수 있는지며, 어떤 이웃과 어울려 살고 싶은 지를 결정해야만 합니다.

지난 주 저는 처와 함께 팔려고 내 놓은 집을 보러 갔었읍니다.

중개인은 그 집은 약간의 수리를 해야 되겠지만, 하여간 우리가 그 집을 보는게 좋을거라고 말했읍니다. 그는 아주 싼 집이라고 말했읍니다. 싼 것이라니! 지붕은 새고 수도관은 고장나 있었읍니다. 앞 계단은 부서졌고, 뒷문에는 자물쇠가 없었읍니다. 그 집은 안 팎으로 페인트를 칠해야 했읍니다. 그 집은 안 밖이 몹시 엉망인 상태였읍니다.

"어떻게 생각하십니까?" 중개인은 물었읍니다.

"우리가 바라던 집이 아니군요." 우리는 그에게 말했읍니다.

"당신네 마음에 들기는 매우 어렵군요." 그는 말했읍니다. "아마 집을 지으시는게 좋겠군요"

*** 새로 나온 단어와 어귀 ***

whether～or… 「～이건 …이건」 **can afford to～** 「～할 여유가 있다」 **inside** 「안쪽이나」 **outside** 「바깥쪽이나」 **the plumbing didn't work** 「수도관이 작용이 되지 않는다」 **in terrible condition** in bad condition보다 더 강한 뜻. **have one's house custom built** 「집을 맞추어 짓다」 「have+명사+과거분사」는 「～을 ～하게 하다」의 뜻.

CONVERSATION

Asking About Furniture and Places To Live

AGENT: Good morning! May I help you?

MR. PITT: Yes, you may. My wife and I are interested in renting a house for the summer.

MRS. PITT: We want something near the beach, if you have it.

AGENT: Do you want a furnished house or an unfurnished one?

MRS. PITT: Furnished. But we have our own sheets and towels.

AGENT: Very well. How long do you want the house? All summer?

MR. PITT: No, not all summer. Just for six weeks.

AGENT: I'm afraid I can only rent it for two months.

MR. PITT: My vacation is only for six weeks, but I think my brother and his family would take it for the other two weeks.

MRS. PITT: Is the house in good condition?

AGENT: Yes, it is. It was just painted and it has all the modern conveniences, including air conditioning.

MRS. PITT: Wonderful. Let's take it, John.

MR. PITT: Not so fast, Eva. We haven't seen it yet, and we have no idea how much it costs.

CONVERSATION

(가구와 살림집에 관한 대화)

Agent: 안녕하십니까? 도와 드릴까요?

Mr. Pitt: 예, 감사합니다. 내 처와 나는 이번 여름에 집을 하나 세 들고자 하는데요.

Mrs. Pitt: 바닷가 근처에 있는 것이면 좋겠어요. 그런 집이 있다면요.

Agent: 댁에서는 가구가 딸린 집을 원합니까? 아니면 가구가 없는 집을 원하시나요?

Mrs. Pitt: 가구가 달린 집을요. 하지만 침구와 수건은 가지고 있어요.

Agent: 좋습니다. 그 집에 얼마나 사실 건가요? 여름 내내인가요?

Mr. Pitt: 아니예요. 여름내는 아니예요. 꼭 6주일동안 머물거예요.

Agent: 그 집을 두 달동안 세 놓으려 했는데 곤란한데요.

Mr. Pitt: 내 휴가가 6주일 뿐 이거든요. 하지만 나머지 두 주일은 내 동생과 그 가족이 쓰게 될 지도 모르겠군요.

Mrs. Pitt: 집은 깨끗한가요?

Agent: 예 그렇고 말고요. 그 집은 새로 칠했고, 에어콘을 포함한 모든 현대식의 편리한 설비를 갖추고 있읍니다.

Mrs. Pitt: 좋아요. 죤, 그 집을 들기로 해요.

Mr. Pitt: 에바, 너무 서두르지 말아요. 우린 아직 그 집을 보지도 않았고, 그 집 가격이 얼마인지도 모르지 않소.

*** 새로 나온 단어와 어귀 ***

beach「해변」 **near the beach**「해변가의」 **sheet**「침구」 **vacation**「휴가」 **in good condition** in bad condition의 반대. **conveniences**「문명의 이기(利器)」 **including ~**「~을 포함해서」 **have no idea**「알지 못하다」

PARTICIPATION DRILLS

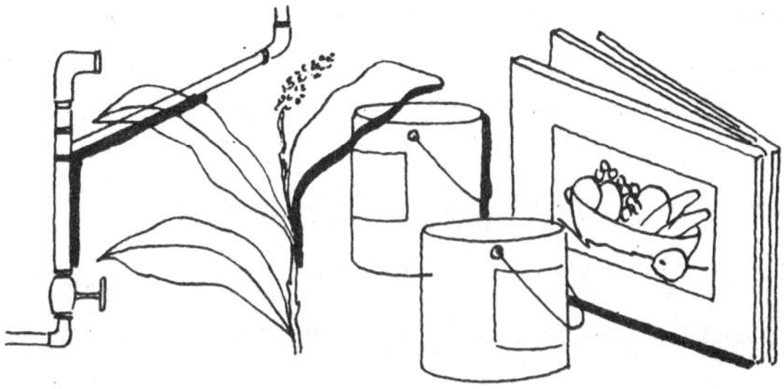

STUDENT A	STUDENT B
(1) (2) Would you like to *see* the *basement?*	Yes, I would. (1) I would like to *see it* now.

(1)	(2)
see	basement
wax	floor
see	attic
sell	cottage
turn on	electricity
install	telephone
put in	plumbing
carpet	floors
repair	side door
cut	grass
paint	house
weed	flower beds
fix	front steps
buy	lamp
have	wastebasket
hang	pictures
scrub	walls
rent	cabin
buy	house

EXERCISES

Noun Modifiers (1)

1. The articles "a", "an", and "the" are **modifiers of nouns.** In the following sentences, insert "a", "an" or "the" in the blank space if it is necessary. Note that some nouns or noun phrases do not require an article.

   Example: We need *a* house or *an* apartment.

   a. We're looking for ______ house to rent.

   b. Expensive houses have ______ air conditioning.

   c. We wish to rent ______ inexpensive house.

   d. We prefer ______ furnished house.

   e. We have ______ few pieces of furniture and some antiques.

   f. This old house has ______ leaky roof and ______ front steps are broken.

   g. We need ______ pictures to hang on ______ living room walls.

   h. I'm also worried about ______ condition of ______ stairway.

   i. ______ remodeling a house is expensive.

   j. I think we'd better rent ______ house instead of ______ apartment.

2. Complete the sentences below by inserting the proper modifier in the space provided.

   a. ______ people prefer new houses with modern conveniences. (*Many, Much*)

   b. The old house needed ______ remodeling. (*a lot of, many*)

   c. The split-level house only had ______ steps. (*a few, a little*)

   d. Do you need ______ sheets? (*a few, a little*)

   e. We have to buy ______ furniture for the living room. (*a few, a little*)

   f. Does a summer cottage cost ______ money? (*much, many*)

3. Complete the following sentences by inserting the modifier "some" or "any" in the space provided.

   Examples: *Some* students work hard. They don't waste *any* time.

   a. ______ houses have a double garage.

b. My house is furnished so I don't need ______ furniture.

c. We still need ______ kitchen curtains.

d. We've already bought ______ living room drapes.

e. We don't have ______ vacant apartments in this building.

f. Are there ______ vacant apartments in the other building?

g. I never buy ______ antiques.

4. Complete the sentences with the **comparative form** of the adjective in parentheses. Use the "-er" form or "more" + base form of the adjective.

Examples: A house is *larger* than a cabin. (*large*)

This floor plan is *more interesting* than that one. (*interesting*)

a. A split-level house is ______ than a cottage. (*big*)

b. Modern furniture is ______ in design than traditional furniture. (*simple*)

c. The old colonial house was in ______ condition than the other houses on the street. (*bad*)

d. An efficiency apartment is ______ than a two-bedroom apartment. (*small*)

e. It's ______ to wash clothes with an automatic washing machine than by hand. (*easy*)

f. Nothing can be ______ than an air-conditioned apartment in the summer. (*good*)

g. A new house is usually ______ than an old one. (*expensive*)

h. A first-floor apartment is ______ than an apartment on the third floor. (*convenient*)

5. Complete the following sentences with the "-est" form or "most" + base form of the adjective in parentheses.

Examples: This antique table is the *oldest* piece of furniture in my house. (*old*)

This is the *most interesting* floor plan I've ever seen. (*interesting*)

a. The three-bedroom house had the ______ back yard in the neighborhood. (*big*) *b*. The colonial house was the _____ house on the block. (*old*)

c. This house has the _____ floor plan of all the houses we've seen. (*bad*)

d. The split-level house had the _____ floor plan. (*good*)

e. In my opinion, a split-level house has the _____ style. (*nice*)

f. A new house usually has the _____ conveniences. (*modern*)

WORD LIST

air conditioning
antique
appearance
attic
automatic
back
bargain
bedroom
beside
cabin
central heating
colonial
condition
convenience
cottage
curtain
den
double
drapes
drawer
dresser
duplex
efficiency
electricity
fireplace
floor plan
flower bed
front
furnished
garage
grass
hallway
inexpensive
interior
laundry
leak
linen
lock
looks
mirror
modern
paint
paper clip
period
plumbing
porch
rattan
refrigerator
roof
room
scissors
set
sheet
sink
sliding
sofa
split-level
stairway
stand
step
stove
style
towel
traditional
trunk
unfurnished
washing machine
wastebasket
woodwork
yard

Verb Forms

carpet
cut, cut (*p. and p. part.*)
hang, hung (*p. and p. part.*)
install
need
paint
put in
remodel
rent
repair
scrub
wax
weed

Expressions

for rent
for sale
have got to

Supplementary Word List
(Conversation and Reading Practice)

agent
vacation
custom built

UNIT 3 TALKING ABOUT THINGS TO WEAR

631 **What are you going to wear today?**
632 **I'm going to wear my blue suit. Is that all right?**
633 **I have two suits to send to the cleaners.**
634 **I have some shirts to send to the laundry.**
635 **You ought to have that coat cleaned and pressed.**
636 **I've got to get this shirt washed and ironed.**
637 **All my suits are dirty. I don't have anything to wear.**
638 **You'd better wear a light jacket. It's chilly today.**
639 **This dress doesn't fit me anymore.**
640 **I guess I've outgrown this pair of trousers.**
641 **These shoes are worn- out. They've lasted a long time.**
642 **I can't fasten this collar button.**
643 **Why don't you get dressed now? Put on your work clothes.**
644 **My brother came in, changed his clothes, and went out again.**
645 **I didn't notice you were wearing your new hat.**

UNIT 3 TALKING ABOUT THINGS TO WEAR

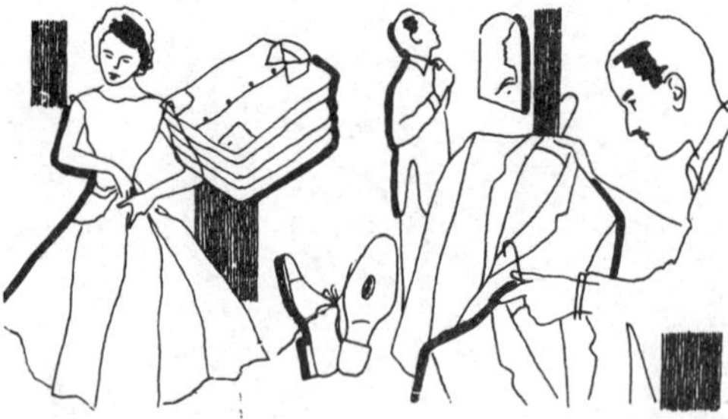

631. 오늘은 무엇을 입으렵니까?
632. 나는 푸른 옷을 입으려고 합니다. 괜찮읍니까?
633. 세탁소에 보내야 할 옷이 두 벌이 있읍니다.
634. 나는 세탁소에 보내야할 샤쓰가 몇벌 있읍니다.
635. 당신은 저 코우트를 깨끗이 세탁해서 다려야 합니다. (you가 하는 것이 아님)
636. 나는 이 샤쓰를 빨아서 다려야만 합니다. (I가 하는 것이 아님)
637. 내 옷은 모두 더럽읍니다. 입을만한 것이 하나도 없읍니다.
638. 당신은 가벼운 자켓을 입는 편이 좋겠읍니다. 오늘은 쌀쌀합니다.
639. 이 드레스는 이젠 내게 맞지 않읍니다.
640. 나는 이 바지가 작어서 못 입을만큼 컸나봅니다.
641. 이 구두는 낡았읍니다. 그 구두는 참 오래 신었읍니다.
642. 나는 이 칼라 단추를 채울 수가 없읍니다.
643. 인제 옷을 입지 그러세요. 작업복을 입으세요.
644. 내 남동생이 들어와서 옷을 갈아입고 다시 밖으로 나갔읍니다.
645. 당신이 새 모자를 쓰고 있는 것을 미처 몰랐읍니다.

*** 새로 나온 단어와 어귀 ***

suit「옷」 **cleaner**「세탁업소」 **laundry**「세탁소」 **clean**「깨끗이 하다」 **press**「누르다, 다리다」 **wash**「세탁하다」 **iron**「다리미질 하다」 **dirty**「더러운」 **light**「가벼운」 **jacket**「자켓」 **chilly**「오싹오싹하는, 쌀쌀한」 **fit**「어울리다, 맞다」 **outgrow**「(옷을 못입을 정도로)성장하다」 **trousers**「바지」 **worn-out**「닳아 빠진」 **last**「지속되다, 견디어내다」 **fasten**「(단추를)채우다」 **collar**「칼라, 깃」 **button**「단추」 **work clothes**「작업복」 cleaner는「드라이 클리닝」을 뜻하고 laundry는「물빨래를 하는 세탁소」를 뜻한다.

문 법

633. I have two suits to send～ : 글자 그대로는 「보내야 할 두 벌의 옷을 가지고 있다」의 뜻이지만 의역하면 「두 벌의 옷을 보내야 한다」의 뜻.

I have *a dress to send* to the cleaners.
(세탁소에 드레스를 보내야 한다)

I have *a pair of slacks to send* to the cleaners.
(세탁소에 슬랙스 한 벌을 보내야 한다)

635. You ought to have that coat cleaned and pressed.

{① I clean and press this coat.
{② I have this coat cleaned and pressed.

위의 ①, ②번이 다 같이 주어는 I로서 동일하지만, ①번은 「빨고 세탁하는」 것은 I 즉 「나」이고 ②번은 「내」가 빨고 세탁하는 것이 아니고, 「제 3 자」(이를테면 세탁소의 세탁부 등)이 하는 것이다. 즉 「have＋목적(명사)＋과거분사」는 「목적(명사)를 ～하게 시키다」의 뜻을 갖는다. 이 때 636번과 같이 「get＋목적＋과거분사」라고 해도 같은 뜻이 된다.

I *change* the tire.
(내가 타이어를 갈다)

I *have* the trie *changed.* ＝I *get* the tire *changed.*
(내가 타인에게 타이어를 갈게 하다)

한편 ought는 should와 마찬가지로 「～해야 한다」는 의무·책임 같은 것을 뜻하는 말이지만, should보다 다소 강조적인 느낌이 있다. 특히 ought는 should와 달리 「to＋동사」를 대동한다.

636. I've got to get this shirt washed and ironed. : have got to는 must의 뜻. 「get＋명사＋과거분사」는 635번의 「have＋명사＋과거분사」와 같다.

I've got to *get* these tablecloths *washed* and *ironed.*
(이 테이블 글로스를 빨아서 다리게 하여야 합니다)

I've got to *get* this dress *washed* and *ironed.*
(이 드레스를 빨아서 다리게 하여야 합니다)

639. This dress doesn't fit me any more. : fit는 「～에게 어울리다, 알맞다」의 뜻. 이외에 appeal to～나 look good on～도 같은 뜻.

640. ～I've outgrown this pair of trousers. : outgrow는 「(옷을 입지 못할 정도로) 성장하다」의 뜻.

I'*ve outgrown* these old clothes.
(작아져서 이 옛날 옷은 못입겠다)

I'*ve outgrown* this bathing suit.
(수영복은 작아져서 못입겠다)

I'*ve outgrown* these boots.
(작아져서 이 부츠는 못 신겠다)

INTONATION

631 What are you going to wear today?

632 I'm going to wear my blue suit. Is that all right?

633 I have two suits to send to the cleaners.

634 I have some shirts to send to the laundry.

635 You ought to have that coat cleaned and pressed.

636 I've got to get this shirt washed and ironed.

637 All my suits are dirty. I don't have anything to wear.

638 You'd better wear a light jacket. It's chilly today.

639 This dress doesn't fit me anymore.

640 I guess I've outgrown this pair of trousers.

641 These shoes are worn out. They've lasted a long time.

642 I can't fasten this collar button.

643 Why don't you get dressed now? Put on your work clothes.

644 My brother came in, changed his clothes, and went out again.

645 I didn't notice you were wearing your new hat.

VERB STUDY

1. **wear**
   a. What are you going to wear today?
   b. She wore her blue dress yesterday.
   c. What is Mr. Cooper wearing today?

2. **clean, press**
   a. You ought to have that coat cleaned and pressed.
   b. I'm cleaning the kitchen because it looks dirty.
   c. She presses her skirts and cleans her dresses every week.
   d. She cleans the house about two or three times a week.

3. **wash, iron**
   a. I've got to get this shirt washed and ironed.
   b. She washes and irons the clothes every week.
   c. Do you wash and iron shirts here?

4. **outgrow**
   a. I guess I've outgrown this pair of trousers.
   b. He's growing fast. He outgrows all of his clothes in a very short time.
   c. Have you outgrown your blue suit already?
   d. I outgrew this pair of shoes in three months.

5. **fasten**
   a. I can't fasten this collar button.
   b. He never fastens the top button of his shirt.
   c. Would you please fasten your seat belts?
   d. Please wait. I haven't fastened my seat belt yet.

6. **come in**
   a. My brother came in at 8 o'clock.
   b. She comes in here every day at 3 o'clock.
   c. Come in please, and sit down.

7. **change**
   a. My brother came in, changed his clothes, and went out again.
   b. She changes her clothes two or three times a day.
   c. You certainly haven't changed very much. You look the same.
   d. The tire is flat. You'll have to change it.

8. **notice**
   a. Have you noticed anything new about me?
   b. I should have noticed your new hat, I guess.
   c. Did you notice the number of that house?
   d. Notice how well this suit fits!

VERB STUDY

1. **wear** (입다, 신다)
   a. 오늘은 무엇을 입으시겠읍니까?
   b. 그녀는 어제 푸른 드레스를 입었읍니다.
   c. 쿠우퍼 씨는 오늘 무엇을 입고 있읍니까?
2. **clean, press** (세탁하다, 다리다)
   a. 당신은 저 코오트를 세탁해서 다리게 해야 합니다.
   b. 나는 부엌이 더러워 보여서, 청소하고 있는 중입니다.
   c. 그녀는 매주 그녀의 스커어트를 다리고 드레스를 세탁합니다.
   d. 그녀는 일주일에 두 세번 정도 집을 청소합니다.
3. **wash, iron** (빨다, 다리미질 하다)
   a. 나는 이 샤쓰를 빨아서 다리게 해야 합니다.
   b. 그녀는 매주 옷을 빨고 다립니다.
   c. 당신은 여기서 스커어트를 빨고 다립니까?
4. **outgrow** (「옷이작아 못입을 정도로」 성장하다)
   a. 이 바지는 작아서 못 입을 것 같읍니다.
   b. 그는 빨리 자라고 있읍니다. 그는 얼마안에 그의 옷 모두가 작아서 못입을 정도로 자랍니다.
   c. 당신의 푸른 옷이 벌써 작아서 못 입을 정도로 자랐읍니까?
   d. 나는 석달 동안에 이 구두가 작아서 못 신을 정도로 자랐읍니다.
5. **fasten** (채우다)
   a. 나는 이 칼라 단추를 채울 수가 없읍니다.
   b. 그는 결코 샤쓰의 맨 위 단추는 채우지 않읍니다.
   c. 좌석 벨트를 채워 주실까요?
   d. 기다려 주십시오. 나는 아직 좌석 벨트를 채우지 않았읍니다.
6. **come in** (들어오다)
   a. 내 남동생은 8시에 들어왔읍니다.
   b. 그녀는 매일 3시에 여기에 옵니다.
   c. 들어와서 앉으십시오.
7. **change** (바꾸다, 변하다, 갈아입다)
   a. 내 남동생은 들어와서 옷을 갈아입고 다시 나갔읍니다.
   b. 그녀는 하루에 두 세번 옷을 갈아 입읍니다.
   c. 당신은 확실히 그리 변하지 않았읍니다. 예나 다름없읍니다.
   d. 그 타이어는 바람이 빠졌읍니다. 당신은 그것을 갈아야 할 것입니다.
8. **notice** (알아채다, 주시하다)
   a. 내게서 어떤 새로운 것을 느끼셨읍니까?
   b. 나는 당신의 새 모자를 알아봤어야만 했는데요.
   c. 저 집의 번호를 알았읍니까?
   d. 이 옷이 얼마나 잘 맞는지 보십시오!

*** 새로 나온 단어와 어귀 ***

in a very short time「얼마 안있으면, 곧」 **seat belt**「좌석 벨트」
should+have+과거분사「~했어야만 했다」

SUBSTITUTION DRILLS

1. What are you going to | wear / put on | today?

2. I'm going to wear my | blue suit / aqua skirt / tuxedo / skirt and blouse / new dress | . Is that all right?

3. I have | two suits / a dress / a pair of slacks | to send to the cleaners.

4. I have | some shirts / some underwear / shirts and socks / some dirty clothes | to send to the laundry.

5. You ought to have that coat | cleaned and pressed / taken up in the sleeves / let down in the sleeves / tailored to fit you | .

6. I've got to get | this shirt / this dress / these clothes / these sheets and towels / these tablecloths / these linens | washed and ironed.

7. All my suits are

dirty
wrinkled
too short
too small for me
out of style

. I don't have anything to wear.

8. You'd better wear

a light jacket
a heavy jacket
something warm
a lightweight suit
a raincoat
gloves

. It's

chilly
cold
freezing
hot
rainy
below zero

today.

9. This dress doesn't

fit
appeal to
look good on

me anymore.

10. I guess I've outgrown

this pair of trousers
these old clothes
these swimming trunks
this bathing suit
these boots
my old house slippers
my bathrobe

.

11. These shoes are worn-out.

They've lasted
I've worn them
I've had them
They've been used for

a long time.

12. I can't

fasten this collar button
buckle this belt
tie these shoestrings
tie this tie
unbutton this shirt
tie these shoelaces

. Will you help me?

13. Why don't you get dressed now? Put on your

work clothes good clothes shirt and tie evening dress white tie and tails best suit	.

14. My brother came in,

changed his clothes undressed put on his best suit	, and	went out again went to bed left for the party	.

15.

I didn't notice I hadn't noticed that It didn't occur to me that I didn't realize that I hadn't realized	you were wearing your new hat.

16.

You'd better You should You ought to I suggest that you	wear something warm. It's cold today.

17. These clothes are

wrinkled dirty too long too short	. They need to be	pressed washed taken up let down	.

18. These shoes are

old fairly new	. They're	worn-out in good condition	.

SUBSTITUTION DRILLS

1.
입다
입다

2.
청색 옷
물색 스커어트
택시이도우
스커어트와 불리우스
새 드레스

3.
두벌
드레스 한 벌
슬랙스 한 벌
(바지 통이큰 옷)

4.
몇개의 샤쓰
몇개의 속옷
샤쓰와 양말
더러운옷 몇벌

5.
세탁해 다려야
소매를 올려야
소매를 내려야
당신에게 맞도록 고쳐야

6.
이샤쓰
이드레스
이 옷들
이 이불보와 수건들
이 테이블보들
이 린네르제품들

7.
더러운
구겨진
너무짧은
내게 너무 작은
구식인

8.
가벼운 자켓
두꺼운 〃
따뜻한 옷
가벼운 옷
비 옷(우비)
장갑

냉냉한
추운
얼음이 만한
더운
비가 오는
영하의 날씨

9.
맞다
마음에 들다
좋아 보이다

10.
이 바지 한 벌
이 낡은 옷들
이 수영 가방들
이 수영복
이 장화들
내 낡은 실내화
내 화장복

11.
오래가다
오래신다
오래간직하다
오래사용되다

12.
칼라단추를 채우다
벨트를 조이다
이 구두끈을 매다
이 샤쓰 단추를 풀다
이 구두끈을 매다

13.
작업복
좋은 옷
샤쓰와 타이
이브닝 드레스
하얀 타이와 예복
가장 좋은 옷

16.
더 낫다
그래야만 한다
반드시 그래야만 한다
있었으면 한다

14.
옷을 갈아 입다
옷을 벗다
제일 좋은 옷을 입다

나갔다
자러갔다
파아티에 갔다

15.
몰라 보았다
미처 몰라 보았다
생각나지 않았다
알아채지 못했다
알아채지 못했다

17.
구겨진
더러운
너무 긴
너무 짧은

다려야
빨아야
주려야
늘려야

18.
낡은
아주 새 것인

다 떨어지다
양호한 상태이다

READING

Talking About Things to Wear

Have you noticed that men and women have very different opinions about clothing? Mr. Harper, for example, has probably been wearing the same clothes for several years and intends to wear them for several more. He's very happy if his clothes last for a long time. He only needs a couple of suits and a sports coat and slacks. Occasionally he buys a shirt, a pair of socks, some underwear, or a new tie. Mr. Harper is confident that he has enough clothing.

He thinks that his wife has plenty of clothes, too. She has several dresses, some skirts and blouses, and a few pairs of shoes. But whenever they plan to go out for the evening she says, "I don't know what to do. I have nothing to wear."

"What about all the things in your closet?" Mr. Harper asks his wife. But he knows what the answer will be. One dress is out of style, another is too small or too short, and the third just doesn't appeal to her anymore. Sometimes Mr. Harper can persuade his wife that something from her closet looks good on her. But once in a while she insists on going shopping for a new dress and new shoes.

Mr. Harper talks a lot, but he doesn't really mind if his wife buys new clothes once in a while. Actually, he likes her to look attractive when they go to the theater or to a party.

Questions

1. Why do you think women need more clothing than men?
2. How long does Mr. Harper wear the same clothes?
3. What does he buy occasionally?
4. What does his wife have in her closet?
5. Why does she frequently say that she has nothing to wear?
6. Why doesn't Mr. Harper mind if his wife buys new clothes once in a while?
7. Do you think men worry about styles as much as women do?

READING

(의복에 관한 대화)

남자와 여자가 의복에 대하여 매우 다른 견해를 갖고 있다는 것을 알고 계십니까? 예를 들면, 하아퍼 씨는 여러해 동안 똑같은 옷만을 입었는데도 앞으로도 여러해 그 옷들을 입을 생각입니다. 그는 옷이 오래 가면 아주 좋아합니다. 그에게는 단지 양복 두 세 벌과 스포오츠용 웃옷과 슬랙스가 있으면 됩니다. 가끔 그는 샤쓰 한 벌, 양말 한 켤레, 몇 벌의 속옷, 아니면 새 넥타이 하나를 삽니다. 하아퍼 씨는 옷이 충분하다고 믿고 있읍니다.

그는 아내에게도 옷이 충분히 많다고 믿고있읍니다. 아내는 여러벌의 드레스와 몇 벌의 스커어트와 블라우스, 또한 구두가 여러 켤레 있읍니다. 그러나 부부가 밤에 외출하려고 계획할 때 마다, 그녀는 말합니다. "어쩌면 좋죠? 입을 것이 아무 것도 없어요." 라고.

"장농에 있는 저 모든 것들은 다 뭐야?"라고 하아퍼씨는 아내에게 묻지만, 대답이 어떠리라는 것을 그는 환히 알고 있읍니다. 하나는 구식이고, 또 하나는 너무 작거나 짧고, 그리고 또 세 번째의 것은 이제 맘에 들지 않는다는 것입니다. 때때로 하아퍼 씨는 장농속의 어느것이 그녀한테 잘 어울린다고 설득할 수도 있읍니다. 그러나 그녀는 가끔 새 드레스와 새 구두를 사러 가겠다고 고집을 피웁니다.

하아퍼 씨는 말을 많이 하지만, 아내가 가끔 새 옷을 산다 해도, 실상은 별로 개의치 않읍니다. 사실 그는 둘이 극장이나 파티에 나갈 때 아내가 예뻐 보이는 것을 좋아하니까요.

*** 새로 나온 단어와 어귀 ***

underwear「속옷」 **tie**「넥타이」 **plenty of**「많은」 **blouse**「브라우스」 **out of style**「구식의」 **appeal to**「~의 마음에 들다」 **look good on**「~에게 어울리다」 **insist on~**「~을 고집하다」

CONVERSATION

Talking About Things to Wear

Dialog 1

BILL: I don't know what to wear today. Is it going to be cold or warm?

BILL'S BROTHER: It looks like it's going to rain today. You'd better take your raincoat.

BILL: I can't decide whether to wear my grey suit or the brown one.

BILL'S BROTHER: Why don't you wear the grey one? It's not as heavy as the brown one. It may rain today, but it won't be very cold.

BILL: All right. What are you going to wear?

BILL'S BROTHER: I think I'll wear my new jacket and dark blue trousers. And if I can borrow your blue tie, I'll wear that. I don't have a blue tie.

BILL: Of course you can have it. All of my shirts are at the laundry, so I borrowed one of yours. I was sure you wouldn't mind.

Dialog 2

ALICE: What kind of dress are you looking for?

MARY: Since it's getting warmer this time of year, I want something lightweight. What material do you think would be best?

ALICE: Let's see what there is. We can go to several stores. Personally, I like a cotton dress for spring.

MARY: So do I. And I could wear it all summer, too. I want something I can use for a long time.

ALICE: What color would you like? Yellow or green would be good colors for you.

MARY: Oh! I want a white dress.

ALICE: Are you sure? It's not a very practical color. It gets dirty so fast.

MARY: I know. But I'm getting married on Saturday, and white is the traditional color for a wedding dress.

CONVERSATION

(의복에 관한 대화)

대 화1.

Bill : 오늘은 무엇을 입어야 할지 모르겠는데. 추워질까? 따뜻해 질까?

Bill's Brother. 오늘은 비가 올것 같애. 비옷을 입는 편이 좋을거야.

Bill : 회색 옷을 입어야 할지, 갈색 옷을 입어야 할지 모르겠어.

Bill's Brother: 회색 옷을 입지 그래? 그 옷은 갈색 옷처럼 무거운(두꺼운) 옷은 아나니까. 오늘은 비가 올지 모르지만 그리 춥지 않을꺼야.

Bill : 됐어. 형은 무엇을 입을려고 그래?

Bill's Brother: 난 새 쟈켓에다 푸른 바지를 입을려고 해. 또 네 푸른 넥타이를 빌릴 수 있으면 그것을 매려하는데, 난 푸른 넥타이가 없어.

Bill's Brother: 매구려. 내 샤쓰는 모두 세탁소에 있어서, 나 역시 형것을 빌려야겠는데 뭘, 괜찮겠지?

대 화2.

Alice : 어떤 드레스를 찾니?

Mary : 요즘은 날씨가 점점 따뜻해져서 가벼운 것이 있으면 해. 어떤 천이 제일 좋을까?

Alice : 가보지 뭘. 여러 상점엘 가 보자구. 난 봄에는 면직 드레스가 좋아.

Mary : 나도 그래. 그건 또 여름 내내 입을 수도 있고. 나는 오래 입을수 있는 옷이 좋아.

Alice : 좋아하는 색이 무엇이지? 노랑이나 초록색이 너에게 잘 어울릴것 같은데.

Mary : 오! 나는 흰 드레스가 좋아.

Alice : 그래? 그것은 실용적인 빛깔이 못돼. 너무 빨리 더러워져.

Mary : 알고있어, 하지만 토요일에 결혼을 해. 흰 색은 결혼 예복에 전통적인 색깔이야

* 새로 나온 단어와 어귀 *

heavy suit「무거운 옷」이란 겨울에 입는 옷이므로 「두꺼운 옷」이라 해도 된다. 반대로 light suit는 「얇은 옷」이라 번역할 수도 있다.

material「원료, 재료, 천」 **cotton**「면직, 솜」 **practical**「실용적인」 **traditional**「전통적인」 **wedding dress**「결혼식 예복」

PARTICIPATION DRILLS

Drill 1

STUDENT A	STUDENT B
Have you *pressed the suit* yet?	Not yet. I don't feel like *pressing it* now.

pressed the suit
cleaned the floor
fastened the seatbelt
changed your clothes
ironed the clothes
changed the tire
put on a shirt
washed my skirt

Drill 2

STUDENT A	STUDENT B
Do you think I ought to *wash the clothes?*	Yes, I do. I think you should *wash them.*

wash the clothes
fasten the shirt
change my clothes
fasten the seatbelt
iron the shirts
press the pants
wear the coat

EXERCISES

Noun Modifiers (2)

1. Single-word modifiers can often be used in place of adjective phrases. Correct the following sentences by changing the italicized phrases to single-word adjectives. Place the adjective *before* the noun as shown in the example.

   Example: You'd better wear a coat *for winter.*
   You'd better wear a *winter coat.*

   a. A suit *that is lightweight* is comfortable on a hot day.
   b. I send clothes *that are dirty* to the laundry.
   c. It's cloudy,so you'd better put on a coat *for the rain* today.
   d. This suit,*which is wrinkled,*will have to be pressed.
   e. My skirt,*which is aqua,*is the same color as my blouse.
   f. If you're going to clean the basement, you'd better wear your clothes *for work.*
   g. I can't fasten this button *for my collar.* Will you help me?
   h. Those trunks *for swimming* are too small.
   i. I didn't realize that I had outgrown my suit *for bathing.*

Adjective clauses (with "who", "which", "whose") function as noun modifiers. These clauses are placed *after* the noun they modify.

2. Combine the following pairs of sentences as shown in the example.

   Example: The students work hard. They are learning English.
   The students *who are learning English* work hard.

   a. The tailor cleaned and pressed my coat. The tailor is on Main Street.
   b. The men wore dress clothes. The men came to the party.
   c. My husband wears slippers and a bathrobe in the house. My husband likes to be comfortable.
   d. The man is chilly. The man forgot his jacket.

3. Using the sentences in Exercise 2, combine the pairs of sentences as shown in the example.

   Example: The students work hard. They are learning English.
   The students *who work hard* are learning English.

4. Combine the following sentences as shown in the example.

Example: This book is interesting. This book is written in English.
This book *which is written in English* is interesting.

a. These shoes lasted for a long time. These shoes are worn-out.

b. This dress doesn't look good. This dress doesn't fit me anymore.

c. These sleeves have to be let down. These sleeves are too short.

d. This dress has to be taken up. This dress is too long.

5. Combine the sentences from Exercise 4 as shown in the example.

Example: This book is very interesting. This book is written in English.
This book, *which is very interesting,* is written in English.

6. From each of the following sentences, form two independent sentences as shown in the example.

Example: The professor, *whose* classes are interesting, teaches English.
(1) *The professor's classes are interesting.* (2) *He teaches English.*

a. My children, *whose* shoes are too small, need larger ones.

b. My brother, *whose* dress suit is out of style, borrowed mine.

c. The girl, *whose* dress was worn out, needed a new one.

d. The woman, *whose* hat was new, showed it to all her friends.

e. The man, *whose* clothes were dirty, took them to the cleaners.

7. Complete the following sentences with "who", "whose", or "which".

a. I need the suit ______ is in the cleaners.

b. The boy ______ needed new clothes went shopping.

c. This jacket, ______ is too small for me, needs to be tailored.

d. Teachers ______ classes are interesting have many students.

e Students ______ study hard are usually successful.

WORD LIST

anymore
aqua
bathing suit
bathrobe
below
blouse
boot
button
cleaners
collar
evening dress
glove
lightweight
linens
rainy
shoelaces
shoestrings
skirt
slacks
sleeve
slipper
swimming trunks
tablecloth
tails
trousers
tuxedo
underwear
wrinkled

Verb Forms

appeal (to)
buckle
clean
fasten
iron
let down
notice
occur
outgrow, outgrew (*p.*),
outgrown (*p. part.*)
press
suggest
tailor
take up
tie
unbutton
undress
use

Expressions

all right
out of style

Supplementary Word List
(Conversation and Reading Practice)

borrow
clothing
for example
sports coat

UNIT 4 DISCUSSING DIFFERENT POINTS OF VIEW

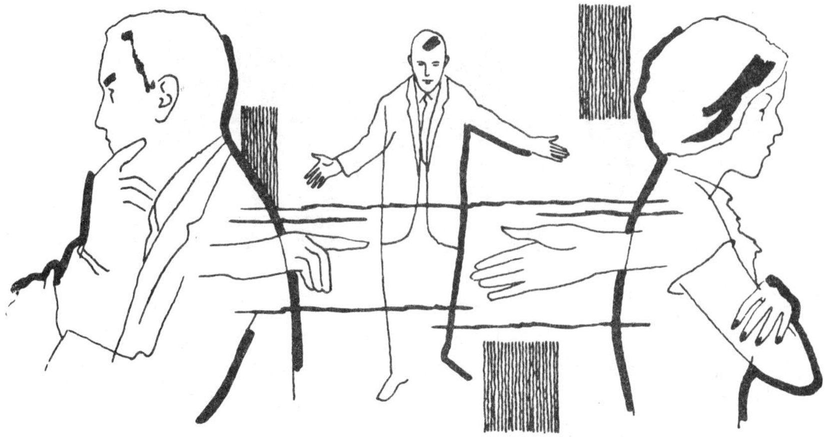

646 You have your point of view, and I have mine.
647 You approach it in a different way than I do.
648 I won't argue with you, but I think you're being unfair.
649 That's a liberal point of view.
650 He seems to have a lot of strange ideas.
651 I don't see any point in discussing the question any further.
652 What alternatives do I have?
653 Everyone is entitled to his own opinion.
654 There are always two sides to everything.
655 We have opposite views on this.
656 Please forgive me. I didn't mean to start an argument.
657 I must know your opinion. Do you agree with me?
658 What point are you trying to make?
659 Our views are not so far apart, after all.
660 We should be able to resolve our differences.

UNIT 4 DISCUSSING DIFFERENT POINTS OF VIEW

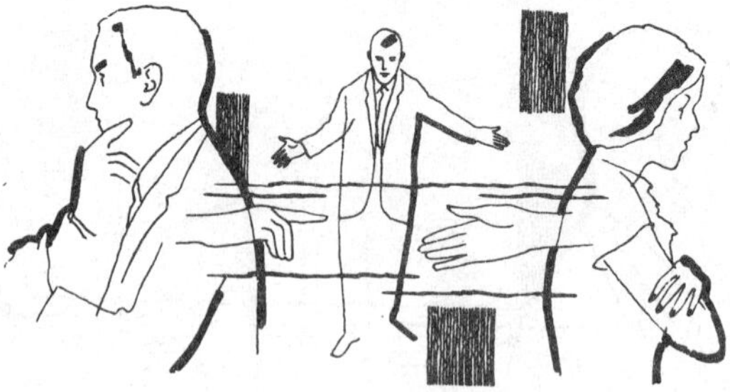

646. 당신은 당신의 견해가 있고, 나도 나대로의 견해가 있읍니다.
647. 당신은 나와는 다르게 그것을다루고 있읍니다.
648. 나는 당신과 논쟁을 하려고는 안하지만 당신이 옳지 못하다고 생각하고 있읍니다.
649. 그것은 진보적인 관점입니다.
650 그는 여러가지 이상한 생각을 가진것 같읍니다.
651. 그 문제를 더 이상 토론한다는 목적을 모르겠읍니다.
652. 나는 어떤 대안을 택해야 합니까?
653. 누구나 자기의 의견을 가질 자격이 있읍니다.
654. 모든 일엔 항상 양면이 있기 마련입니다.
655. 우리는 이에 대해서 서로 반대 의견을 가지고 있읍니다.
656. 용서하십시오. 논쟁을 할 생각은 아니었읍니다.
657. 당신의 견해를 알아야 합니다. 내게 동의하는 겁니까?
658. 어떤 주장을 하시려는 겁니까?
659. 결국, 우리의 견해가 아주다른 것은 아닙니다.
660. 우리는 우리들의 견해차를 해결할 수 있을겝니다.

* 새로 나온 단어와 어귀 *

point of view「견해, 관점」 **approach**「접근하다, (어떤문제를) 다루다」 **in a different way**「다르게」 **argue**「논쟁하다, 주장하다」 **unfair**「부당한, 옳지 않은」 **liberal**「진보적인, 자유로운」 **see a point**「목적이 있다, 견해가 있다」 **discuss**「토의하다」 **further**「더욱」 **alternative**「대안」 **be entitled to~**「~게 대해서 권리·자격이 있다」 **opposite**「반대의」 **view**「견해, 관점」 **mean to~**「~할 의도이다, 생각이다」 **argument**「논쟁」 **agree with**「~에게 동의하다, ~와 일치하다」 **make a point**「주장을 하다」 **apart**「다른, 벗어나는」 **after all**「결국」 **resolve**「해결하다, 결심하다」 **difference**「(견해) 차」

문 법

647. **You approach it in a different way than I do.** : in a different way「다르게」, than I do의 do는 approach를 대신한 것.

You view it *in a different way* than I *do*.
(너는 나와는 다르게 그것을 관찰하고 있다)
You look at it *in a different way* than I *do*.
(너는 나와는 다르게 그것을 보고 있다)
You conceive of it *in a different way* than I do.
(너는 나와는 다르게 그것을 이해하고 있다)

65 . **I don't see any point in discussing~**: see a point in~ing「목적이 있다」의 뜻.

I *don't see any point in* considering the question any further.
(그 문제를 더이상 토론한다는 목적을 모르겠읍니다)
I *don't see any point in* arguing the question any further.
(그 문제를 더 이상 주장한다는 목적을 모르겠읍니다)

653. **Everyone is entitled to his own opinion.** : be entitled to~「~에 대해서 권리·자격이 있다」와 같은 뜻으로 have a right to~, deserve the right to~가 있다.

Everyone *has a right to* his own opinion.
(누구나 자신의 견해에 대한 권리가 있다)
Everyone *deserves the right to* his own opinion.
(누구나 자신의 견해에 대한 권리를 가져 마땅하다)

657. **Do you agree with me?** : agree with~와 유사한 표현으로 다음 여러가지가 있다.

Are you *on my side*? (내편입니까?)
Do you *disagree with* me? (나와 견해가 다릅니까?)
Are you *against me*? (내게 반대합니까?)
Are you *for* or *against* me?
(내게 찬성합니까? 반대합니까?)
Are you *in agreement with* me?
(내게 찬성하고 있읍니까?)
Do you more or less *argee with* me?
(내게 다소나마 찬성합니까?)

659. **Our views are not so far apart~** : be not so far apart「그렇게 멀리 동떨어진건 아니다 → 그렇게 다르지는 않다」

Our views are *not so close together*.
(우리의 견해는 아주 가까운 것은 아니다)
Our views are *not so much alike*.
(우리의 견해는 아주 닮은건 아니다)
Our views are *not so widely different*.
(우리의 견해는 차이가 심한것은 아니다)

INTONATION

646 You have your point of view, and I have mine.

647 You approach it in a different way than I do.

648 I won't argue with you, but I think you're being unfair.

649 That's a liberal point of view.

650 He seems to have a lot of strange ideas.

651 I don't see any point in discussing the question any further.

652 What alternatives do I have?

653 Everyone is entitled to his own opinion.

654 There are always two sides to everything.

655 We have opposite views on this.

656 Please forgive me. I didn't mean to start an argument.

657 I must know your opinion. Do you agree with me?

658 What point are you trying to make?

659 Our views are not so far apart, after all.

660 We should be able to resolve our differences.

VERB STUDY

1. **approach**
   - *a.* You approach it in a different way than I do.
   - *b.* She approaches everything in a peculiar way.
   - *c.* When you approached the house, did you notice anything different?
   - *d.* We're approaching the river now.

2. **argue, discuss**
   - *a.* I won't argue with you, but I think you're being unfair.
   - *b.* She always argues about everything.
   - *c.* Why are you arguing with me now?
   - *d.* He argued with me for two hours last night.
   - *e.* I don't see any point in discussing the question any further.
   - *f.* He discusses most of his problems with me.
   - *g.* Have you ever discussed this with anybody else?

3. **be entitled (to)**
   - *a.* Everyone is entitled to his own opinion.
   - *b.* She's entitled to have her own opinion, isn't she?
   - *c.* They were entitled to have their own opinion.

4. **forgive**
   - *a.* Please forgive me.
   - *b.* I've already forgiven you.
   - *c.* I hope he forgives me. I didn't mean to start an argument.

5. **mean to**
   - *a.* I didn't mean to start an argument.
   - *b.* I haven't meant to bother you.
   - *c.* So you think she means to start an argument?
   - *d.* I've been meaning to call you, but I've been busy.

6. **agree**
   - *a.* I must know your opinion. Do you agree with me?
   - *b.* She agrees with me most of the time.
   - *c.* He agreed with me at first; then he changed his mind.
   - *d.* I'm agreeing with you now, but I may change my mind later.

7. **resolve**
   - *a.* We should be able to resolve our differences.
   - *b.* They resolved their differences and became good friends again.
   - *c.* How did he resolve his problem?
   - *d.* I resolved not to start any arguments.

VERB STUDY

1. **approach** (접근하다, (문제를) 다루다)
   a. 당신은 나와는 다르게 그것을 다루고 있읍니다.
   b. 그녀는 괴상하게 모든 것을 다루고 있읍니다.
   c. 당신은 그 집에 접근했을 때 다른 어떤 것을 보았읍니까?
   d. 우리는 지금 그 강에 접근하고 있읍니다.
2. **argue, discuss** (논쟁하다, 토의하다)
   a. 난 당신과 논쟁하진 않겠지만, 당신이 옳지 못하다고 생각하고있읍니다.
   b. 그녀는 항상 무엇에나 논쟁하려 듭니다.
   c. 당신은 지금 왜 나와 논쟁하고 있읍니까?
   d. 어젯밤 그는 나와 두 시간 동안이나 논쟁을 했읍니다.
   e. 나는 그 문제에 대해서 더 이상 토론할 목적을 모르겠읍니다.
   f. 그는 그의 대부분의 문제들을 나와같이 의논합니다.
   g. 당신은 이 문제를 다른 어떤 사람과 토의해 본적이 있읍니까?
3. **be entitled (to)** (…할 권리가 있다)
   a. 누구나 자기의 견해를 지닐 권리가 있읍니다.
   b. 그녀는 자신의 견해를 가질 자격이 있읍니다. 안 그런가요?
   c. 그들은 그들 자신의 의견을 지닐 자격이 있었읍니다.
4. **forgive** (용서하다)
   a. 저를 용서하십시요.
   b. 난 이미 당신을 용서했오.
   c. 그의 용서를 바랍니다. 논쟁을 시작할 의도는 아니었어요.
5. **mean to** ((생각을) 품다, …할 의도이다)
   a. 난 논쟁을 시작하려는 의도는 아니었읍니다.
   b. 당신을 괴롭힐 생각은 아니었읍니다.
   c. 그래서 당신은 그녀가 논쟁을 할 생각이라고 여깁니까?
   d. 당신에게 전화나 할 작정이었으나(실은) 바빴읍니다.
6. **agree** (동의하다)
   a. 나는 당신 의견을 알아야 합니다. 내게 동의하는 겁니까?
   b. 그녀는 대개 내게 동의합니다.
   c. 그는 처음엔 내게 동의했지만, 나중에는 마음이 변했읍니다.
   d. 지금은 내가 당신에게 동의하고 있지만, 후에는 내 마음이 변할지도 모릅니다.
7. **resolve** (해결하다, 결심하다)
   a. 우리는 우리들의 견해차를 해결할수 있을 것입니다.
   b. 그들은 그들의 견해차를 해결해서 다시 친한 친구가 됐읍니다.
   c. 그는 어떻게 그의 문제를 해결했을까요?
   d. 나는 어떤 논쟁도 시작하지 않기로 결심했읍니다.

＊ 새로 나온 단어와 어귀 ＊

in a peculiar way「괴상하게, 특이하게」
bother「괴롭히다」 **at first**「처음에는」

SUBSTITUTION DRILLS

1. You have your | point of view | , and I have mine.
 viewpoint
 belief
 opinion
 ideas

2. You | approach | it in a different way than I do.
 view
 look at
 conceive of
 visualize

3. Are you being fair? Have you | listened to | both sides of the
 considered | question?
 thought over

4. I won't argue with you, but I think you're being | unfair |.
 stubborn
 narrow-
 minded
 impractical
 childish

5. That's a | liberal | point of view.
 conservative
 radical
 selfish
 narrow

6. He seems to have a lot of | strange | ideas.
 funny
 peculiar
 bright
 clever
 practical

7. I don't see any point in	discussing considering arguing debating	the question any further.

8. What	alternatives choice other choice	do I have?

9. Everyone	is entitled to has a right to deserves the right to	his own opinion.

There are always	two sides to everything two sides to every argument several different points of view differences in people's viewpoints

11. We have	opposite conflicting widely different opposing	views on this.

12. Please forgive me. I didn't mean to start	an argument a long discussion a debate a quarrel a conflict a fight a riot a revolution	.

13. I must know your opinion. ___ ?
    - Do you agree with me
    - Are you on my side
    - Do you disagree with me
    - Are you against me
    - Are you for or against me
    - Are you in agreement with me
    - Do you more or less agree with me

14. What point are you trying to ___ ?
    - make
    - prove
    - get across
    - put across

15. Our views are not so ___ , after all.
    - far apart
    - close together
    - much alike
    - widely different

16. We should be able to ___ our differences.
    - resolve
    - settle
    - reconcile
    - discuss
    - talk about

17. The debate was fair.
    Each opponent had a chance to ___ .
    - speak
    - present his argument
    - answer all questions
    - present his point of view

SUBSTITUTION DRILLS

1.
견해
관점
신념
의견
아이디어

2.
접근하다
관찰하다
고찰하다
느끼다
그리다

3.
듯다
고려하다
생각하다

4.
정당치 못한
고집이 있는
편협한
비 실제적
유치한

5.
너그러운
보수적인
급진적인
이기적인
좁은

6.
이상한
재미있는
독특한
멋진
영리한
실제적인

7.
토의할
생각할
논의할
토론할

8.
대안
선택
다른 묘안

9.
자격이 있다
권리가 있다
할 권리가 있다

10.
만사에는 두 편이
모든 토론엔 두 쪽이
여러 견해차
사람의 견해에는 차이가

11.
반대되는
모순된
차이가 큰
상충하는

12.
논쟁
장시간의 토론
토론
말다툼
충돌
투쟁
폭동
혁명

13.
내게 동의하는가
내 편인가
내게 불찬성인가
내게 반대하는가
내게 찬성인가 불찬성인가
내게 찬성하는 것인가
다소나마 찬성하는가

14.
주장 하려고
증명 하려고
이해 시킬려고
해 낼려고

15.
아주 벗어난
가까운
비슷한
차이가 심한

16.
해결하다
화해하다
일치시키다
토론하다
이야기하다

17.
발언할
논점을 제시할
문답할
견해를 밝힐

READING

Discussing Different Points of View

Some people are always starting an argument. They often have very little information on the subject, but this doesn't matter. They have strong beliefs, anyway. There's no point in debating with people like this because you can never resolve anything.

But with other people a difference of opinion can start an extremely interesting discussion. Each person tries to explain his point of view, but he listens to other arguments, too. This type of conflict becomes an exchange of ideas instead of a quarrel. Whether or not their differences are reconciled, each person learns something from the experience.

In New England and in some other parts of the United States, citizens of the town meet and talk over all local problems. The people sometimes disagree with each other, and there may be some arguments. Each side will try to persuade others that its point of view is the best. But frequently the two sides are not really far apart in their views, and this kind of public discussion helps to settle their differences. This is a healthy situation.

Questions

1. Why shouldn't you argue with people who have little information on a subject?
2. What is a quarrel? What is a discussion? How are they different?
3. When does a conflict become an exchange of ideas instead of a quarrel?
4. What do the citizens do in New England?
5. Do you think public discussion of local problems is a good idea? Why.
6. Do you know of other places where citizens meet for public discussion of local problems?

READING

(견해 차에 대한 토론)

어떤 사람들은 언제나 논쟁을 시작하곤 합니다. 그들은 흔히 그 문제에 대한 지식을 별로 갖고 있지 못하지만 상관치 않읍니다. 그들은 여하튼 강력한 신념을 지니고 있읍니다. 이와같은 사람들과는 토론을 해 봤자 별 소용이 없읍니다. 어떤 결론에 도달할 수 없기 때문입니다.

하지만 그렇지 않은 사람들과는 견해 차이로 인해서 아주 재미있는 토론이 시작될 수도 있읍니다. 각자가 자신의 견해를 설명하려고 들기도 하지만 또한 남의 주장에 귀를 기울이기도 합니다. 이러한 충돌은 싸움이 아니라, 하나의 의견 교환이 될 수도 있는 것입니다. 그들의 견해 차가 화해가 되든 안되든간에 각자는 그 경험에서 무언가 배우는 것이 있을 것입니다.

뉴우 잉글랜드 및, 미국의 또 다른 일부 지역에서는 한 고장 사람들이 서로 만나 그 고장의 모든 문제들을 토의합니다. 때로는 그들끼리 서로 의견이 상충되기도 하고 논쟁이 있을 수도 있읍니다. 또한 양쪽이 서로 자기네 견해가 제일이라고 상대방을 설득하려 들기도 합니다. 그렇지만 양쪽의 견해가 그렇게 크게 동떨어진건 아닌 때도 빈번히 있고, 대개는 이러한 공개토론을 함으로써 그네들 상호간의 견해차는 좁힐 수 있읍니다. 이것은 하나의 건전한 상태라 하겠읍니다.

＊ 새로 나온 단어와 어귀 ＊

information「지식, 정보」 **subject**「문제, 주제」 **matter**「중요하다」 **belief**「신념, 신앙」 **debate**「토론, 논쟁하다」 **conflict**「상충, 충돌」 **reconcile**「화해시키다」 **citizen**「시민」 **local**「그 지방 특유의」 **talk over**～「～에 대해서 토론하다」 **healthy**「건전한」 **situation**「상태」

CONVERSATION

Discussing Different Points of View

FRED: Do you mean to tell me you don't care for modern art? Not any of it?

JOAN: That's right. I don't understand it and I don't like it.

FRED: That's a very narrow-minded viewpoint. If you don't understand it, how can you say that you don't like it?

JOAN: Perhaps I am a little conservative. I just can't imagine that the modern artist is really serious.

FRED: I won't argue with you, but I think you're being unfair. The modern artist has a different approach to his work than the more traditional artist.

JOAN: Are you trying to tell me that these peculiar paintings mean anything? A child could paint better than that.

FRED: I guess there's no point in discussing the matter any further. You have your opinion and I have mine.

JOAN: I agree there are two sides to everything, but this time I see only one of them.

FRED: Well, I'm attempting to explain that the modern artist is trying to get across his personal feelings about the world around him.

JOAN: Then he should keep his feelings to himself.

CONVERSATION

Fred : 당신은 현대미술에 전혀 마음을 쓰지 않는다는 말씀을 하려고 하는 겁니까? 전혀 마음에 드는게 없으시다는 겁니까?

Joan : 그래요. 현대미술은 이해도 할 수 없거니와, 마음에 들지도 않아요.

Fred : 매우 편협한 견해군요. 이해를 못 한다고 해서, 어떻게 싫다고야 말할 수 있읍니까?

Joan : 아마 전 좀 보수적일런지 모르죠. 전 현대 미술가들이 정말 진지하다고는 생각지 않아요.

Fred : 당신과 논쟁하고 싶지는 않지만, 당신이 정당치 못하다고 생각합니다. 현대 미술가들은 전통적인 미술가들 보담 다른 각도로 작품을 대하는것 같애요.

Joan : 당신은 이 괴상한 그림들이 무언가 진지한 뜻이 있다는 말씀입니까? 아이들이라도 저 보다는 낫게 그릴 수 있을거에요.

Fred : 더 이상 그 문제를 갖고 논해봤자 소용이 없을겁니다. 당신도 당신의 견해가 있고 나도 나대로의 견해가 있으니까요.

Joan : 모든 일엔 양 면이 있기 마련이지만 이 경우는, 오로지 일면 밖에 없는것 같읍니다.

Fred : 제말은, 현대 미술가들이 자기 주위의 세계에 대한 각자의 개인적 감성을 세상사람에게 알리고자 한다는 거죠.

Joan : 그렇다면, 미술가는 자신의 감정을 남에게 알리지 말아야 할거에요.

* 새로 나온 단어와 어귀 *

don't care for～＝don't like～ **conservative**「보수적인」 **get across**「세상사람에게 알리다」 **keep his things to himself**「세상 사람에게 알리지 않고 혼자만이 간직하다」

PARTICIPATION DRILLS

Drill 1

STUDENT A	STUDENT B
Doesn't he have *strange* ideas?	Not really. They don't seem so *strange* to me.

strange
funny
peculiar
bright
clever
practical

Drill 2

STUDENT A	STUDENT B
Don't you see my *point of view?*	Certainly. Of course, I see your *point of view*.

point of view
view
argument
problem
side of the argument

EXERCISES

The Complement of the Sentence

The **complement** of the sentence consists of a word or group of words occurring after the verb. Nouns, pronouns, prepositional phrases, included clauses, direct and indirect objects occur in complement position in the following sentences.

1. Complete the complement in the sentences below by selecting the appropriate **noun** or **noun form** from the list.

conflict	viewpoints	side
agreement	conservative's	argument

a. We do not agree. We have conflicting ______.

b. Our points of view are close together; we are more or less in ______.

c. The liberal's opinion did not agree with the ______.

d. I must know if you're on my ______.

e. You are entitled to your opinion. I do not wish to start an ______.

f. If you agree with me, there is no reason for a ______.

2. Complete the following sentences by selecting the appropriate **pronoun** from the list.

theirs	mine	our	my
ours	his	their	your
yours	hers	her	

a. You have your opinion, and they have ______.

b. The speaker had his point of view, and I had ______.

c. Just as you have a right to your ideas, we have a right to ______.

d. I presented my beliefs, and he presented ______.

e. If you'll think about my viewpoint, I'll consider ______.

f. The man and woman were able to settle their quarrel, but his views were different from ______.

g. We are entitled to ______ own opinions.

h. They finally resolved ______ differences.

i. She presented ______ point of view.

j. I have ______ own ideas.

k. You've already presented ______ view, haven't you?

3. Complete each of the following sentences with an **included clause** (question word + noun or pronoun + verb) as shown in the example. Be sure to use the correct word order.

Example: Where is the English book?
I'm not sure *where the English book is.*

a. What is John's point of view? I learned ______.

b. Why are they arguing? I don't understand ______.

c. How many answers are there to this question? I can't say ______.

d. What point are you trying to prove? Please explain ______.

e. What is the discussion all about? I would like to know ______.

f. How long has this conflict been going on? I can't imagine ______.

g. Who is the speaker? Please tell me ______.

h. Why is he so narrow-minded? I've found out ______.

i. What is a radical? I don't know ______.

j. What did the speaker say about revolution? Please repeat ______.

4. Include the **indirect object** in parentheses in each of the statements below as shown in the examples. (With verbs such as "give", "tell", "ask", the indirect object occurs immediately after the verb. With other verbs, "to", or "with" precede the indirect object and the entire phrase is placed at the end of the sentence.)

Example: The teacher asked a question. (*the student*)
The teacher asked *the student* a question.

The teacher debated the question. (*him*)
The teacher debated the question *with him.*

The teacher repeated the sentence. (*them*)
The teacher repeated the sentence *to them.*

a. He explained his point of view. (*me*)

b. I'm going to ask for some practical arguments. (*him*)

c. I asked for his opinion. (*my opponent*)
d. The teacher told about the revolution in ideas. (*us*)
e. I talked over our differences. (*him*)
f. He tried to put his peculiar viewpoint across. (*me*)
g. The conservative student debated the question. (*the liberal*)
h. The teacher gave alternative answers to the question. (*him*)
i. The speaker couldn't give answers to our questions. (*us*)
j. I asked for proof of his strange statements. (*my opponent*)

WORD LIST

alike
alternatives
apart
argument
belief
bright
childish
clever
close
conflict
conflicting
conservative
debate
discussion
everything
fair
fight
for
further
impractical
liberal
narrow-minded
opponent
opposing
opposite
point
quarrel
radical
revolution
right
riot
selfish
stubborn
unfair
viewpoint
widely

Verb Forms

approach
conceive (of)
debate
deserve
disagree (with)
discuss
forgive, forgave (*p.*), forgiven (*p. part.*)
get across
mean to
present
prove, proved (*p. and p. part.*)
put across
reconcile
resolve
settle
view
visualize

Expressions

after all
be entitled to
in agreement
more or less
point of view
see a point in

Supplementary Word List
(Conversation and Reading Practice)

artist
citizen
painting

UNIT 5 THINKING ABOUT POSSIBLE FUTURE ACTIVITIES

661 **If it doesn't rain tomorrow, I think I'll go shopping.**

662 **There's a possibility we'll go, but it all depends on the weather.**

663 **If I have time tomorrow, I think I'll get a haircut.**

664 **I hope I remember to ask the barber not to cut my hair too short.**

665 **My son wants to be a policeman when he grows up.**

666 **If I get my work finished in time, I'll leave for New York Monday.**

667 **Suppose you couldn't go on the trip. How would you feel?**

668 **What would you say if I told you I couldn't go with you?**

669 **If I buy that car, I'll have to borrow some money.**

670 **If I went with you, I'd have to be back by six o'clock.**

671 **One of these days, I'd like to take a vacation.**

672 **As soon as I can, I'm going to change jobs.**

673 **There's a chance he won't be able to be home for Christmas.**

674 **We may be able to help you in some way.**

675 **If you were to attend the banquet, what would you wear?**

UNIT 5 THINKING ABOUT POSSIBLE FUTURE ACTIVITIES

661. 내일 비가 안 오면, 장보러 갈 생각입니다.
662. 우리들이 가게 될 가능성은 있으나 모든 것은 날씨에 달려 있읍니다.
663. 내일 시간이 나면, 나는 이발을 할 생각입니다.
664. 나는 내 머리를 너무 짧게 깍지 않도록 잊지 말고 이발사에게 부탁하게 되길 바랍니다.
665. 내 아들은 커서, 경찰관이 되기를 원하고 있읍니다.
666. 예정대로 일을 끝내면, 월요일에 뉴욕으로 떠나려고 합니다.
667. 당신이 여행을 떠날 수 없다고 상상해 보세요. 그러면 당신의 기분은 어떨까요?
668. 만일 내가 당신과 동행할 수 없다고 당신에게 말한다면 당신은 뭐라고 말씀하시겠읍니까?
669. 만일 내가 저 차를 산다면, 돈을 좀 빌려야겠읍니다.
670. 만일 당신과 동행한다면, 나는 6시까지는 돌아와야합니다.
671. 금일 중으로 휴가를 얻고 싶읍니다.
672. 가급적 빨리 직장을 옮기고 싶읍니다.
673. 그는 크리스마스 때 집에 오지 못할 가능성도 있읍니다.
674. 우리들은 어떻게 해서든지 당신을 도와줄 수가 있을런지 모르겠읍니다.
675. 당신이 연회에 참석하게 된다면 어떤 옷을 입겠읍니까?

*** 새로 나온 단어와 어귀 ***

possibility「가능성」 **depend on～**「～에 좌우되다」 **get a haircut**「이발하다」 **barber**「이발사」 **not to cut～**「～깍지 말도록」 **cut～ too short**「너무나 짧게 깍다」 **grow up**「성인이 되다」 **in time**「조만간, 알맞게」**leave for～**「～로 향해서 떠나다」 **suppose**「생각하다, 상상하다」 **go on the trip**「여행을 가다」 **borrow**「빌리다」 **be back**=come back **take a vacation**「휴가를 얻다」 **chance**「가능성, 기회」 **be able to**=can **attend**「참석하다」 **banquet**「연회」

문 법

661 If it doesn't rain tomorrow, I think I'll go shopping. :

If you *wish*, I *will help* you.

If you *are* honest, you *are loved* by every body.

이 두가지 문장의 경우와 같이 If~절에 현재형 동사, 본문에는 내용에 따라 현재동사나 미래조동사를 써서, 미래 또는 현재에 대한 불확실한 가정을 나타낸다. 뜻은 「만일(if)…한다면, ~할텐데 (혹은 ~하다)」로 번역한다.

If it *doesn't rain* tomorrow, I think I'*ll go* to the market.
(만일 내일 비가 안오면 장보러 갈 생각이다)

If I *have* time tomorrow, I think I'*ll go* to the barbershop.
(내일 시간이 있으면, 이발소에 갈 생각이다)

If I *buy* that car, I'*ll have to pay* for it over 36 months.
(내가 그 차를 사면 36개월 이상 그 차 값을 치루어야할 것이다)

662. There's a possibility we'll go, ~ : we'll go와 a possibility가 동격관계를 이루어 「우리가 가게 될 가능성」이라 번역한다. 673번의 There's a chance he won't be able to~ 「그가 ~할 수 없게 될 가능성(혹은, 기회)」도 마찬가지 경우이다.

There's *a possibility* we'll buy that car.
(우리가 그 차를 사게 될 가능성이 있다)

There's *a chance* he will be able to help you.
(그가 너를 도울 수 있는 가능성도 있다)

666. If I get my work finished in time, ~ : get my work finished는 「일을 끝내다」란 구어적인 표현이다.

Where can I *get* this *printed*? (어디서 이것을 인쇄할 수 있을까?)

667. Suppose you couldn't go on the trip. : suppose는 「…라 상상해 보라」 혹은 「…라 친다면」의 뜻으로 if와 같다. supposing도 같은 뜻이다. 그러나 suppose가 일단 문장을 끊고 다시 본문을 계속하지만, supposing은 if ~를 쓸 때와 같이 문장은 comma로 계속된다.

Suppose we go for a walk.
(산보가는게 어때?)

Supposing it were true, what would happen?
(그것이 사실이라면 어떻게 될까?)

670. If I went~, I'd have~. :

675. If you were to attend~, what would you wear? : If~절에 과거동사(be동사의 경우 were),본문에「would(혹은 should, could, might)+동사」를 쓰면 「사실과는 반대되는 가정」을 나타낸다. 특히 「If~ were to동사」는 절대로 있을 수 없는 미래의 가정을 나타낸다.

If I *were* a bird, I *would fly* to you.
(내가 새라면 너에게 날아 갈텐데)

If I *had* money, I *could buy* the car.
(나에게 돈이 있다면, 그 차를 살 수 있을텐데)

If the sun *were to rise* in the west, I *would* not *change* my mind.
(태양이 서쪽에서 뜨더라도 나는 마음을 변치 않겠다) 현실적으로는 나는 새도 아니고, 돈도 없고, 태양이 서쪽에서 뜰 수도 없다.

INTONATION

661 If it doesn't rain tomorrow, I think I'll go shopping.

662 There's a possibility we'll go, but it all depends on the weather.

663 If I have time tomorrow, I think I'll get a haircut.

664 I hope I remember to ask the barber not to cut my hair too short.

665 My son wants to be a policeman when he grows up.

666 If I get my work finished in time, I'll leave for New York Monday.

667 Suppose you couldn't go on the trip. How would you feel?

668 What would you say if I told you I couldn't go with you?

669 If I buy that car, I'll have to borrow some money.

670 If I went with you, I'd have to be back by six o'clock.

671 One of these days, I'd like to take a vacation.

672 As soon as I can, I'm going to change jobs.

673 There's a chance he won't be able to be home for Christmas.

674 We may be able to help you in some way.

675 If you were to attend the banquet, what would you wear?

VERB STUDY

1. **depend (on)**
   - *a.* It all depends on the weather.
   - *b.* You can depend on me to help you.
   - *c.* He's depending on me to show him the house this afternoon.

2. **remember**
   - *a.* I hope I remember to go to the barbershop.
   - *b.* I remembered it just in time.
   - *c.* Does he remember where he put the book?
   - *d.* He remembers my name, but he doesn't really know me.

3. **cut**
   - *a.* I hope the barber doesn't cut my hair too short.
   - *b.* The barber cut my hair too short the last time.
   - *c.* My brother likes the way the barber cuts his hair.

4. **suppose, assume**
   - *a.* Supposing the weather was bad, where would you go?
   - *b.* Suppose you couldn't go on the trip. How would you feel?
   - *c.* He assumed I wasn't going on the trip.
   - *d.* He's assuming he can make monthly payments on his new car.

5. **borrow**
   - *a.* If I buy that car, I'll have to borrow some money.
   - *b.* She often borrows money from her brother.
   - *c.* I've borrowed money from you several times, haven't I?
   - *d.* I'm borrowing this book for a few days, if you don't mind.

6. **change (jobs)**
   - *a.* As soon as I can, I'm going to change jobs.
   - *b.* He changes jobs every two or three months.
   - *c.* Mr. Green changed jobs a month ago.

7. **attend**
   - *a.* If you were to attend the banquet, what would you wear?
   - *b.* He always attends the weekly meetings.
   - *c.* I've attended most of the meetings.
   - *d.* Why don't you plan to attend the banquet with me?

VERB STUDY

1. **depend** (**on**) (…에 좌우되다, …에 의존하다, …에 부탁하다)
   a. 모든 것은 날씨에 달려 있다.
   b. 당신을 돕는 건, 나에게 달려있다.
   c. 오늘 오후 그 집을 안내해 달라고, 그는 내게 부탁하고 있다.
2. **remember** (기억하다, 잊지 않고 …하다)
   a. 나는 잊지 않고 이발소에 갈 수 있으면 한다.
   b. 나는 마침 알맞은 때에 그것을 생각해 냈다.
   c. 그는 책을 어디에 놓아 두었는지 기억하고 있느냐?
   d. 그는 내 이름을 기억하고 있으나, 실제로 나를 알지는 못한다.
3. **cut** (자르다, 깎다)
   a. 이발사가 내 머리를 너무 짧게 깎지 않기를 바란다.
   b. 지난 번에 이발사가 내 머리를 너무 짧게 깎았다.
   c. 내 동생은 이발사가 그의 머리를 깎는 방식을 좋아한다.
4. **suppose, assume** (상상하다, 가정하다)
   a. 만일 날씨가 나빴다고 가정한다면 당신은 어디에 갔을까?
   b. 만일 당신이 여행을 할 수 없다고 가정한다면, 당신의 기분은 어떨까요?
   c. 내가 여행을 떠나지 않을 것으로 그는 생각했다.
   d. 그는 그의 새 차에 대해 월부로 지불할 생각이다.
5. **borrow** (빌리다)
   a. 만일 저 차를 산다면, 나는 얼마간의 돈을 빌려야 할 것이다.
   b. 그녀는 종종 오빠에게서 돈을 빌리곤 한다.
   c. 나는 몇 번 너에게서 돈을 빌렸었지, 안 그랬니?
   d. 당신이 괜찮다면, 이 책을 몇일 동안 빌려야겠다.
6. **change** (**jobs**) (직장을 옮기다)
   a. 가급적 빨리 직장을 옮기고자 한다.
   b. 그는 2, 3개월 마다 직장을 옮긴다.
   c. 그리인 씨는 한달 전에 직장을 옮겼다.
7. **attend** (참석하다, 참가하다)
   a. 만일 연회에 참석하신다면, 당신은 어떤 옷을 입으시겠읍니까?
   b. 매주 있는 회합에 그는 항상 참석한다.
   c. 나는 그 회합에 대개 다 참석해 왔다.
   d. 왜 당신은 나와 함께 연회에 참석하지 않으려고 합니까?

*** 새로 나온 단어와 어귀 ***

the last time 「지난 번」
the way~ 「~하는 방식」
weekly meetings 「주 1 회의 회합」

SUBSTITUTION DRILLS

1. If it doesn't rain tomorrow, I think I'll

go shopping
run some errands
go to the market
attend the club meeting

2. There's a possibility we'll go, but it all depends on

the weather
how we feel
how much it'll cost

3. If I have time tomorrow, I think I'll

get a haircut
go to the barbershop
go get my hair cut
shampoo my hair
go to the beauty parlor
get my hair set

4. I hope I remember to ask the barber not to

cut my hair too short
give me a short haircut
put tonic on my hair

5. My son wants to be

a policeman
an electronic engineer
an astronaut
a physicist
a highway engineer
an architect

when he grows up.

6. If I get my work finished in time, I'll

leave
be off
depart
head

for New York Monday.

7.

Suppose
Supposing
Let's say
Assuming

you couldn't go on the trip. How would you feel?

8. | What would you say | if I told you I couldn't go with you?
 | How would you react |
 | What would be your reaction |
 | How would you feel |

9. If I buy that car, I'll have to | borrow some money
 | pay for it over 36 months
 | make monthly payments
 | use all my savings
 | get somebody to lend me money

10. If I went with you, I'd have to | be back by six o'clock
 | get my father's permission
 | take an overnight bag

11. One of these days, I'd like to | take a vacation
 | take a trip around the world
 | go off on a vacation
 | trade my old car in
 | get rid of my old car

12. As soon as I | can | , I'm going to change jobs.
 | am able to |
 | have an opportunity |
 | find it possible |

13. There's a chance he won't be able to | be home for Christmas
 | get any time off for the holidays
 | get leave in December
 | make it home at Christmastime

14. We may be able to | help you | in some way.
 | assist you |
 | aid you |
 | help you out |

15. If you were to attend the | banquet | , what would you wear?
 | formal dance |
 | reception |
 | ceremony |
 | wedding |

SUBSTITUTION DRILLS

1.
장보러 가다
심부름 가다
시장에 가다
클럽 회의에 참석하다

2.
날씨에
우리들의 기분여하에
비용에 다소에

3.
이발을 하다
이발소에 가다
머리를 깍게하다
머리를 감게하다
미장원에 가다
머리 손질을 하다

4.
너무 짧게 깍지
짧게 깍지
머리에 토닉을 바르지

5.
경찰
전기 기술자
우주 비행사
물리학자
고속도로 엔지니어
건축가

6.
떠나가다
출발하다
떠나다
향하다

7.
가정하자
상상하자
말하자
가정하자

8.
뭐라고 말하겠는가
어떠한 반응을 보이겠는가
당신의 반응은 어떻겠는가
당신의 기분은 어떻겠는가

9.
약간의 돈을 빌려야
36개월 이상 지불해야
월부로 지불해야
저축한 돈 전부를 써야
누구에게 돈을 빌려야

10.
6 시까지 돌아와야
아버지의 허락을 얻어야
여행용 가방을 휴대해야

11.
휴가를 얻다
세계 일주 여행을 하다
휴가를 떠나다
내 낡은 차를 교환하다
내 낡은 차를 처분하다

12.
가능한한
될 수 있는한
기회가 있는대로
가능성이 있는한

13.
크리스마스에 집에 있을
휴가기간 중에 어느때나 쉴 수 있는
12월에 출발할
크리스마스에 편히 쉴

14.
당신을 도웁다
협조하다
원조하다
당신을 구해 주다

15.
연회
당신
환영회
식
결혼식

READING

Thinking About Future Activities

There are some people who just can't make up their minds by themselves. They frequently ask the advice of their friends and then do the opposite of what their friends have suggested.

My brother Tom is such a person. He can never decide what to do, and is always asking my opinion. I try to help him as well as I can, but he never takes my advice. Yesterday I answered his question in a different way.

"Look," he said, showing me a letter. "What do you think I ought to do?"

The letter was an offer of a job. It seemed to be an excellent opportunity for a young engineer. Tom would be sent to Africa to work. The job would pay very well, and he would be able to travel and visit many interesting places.

"What do you think, Bill?" he asked. "Should I go? If I were to accept the job, I'd have to stay in Africa for two years. I might have to stay longer. But it would be wonderful experience for me. What should I do?"

"Don't go," I told him. "You'd be very unhappy."

"Don't go?" he looked very surprised at my answer.

As you've probably guessed, Tom accepted the offer. I don't know if it has occurred to him that I actually wanted him to take the job.

Questions

1. What do some people do when they can't make up their minds?
2. What was in the letter that Tom showed to Bill?
3. Where would Tom be sent?
4. What did Bill advise Tom to do?
5. Why did Bill tell Tom *not* to take the job?
6. Do you think Bill did the right thing?

READING

(장래에 있을 활동에 관한 생각)

스스로 결정하지 못하는 사람들이 있읍니다. 그들은 종종 친구들에게 조언을 부탁하고 그리고 나선 친구들이 제의한 것과는 정 반대의 행동을 합니다.

내 동생, 톰 역시 이런 사람입니다. 그는 어떻게 해야 할지 전혀 결정을 못하고, 언제나 내 의견을 묻읍니다. 가능한 한 나는 그를 도와주려고 하지만 그는 내 조언을 전혀 받아들이지 않읍니다. 어제 나는 그의 질문에 대해 전혀 다르게 대답해 주었읍니다.

"자, 이거 봐요" 한 통의 편지를 내보이면서 그는 말했읍니다. "내가 어떻게 했으면 좋겠죠?"

그 편지는 직장을 제의하는 것이었읍니다. 젊은 엔지니어에게는 썩 좋은 기회가 될 것으로 보였읍니다. 톰은 일하러 아프리카로 파견되는 것입니다. 그 직장은 보수도 아주 좋으며 재미있는 여러 곳을 찾아다니며 여행할 수도 있읍니다.

"어떻게 생각하세요, 빌?" 그가 물었읍니다. "가도 괜찮을까요? 만일 그 직장을 받아들인 다면 나는 2년 동안 아프리카에 체류하여야 할거예요. 그 이상 체류해야 할런지도 모르구요. 그러나 나에게는 정말 멋진 경험이 될 거에요. 어떻게 했으면 좋을까요?"

"가지 말아라" 나는 그에게 말했읍니다.

"아주 좋지 않을 것 같다"

"가지 말아요?" 내 대답을 듣고 그는 몹시 놀란듯 했읍니다. 짐작 한 대로, 톰은 그 제안을 받아 드렸읍니다. 사실은 그가 그 직업을 택하기를 내가 원하고 있다는 생각이 그에게 떠올랐는지도 모릅니다.

*** 새로 나온 단어와 어귀 ***

by themselves「스스로의 힘으로」 **ask~ of…**「‥에게 ~을 청하다」 **opposite**「반대」 **in a different way**「다르게」 **occur to him that~**「~라는 생각이 그에게 떠오르다」

CONVERSATION

Thinking About Possible Future Activities

Dialog 1

DAVE: Would you like to go to the movies with me tonight, Jean?

JEAN: Thanks, Dave. I'd like to go very much, but there's a possibility I'll have to work at the library.

DAVE: How soon will you know?

JEAN: I should know this afternoon. Why don't you call me up later?

DAVE: All right. If you finish your work early, perhaps we can still go somewhere tonight.

JEAN: Fine. Suppose I don't get finished in time. Would you be able to go tomorrow night?

DAVE: Sure, I can go tomorrow night, too.

Dialog 2

CHUCK: Will you be going home for Christmas this year, Nancy?

NANCY: I want to go, but I don't know if I'll have enough money by then.

CHUCK: You live in Portland, Oregon, don't you?

NANCY: That's right. And the plane fare is very expensive.

CHUCK: Why don't you go by train? It would be cheaper than the plane.

NANCY: Yes, but I don't care for trains very much.

CHUCK: How about the bus? That's not very expensive, either.

NANCY: I'm never comfortable on a bus, and it takes such a long time.

CHUCK: Well, you can do one of two things, then. Either start saving your money for the plane fare, or start walking now.

CONVERSATION

(장래에 있을 활동에 관한 생각)

대 화 1

Dave : 오늘 저녁에 나와 함께 영화보러 가지 않으시렵니까?

Jean : 감사합니다. 데이브. 굉장히 가고 싶긴 하지만, 도서관에서 일해야 하게 될지 모르겠어요.

Dave : 언제 알 수 있을까요?

Jean : 오늘 오후에는 알 수 있을거에요. 나중에 전화해 주세요.

Dave : 알겠읍니다. 당신의 일이 일찌기 끝나면, 우리는 오늘 저녁에 어디엔가 갈 수도 있을 겁니다.

Jean : 좋읍니다. 내가 제시간에 끝내지 못한다고 합시다. 당신은 내일 저녁에 갈 수 있지 않읍니까?

Dave : 물론이죠, 내일 저녁에라도 갈 수 있읍니다.

대 화 2

Chuck : 금년 크리스마스 때 당신은 집에 갈 작정입니까? 낸시?

Nancy : 가고 싶지만. 그때쯤 나에게 충분한 돈이 있을지 모르겠군요.

Chuck : 당신은 오리곤 주 포오틀란드 시에 살고 있죠, 그렇지 않은가요?

Nancy : 맞읍니다. 비행기표 값이 굉장히 비쌉니다.

Chuck : 기차로 가시죠. 비행기보다 쌀 텐데요.

Nancy : 그렇지요. 그러나 나는 기차를 그렇게 좋아하지 않읍니다.

Chuck : 버스는 어떻게 생각하시는지요? 그것 역시 그렇게 비싸지 않읍니다.

Nancy : 버스는 아주 불편하고 너무 시간이 많이 걸려요.

Chuck : 그렇다면 당신은 두 가지 중 하나를 택할 수 있읍니다. 비행기표 값을 위한 돈을 저축하든가 지금부터 걸어서 출발하든가 입니다.

*** 새로 나온 단어와 어귀 ***

why don't you~ 「~해 보세요」 **plane fare** 「비행기 표값」

PARTICIPATION DRILLS

Drill 1

STUDENT A	STUDENT B
What do you plan to do *this afternoon?*	If it doesn't rain, I think I'll *go shopping.*

this afternoon	go shopping
in the morning	get a haircut
tonight	go for a walk
at 2 o'clock	play tennis
after we eat	run some errands

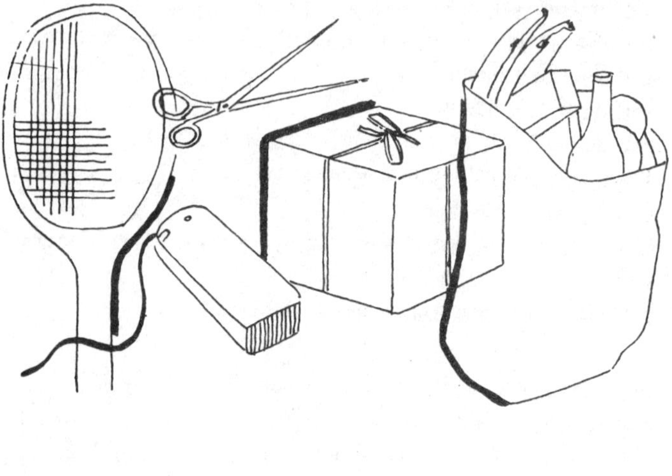

Drill 2

STUDENT A	STUDENT B
Do you think you'll go *shopping?*	There's a possibility we'll go, but it all depends on *the weather.*

shopping	the weather
to San Francisco	how much it'll cost
to the meeting	how I feel
to the bank	what my wife says
to the dance	whether I'm asked

EXERCISES

Verbs and Modifiers of Verbs (1)

Time Expressions: all the time, every day, on Sundays, at night, every year, every month, later, in 1954

past time: last week, a year ago, yesterday, the day before yesterday, last night

future time: next year, tomorrow, next week, in the near future, someday, one of these days

1. Complete the following sentences by selecting the most appropriate time expression.

   Example: I went to class *yesterday.* (*tomorrow, yesterday, every day*)

   a. I think I'll attend the club meeting ______. (*every day, last week, tomorrow*)

   b. Did you wear formal clothes to the banquet ______? (*last night, all the time, later*)

   c. Does he come home for Christmas ______? (*in 1954, every year, next year*)

   d. I think I'll change jobs ______. (*a year ago, one of these days, on Sundays*)

   e. We're going to take a trip around the world ______. (*on Sundays, the day before yesterday, someday*)

   f. I have to borrow some money ______. (*yesterday, in 1954, every month*)

   g. An astronaut will go to the moon ______. (*the day before yesterday, in the near future, all the time*)

   h. I went to the beauty parlor to get my hair set ______ (*the day before yesterday, later, every day*)

   f. I take a vacation ______. (*every year, last year, next year*)

2. Include the time expression in parentheses in each sentence, as shown in the example. Be sure to use the correct form of the verb.

   Example: I go to class every day. (*tomorrow*)
   I will go to class tomorrow.

   a. Highway engineers are building this road. (*last year*)

   b. An architect designed my house. (*next year*)

   c. I went shopping last Saturday. (*every Saturday*)

   d. Do you buy a new car every year? (*a year ago*)

   e. I got somebody to lend me money. (*tomorrow*)

   f. The teacher helped the student out with his problem. (*next week*)

   g. I am trying to get my father's permission to travel. (*yesterday*)

   h. Can you get rid of your old car? (*last year*)

3. Complete the following sentences describing past activities by selecting the appropriate time expression. Follow the example.

   Example: Has the class begun *already?* (*already, yesterday*)

   a. Did you attend the reception ______? (*last week, many times*)

   b. The teacher has assisted me ______. (*many times, yesterday*)

   c. I've ______ changed jobs. (*already, last week*)

   d. I took my vacation ______. (*since, last summer*)

   e. I've made monthly payments ______. (*since 1960, last week*)

   f. I used all my savings to pay for my car ______. (*never, last month*)

   g. I went to the barbershop ______. (*just, last night*)

   h. I've ______ put tonic on my hair. (*never, yesterday*)

4. Use the correct form of the verb in parentheses. Use the past form of the verb with time expressions such as "last week", "a week ago", etc. Use "have" + past participle with the adverbs "never", "already", and time expressions such as "since 1957", "for many years".

Examples: Our instructor *explained* that lesson to us last time. (*explain*)
Our instructor *has already explained* that lesson to us. (*already, explain*)

a. I ______ to the market. (*already, go*)

b. The barber ______ my hair too short last Saturday. (*cut*)

c. The physicist ______ physics since 1957. (*study*)

d. I ______ an overnight bag when I ______ to San Francisco last weekend. (*take*), (*go*)

e. He ______ it impossible to change jobs a year ago. (*find*)

f. The young girl ______ a wedding reception. (*never, attend*)

g. The businessmen ______ an annual banquet for many years. (*hold*)

h. I ______ to trade my old car in yesterday, but nobody ______ it. (*try*), (*want*)

i. I ______ to the beauty parlor. (*never, be*)

j. I ______ shopping last night. (*go*)

5. Insert the time expressions in parentheses in the correct position in the sentence. Follow the examples.

Examples: The professor has *just* explained the lesson. (*just*)
The professor has been teaching *since 1950*. (*since 1950*)

a. I need a haircut because I haven't been to the barber. (*recently*)

b. I've had my vacation. (*already*)

c. I haven't changed jobs. (*for years*)

d. He left for San Francisco. (*just*)

e. I haven't borrowed any money. (*ever*)

f. I've made monthly payments. (*never*)

g. I haven't taken a trip around the world. (*yet*)

h. I haven't been home for Christmas. (*since 1960*)

i. I haven't been to New York. (*for a long time*)

j. I've been to Washington. (*many times*)

WORD LIST

architect
astronaut
bag
banquet
barber
barbershop
beauty parlor
ceremony
Christmas
Christmastime
club
dance
electronic
formal
haircut
help
highway
market
monthly
opportunity
overnight
permission
physicist
policeman
reaction
reception
savings
tonic
vacation

Verb Forms

aid
assist
attend
be back
be off (for)
borrow
depart
depend (on)
go off (on)
head (for)
help out
lend, lent (*p. and p. part.*)
run, ran (*p.*), run (*p. part.*)
shampoo
trade in

Expressions

get finished
get (one's) hair cut
get (one's) hair set
get leave
get rid of
get time off
make payments
run errands

Supplementary Word List
(Conversation and Reading Practice)

comfortable
offer
roommate
save

UNIT 6 TALKING ABOUT PAST POSSIBILITIES

676 **What would you have done last night if you hadn't had to study?**

677 **I would have gone on the picnic if it hadn't rained.**

678 **If you had gotten up earlier, you would have had time for breakfast.**

679 **If I had had time, I would have called you.**

680 **Would he have seen you if you hadn't waved to him?**

681 **If he had only had enough money, he would have bought that house.**

682 **I wish you had called me back the next day, as I had asked you to.**

683 **If you hadn't slipped and fallen, you wouldn't have broken your leg.**

684 **If I had known you wanted to go, I would have called you.**

685 **Had I known you didn't have a key, I wouldn't have locked the door.**

686 **She would have gone with me, but she didn't have time.**

687 **If I had asked for directions, I wouldn't have gotten lost.**

688 **Even if we could have taken a vacation, we might not have wanted to.**

689 **Everything would have been all right if you hadn't said that.**

690 **Looking back on it, I wish we hadn't given in so easily.**

UNIT 6 TALKING ABOUT PAST POSSIBILITIES

676. 어젯밤 당신이 공부할 필요가 없었다면 무얼 했겠읍니까?
777. 비가 오지 않았더라면 피크닉을 갔었을 것입니다.
678. 좀 더 일찍 일어났더라면 아침 식사를 할 시간이 있었을 거예요.
679. 시간이 있었더라면, 당신에게 전화 했을텐데.
680. 당신이 그에게 손짓을 안했던들 그가 당신을 보았을까요?
681. 그에게 돈만 많이 있었더라면, 그는 그 집을 샀을겁니다.
682. 내가 부탁한대로 다음날 나에게 전화를 다시 해 주었더라면 좋았을 걸.
683. 당신이 미끄러져 넘어지지 않았더라면, 다리를 다치지 않았을 텐데.
684. 당신이 가고 싶다는 걸 알았더라면 나는 당신에게 전화해 주었을 텐데.
685. 당신에게 열쇠가 없었다는 것을 알았더라면, 문을 잠그지 않았을 텐데.
686. 그녀에게 시간이 없지 않았다면 그녀는 나와 동행했을 것이다.
687. 내가 방향을 물었더라면, 길을 잃지는 않았을 텐데.
688. 휴가를 얻을 수 있었다 하더라도 우린 원치 않았을 것입니다.
689. 당선이 그 말만 안 했어도, 만사는 잘 되었을 겁니다.
690. 돌이켜 보면, 그처럼 쉽게 양보하지 않았어야 하는 건데.

*** 새로 나온 단어와 어귀 ***

go on a picnic「피크닉 가다」 **wave**「손짓하다」 **slip**「미끄러지다」 **key**「열쇠」 **lock**「잠그다」 **ask for direction**「방향을 묻다」 **get lost**「길을 잃다」 **look back on**「회고하다, 돌이켜 보다」 **give in**「지다, 양보하다」

문 법

676. What would you have done last night if you hadn't had to study? : if~절에 「had+과거분사」 본문에 「would (혹은 should, could, might) +have +과거분사」를 쓰면 「과거의 사실에 반대되는 가정」을 나타내어 「만일 …였더라면, ~했을 텐데」라고 번역한다.

「If~ 과거동사, ~would+동사」가 「현재 사실의 반대의 가정」임에 비추어 「If~had+과거분사, ~ would+have+과거분사」는 「과거 사실의 반대의 가정」을 나타내는 것이다.

What *would* you *have done* last night if you *hadn't had to stay* home?
(어젯밤 당신이 꼭 집에 있어야 되는 것이 아니었다면, 무얼 했겠읍니까?)

I *would have gone* on the picnic if I *had known* about it.
(내가 그것에 대해서 알았더라면 나는 피크닉을 갔을 것이다)

If you *had* not *slept* so late, you *would have had* time for breakfast.
(네가 그렇게 늦잠을 자지 않았더라면, 아침 먹을 시간이 있었을 텐데.

681. If he had only had enough money, ~: only는 「…만 했더라면」으로서 가정의 뜻을 더 강조하고 있다.

If you had *only* slept early. (네가 일찍 잠만 잤어도)

682. I wish you had called me back the next day~. : I wish~도 가정법 동사를 거느린다. 따라서 I wish 다음에 과거동사가 오면 「현재 사실의 반대의 가정」으로 「…라면 좋을텐데」의 뜻이고, I wish다음에 「had+과거분사」가 오면 「과거 사실의 반대의 가정」으로 「…였더라면 좋았을 걸」이라고 번역된다.

I wish I *were* a bird. (새라면 좋겠다)

I wish I *had been* a bird. (새였더라면 좋았을 걸)

I wish I *took* my vacation this summer.
(금년 여름 휴가를 갈 수 있으면 좋겠는데)

I wish I *had taken* my vacation last summer.
(작년에 휴가를 갈 수 있었더라면 좋았겠는데)

685. Had I known you didn't have a key~. : If I had known~에서 if를 생략하면, Had I known~이 된다.

686. She would have gone with me, but she didn't have time. : but she didn't have time. 의 but~는 if not의 뜻이다. 특히 but가 if not를 대신할 경우 동사의 시제는 가정법 시제를 취하지 않고 원래의 시제를 취한다. 따라서 *but she didn't have time*=if she had had time. 의 뜻이다.

If you hadn't had to stay home=*but you had to stay home.*
(네가 꼭 집에 있어야 되는 것이 아니었다면)

If I had known about it=*but I did not know about it.*
내가 그것에 대해 알았더라면)

INTONATION

676 What would you have done last night if you hadn't had to study?

677 I would have gone on the picnic if it hadn't rained.

678 If you had gotten up earlier, you would have had time for breakfast.

679 If I had had time, I would have called you.

680 Would he have seen you if you hadn't waved to him?

681 If he had only had enough money, he would have bought that house.

682 I wish you had called me back the next day, as I had asked you to.

683 If you hadn't slipped and fallen, you wouldn't have broken your leg.

684 If I had known you wanted to go, I would have called you.

685 Had I known you didn't have a key, I wouldn't have locked the door.

686 She would have gone with me, but she didn't have time.

687 If I had asked for directions, I wouldn't have gotten lost.

688 Even if we could have taken a vacation, we might not have wanted to.

689 Everything would have been all right if you hadn't said that.

690 Looking back on it, I wish we hadn't given in so easily.

VERB STUDY

1. wave

a. Would he have seen you if you hadn't waved to him?
b. I waved good-bye to her at the airport.
c. Who is that man over there? He's waving to us.
d. My little daughter always waves to people when they wave to her.
e. Who are you waving to?

2. give in

a. Looking back on it, I wish we hadn't given in so easily.
b. Why don't you give in?
c. My son wanted to go to the party, and I finally gave in and said 'yes'.
d. Did you finally give in and tell him he could go?
e. He usually gives in and takes me out to dinner when I want to go.

3. had had, had said, had known, had had to

a. If I had had time, I would have called you.
b. Had I had time, I would have called you.
c. Everything would have been all right if you hadn't said that.
d. If you had said you wanted to go, I would have waited for you.
e. If I had known you wanted to go, I would have gone by your house.
f. Had she known that I was going, she would have gone with me.
g. If you hadn't had to study, what would you have done last night?
h. If I had had to pay for the car, I would have had to borrow money.

4. would have had, would have bought, would have broken

a. You would have had time for breakfast if you had gotten up earlier.
b. Wouldn't you have had time to study if you had gotten up at 6 a.m.?
c. He would have bought that house, if he had only had enough money.
d. She wouldn't have bought that house even if she had had enough money.
e. If you hadn't fallen down, you wouldn't have broken your leg.
f. Would you have broken your arm if you hadn't slipped and fallen?

VERB STUDY

1. **wave** (손짓하다, 손을 흔들다)
   a. 네가 그에게 손짓을 하지 안했더라면 그가 너를 보았을까?
   b. 난 공항에서 그녀에게 작별인사로 손을 흔들었다.
   c. 저기 저 사람은 누구입니까? 우리에게 손짓하고 있군요.
   d. 내 어린 딸은 사람들이 손짓을 하면 항상 따라 손을 흔든다.
   e. 당신은 누구에게 손을 흔들고 있읍니까?
2. **give in** (굴복하다, 양보하다)
   a. 회고해 보면, 그처럼 쉽게 굴복하지 않았더라면 좋았을 걸.
   b. 넌 왜 굴복하지 않느냐?
   c. 아들이 파티에 가고 싶다고 해서 나는 결국 굴복해서 승락했다.
   d. 네가 결국 져서 그에게 가도 좋다고 말했는가?
   e. 내가 가고 싶다고 하면 언제나 그가 져서 날 데리고 외식하러 간다.
3. **had had, had said, had known, had had to**
   (가졌었더면, 말했더라면, 알았더라면, 해야만 했다면)
   a. 시간이 있었더라면, 네게 전화했을 것이다.
   b. 시간이 있었더라면, 네게 전화했을 것이다.
   c. 네가 그처럼 말하지 않았더라면 만사가 잘 되었을 것이다.
   d. 네가 가고 싶다고 말했더라면, 널 기다렸을 것이다.
   e. 네가 가고 싶다는 것을 알았더라면 네 집에 들렀을 것이다.
   f. 내가 간다는 걸 그녀가 알았더라면, 그녀는 나와 동행했을 것이다.
   g. 네가 공부할 필요가 없었더라면, 넌 어젯밤 무얼 했겠는가?
   h. 내가 그 값을 치루어야 했다면 난 돈을 빌려야 했을 것이다.
4. **would have had, would have bought, would have broken.**
   (…가졌을 것이다, 샀을 것이다, 부러뜨렸을 것이다)
   a. 네가 좀 더 일찍 일어났더라면, 아침 식사를 할 시간이 있었을 것이다.
   b. 네가 6시에 일어났더라면, 공부할 시간이 있지 않았을까?
   c. 그가 돈만 충분히 있었다면, 그 집을 샀을 것이다.
   d. 그녀가 돈이 충분히 있었다 할지라도 그 집은 안 샀을 것이다.
   e. 네가 넘어지지만 않았더라도 네 다리를 다치진 않았을 것이다.
   f. 네가 미끄러져 넘어지지 않았더라면 네 팔을 다쳤을까?

*** 새로 나온 단어와 어귀 ***

wave good-bye「작별인사로 손을 흔들다」
say 'yes'「승락하다」 **take me out to dinner**「데리고 나가 외식하다」
go by「들리다」

SUBSTITUTION DRILLS

1. What would you have done last night
 if you hadn't had to | study | ?
 | work
 | stay home
 | wash your hair
 | do your laundry
 | go to the banquet

2. I would have gone on the picnic if | it hadn't rained .
 | I had known about it
 | there had been time to get
 | ready
 | you had told me about it
 | earlier
 | I had realized you were
 | going

3. If you had | gotten up earlier | , you would have had time for
 | not slept so late | breakfast.
 | set your alarm
 | awakened in time
 | hurried up
 | gotten dressed faster

4. If I had had time, I would have | called you
 | gone on the picnic
 | run some errands for you
 | seen all my old friends
 | visited all the museums

5. Would he have seen you
 if you hadn't | waved | to him?
 | shouted
 | introduced yourself

6. If he had only had enough money, he would have
   - bought that house
   - made the trip
   - paid cash for the car
   - made a lump-sum payment

7. I wish you had
   - called me back
   - stayed in bed
   - gone on the trip
   - finished your work

   the next day, as I had asked you t

8. If you hadn't slipped and fallen,
   - you wouldn't have broken your leg
   - there wouldn't be any broken bones
   - you'd be all right now
   - you wouldn't have sprained your ankle

   .

9. If I had known you wanted to go, I would have
   - called
   - invited
   - included
   - asked

   you.

10. Had I known you didn't have
    - a key
    - time
    - any money
    - training
    - money

    , I wouldn't have
    - locked the door
    - bothered you
    - married you
    - hired you
    - sold you the car

    .

11. She would have gone with me,
    - but
    - except
    - except for the fact that
    - if it hadn't been that

    she didn't have time.

12. If I had asked for directions, I wouldn't have | gotten lost / lost my way / taken the wrong road / gone the wrong way | .

13. Even if we could have | taken a vacation / gone on the picnic / bought a new car / enrolled in a class / attended the banquet | , we might not have wanted to.

14. Everything would have been | all right / agreeable / acceptable / settled / resolved / perfect | if you hadn't said that.

15. | Looking back on it / Now that I think about it / Looking at it now / Come to think of it / Thinking it over carefully | , I wish we hadn't given in so easily.

16. | I took / I wish I had taken | my vacation last winter. | I went / I would have gone | to Florida.

17. | I can go / I wish I could go / I wish I could have gone | with you on the picnic. | We'll have / We would have / We would have had | a good time.

SUBSTITUTION DRILLS

1.
공부할
일 할
집에 있을
머리감을
세탁을 할
연회에 갈

2.
비가 오지 않았드라면
알았드라면
준비할 시간이 있었드라면
더 일찍 내게 얘기해 줬더라면
네가 간다는 것을 알았드라면

3.
일찍 일어 났더라면
그렇게 늦도록 잠자지 않았다면
자명종 시계를 맞췄드라면
제시간에 깼드라면
서둘렀더라면
옷을 빨리 입었드라면

4.
전화 했을 텐데
소풍을 갔을 텐데
네 심부름을 했을 텐데
옛 친구를 모두 만났을 걸
모든 박물관을 구경 했을 걸

5.
손짓 하지 않았으면
외치지 않았으면
너를 소개하지 않았으면

6.
집을 샀을 텐데
여행을 했을 텐데
차 값을 현금으로 지불 했을 텐데
일시불로 했을 텐데

7.
다시 전화하다
침대에 있다
여행을 가다
일을 끝마치다

8.
네 다리를 다치지 않았을 것이다
뼈를 부러트리지 않았을 것이다
지금은 다 나았을 것이다
발목을 삐지 않았을 것이다

9.
전화 했을 텐데
초대 했을 텐데
포함 했을 텐데
물었을 텐데

10.

열쇠	문을 잠그다
시간	널 괴롭히다
돈	너와 결혼하다
훈련	너를 채용하다
돈	너에게 차를 팔다

11.
허나
~이외에는
~는 사실 이외에는
그렇지 않았다면

12.
잃다
길을 잃다
길을 잘못 들다
딴 길로 가다

13.
휴가를 가다
피크닉을 가다
새 차를 사다
학급에 적을 두다
연회에 참석하다

14.
만사가 좋았을
합당했을
받아드릴만 했을
해결 됐을
풀렸을
완전했을

15.
도리 켜 보니
지금 생각 해 보니
도리 켜 보니
생각 해 보니
깊이 생각해 보니

16.

얻다	갔다
바라다	갔었으면 했다

17.
갈 수 있다
갈 수 있었으면 좋을텐데
갈 수 있었으면 좋았을 텐데

READING

Talking About Past Possibilities

The two girls sat drinking their coffee without talking. Finally, Judy asked, "What would you have done if this had happened to you?"

Betty drank some more coffee before she answered. "If this had happened to me, I'd have told Steve exactly what I thought of him. I wouldn't have been so nice to him."

"If I'd had enough time to think about it," Judy agreed, "I'd have given him an argument for causing me so much inconvenience."

They were discussing what had happened that morning. Steve had asked Judy to go to the school dance with him on Saturday night, and she had accepted. Now, it seemed, he wouldn't be able to go.

"He should have told me sooner," Judy said. "I might have been able to go with someone else. I wouldn't have had to stay home while everyone else went to the dance."

"You could have gone with Charles," Betty reminded her.

"Yes, but it's too late now," Judy said. "You'd think that when a boy had invited you to the biggest dance of the year, he'd have realized how important it was."

Betty agreed. "That's right. If he hadn't slipped and fallen, you wouldn't have this problem. He should have broken his leg some other time."

Questions

1. Why is Judy so unhappy?
2. What's the matter with Steve?
3. Do you think Judy should have given him an argument?
4. What would you have done if you had been Steve?
5. Why can't Judy go to the dance with someone else?

READING

(과거에 있을 뻔 했던 일에 관한 대화)

두 소녀는 말없이 커피를 마시며 앉아 있었읍니다. 마침내 쥬디는 "네게 이런 일이 생겼다면 넌 어떻게 했겠니?"하고 물었읍니다.

베티는 커피를 좀 더 마시고나서 대답했읍니다. "내게 그런 일이 생겼다면, 나는 스티브에게 그에 대한 내 생각이 어떠한가를 그대로 이야기 했을거야. 나 같으면 그에게 그렇게 잘해 주지는 않았을거야"

"나도 생각할 시간이 충분히 있었더라면 왜 내게 그런 불편을 주느냐고 따졌을 거야"하고 쥬디는 말했읍니다.

두 소녀는 그날 아침에 일어났던 사건을 이야기하고 있는 것입니다. 스티브가 쥬디에게 토요일 저녁 학교에서의 댄스 파티에 가자고 했고, 쥬디도 승락을 했던 것입니다. 그런데 스티브가 인제는 갈 수 없다는 것 같읍니다.

"그렇다면 그사람이 내게 빨리 알려주었어야 했든거야, 그렇다면 다른 사람 하구나 갔을 것 아니겠니. 모두들 댄스 파티에 가고 나만 집에 있을 수는 없잖아" 하고 쥬디는 말했읍니다.

"너 참 찰즈하고나 갈 걸 그랬다."하고 베티가 쥬디에게 말했읍니다.

"그럼, 그렇지만 너무 늦었어. 어떤 남자가 연중 가장 성대한 파아티에 너를 초대했다고 생각 해봐. 그 사람은 그 파티가 얼마나 중요한 것인 가를 알았을거야." 하고 쥬디가 말했읍니다.

"그렇지, 그 사람이 미끄러져 넘어 지지만 않았더라도 이런 일은 없었을 텐데 …. 다른 때나 다리를 다칠 것이지"하고 베티는 동의했읍니다.

＊ 새로 나온 단어와 어귀 ＊

cause me so much～「내게 많은 ～을 일으키다」 **inconvenience**「불편」
should have told me sooner「좀 더 일찍 나에게 알려 주었어야 했다」

CONVERSATION

Talking About Past Possibilities

STELLA: Don't worry about it, Stanley. There's nothing we can do now.

STANLEY: I can't help it, Stella. If I'd been thinking, this wouldn't have happened.

STELLA: We all make mistakes. I see no point in standing here talking about it.

STANLEY: If I hadn't gone on that trip, I wouldn't have forgotten about it.

STELLA: It's not really your fault. I didn't remember, either.

STANLEY: There's no excuse for it, Stella. I had known about it for several weeks.

STELLA: Well, it's too late to do anything now.

STANLEY: If we had written it down on the calendar, we wouldn't have made this mistake.

STELLA: We can do that next time, but it won't help us now. Let's go home.

STANLEY: I guess you're right. Next time I buy tickets for the theato I'll be sure to look at the date. Then we'll go on the rigl day instead of a day late.

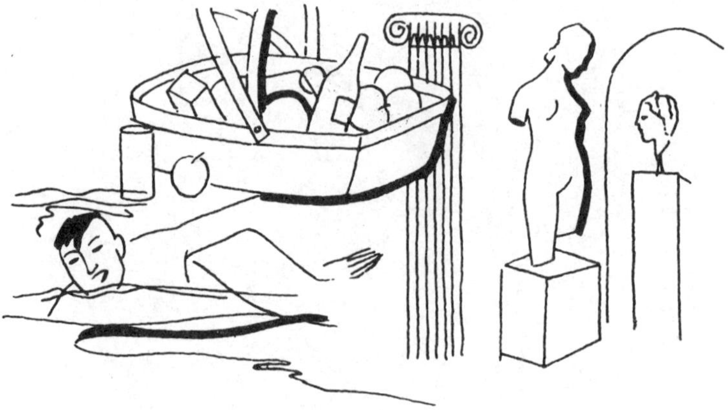

CONVERSATION
(과거에 있을뻔 했던 일에 관한 대화)

Stella : 걱정마세요, 스탠리. 인제는 어쩔 도리가 없잖아요.

Stanley : 어쩔 수 없군 그래, 스텔라. 내가 생각을 하고 있었더라면 이런 일이 없었을 텐데.

Stella : 우리 모두의 실수인 걸요. 여기 서서 떠들어 보아야 소용 없어요.

Stanley : 내가 여행만 안 갔더라면, 그걸 잊지 않았을 텐데.

Stella : 당신 잘못만은 아네요. 저도 잊었는 걸요.

Stanley : 변명 할게 없구먼 스텔라, 몇 주일 전에는 알고 있었는데.

Stella : 글쎄 인제는 늦은거니 어쩔 수 없어요.

Stanley : 달력에다 표시만 해 놨더라도, 실수는 저지르지 않았을 텐데.

Stella : 다음번엔 몰라도 이젠 어쩔 수 없잖아요. 어서 집에나 가십시다.

Stanley : 응, 당신 말이 옳아, 다음엔 극장표를 사면 날짜를 꼭 확인 할테야. 그러면 날짜를 늦지않고 옳바로 갈 수 있겠지.

* 새로 나온 단어와 어귀 *

I can't help it「어찌할 수가 없다」 **fault**「잘못, 실수」 **write down**「기록하다」 **calendar**「달력」

PARTICIPATION DRILLS

Drill 1

STUDENT A	STUDENT B
Why didn't you go *to the museum?*	How could I go? *I had to study.*

to the museum	I had to study.
on the picnic	It rained.
to the store	I had no money.
swimming	It was too cold.
to the laundry	I didn't have time.
to the movie last night	I was too sleepy.
to the banquet	I wasn't invited.
driving	There was too much traffic.

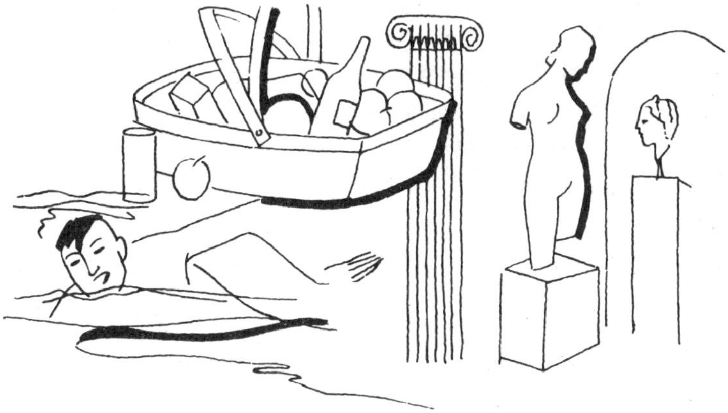

Drill 2

STUDENT A	STUDENT B
Wouldn't you have had time to *study?*	No, I wouldn't. I had to *do my laundry.*

study	do my laundry
go to the movie	wash my hair
make the trip	visit my mother
go to the store	go to the bank

EXERCISES

Verbs and Modifiers of Verbs (2)

1. Use the "had" + past participle construction in each sentence. Follow the example.

   Example: I knew that I *had read* that book before. (*read*)

   a. I heard that you ______ all the museums. (*visited*)

   b. I believed you ______ on the trip. (*go*)

   c. I knew I ______ late. (*sleep*)

   d. I was afraid I ______. (*get lost*)

   e. You said you ______ a new car. (*buy*)

   f. I remembered he ______ in my English class. (*enroll*)

2. Use the "had" + past participle construction in each sentence. Be sure to insert the adverbs "already", "never" in the correct position in the sentence. Follow the example.

   Example: By the time we got to the class, it *had already begun.* (*already, begin*)

   a. By the time we arrived at the picnic, it ______ to rain. (*already, start*)

   b. He couldn't buy the car until he ______ the money. (*borrow*)

   c. When I asked for directions, I ______ my way. (*lose*)

   d. Before you introduced us, we ______. (*never, meet*)

   e. I returned home after I ______ all my old friends. (*see*)

3. Use the base form or the "-s" form of the verb in each of the following sentences denoting a possible future action. Follow the example.

   Example: I will study tonight if I *have* time. (*have*)

   a. I will go on the picnic if there ______ time to get ready. (*be*)

   b. If she ______ enough money, she will pay cash for the car. (*have*)

   c. If I ______ my key, I won't be able to lock the door. (*lose*)

   d. He won't get lost if he ______ for directions. (*ask*)

   e. If they ______ an alarm clock, they will get up on time. (*use*)

4. Use the past form of the verb to indicate a future action which is not certain, improbable, or not true. Follow the example.

   Example: If I *had* a million dollars, I would travel around the world. (*have*)

   a. I would go on the picnic if there ______ time to get ready. (*be*)

   b. If she ______ enough money, she would pay cash for the car. (*have*)

   c. If I ______ my key, I wouldn't be able to lock the door. (*lose*)

   d. He wouldn't get lost if he ______ for directions. (*ask*)

   e. If they ______ an alarm clock, they would get up on time. (*use*)

   f. I wouldn't go to the movies if I ______ study. (*have to*)

5. Use the "had" + past participle construction in each of the following sentences describing a situation or action which was unreal or contrary to the truth. Follow the example.

   Example: If I *had had* a million dollars, I would have traveled around the world. (*have*)

   a. I would have gone on the picnic, if there ______ time to get ready. (*be*)

   b. If she ______ enough money, she would have paid cash for the car. (*have*)

   c. If I ______ my key, I wouldn't have been able to lock the door. (*lose*)

   d. He wouldn't have gotten lost if he ______ for directions. (*ask*)

   e. If they ______ an alarm clock, they would have gotten up on time. (*use*)

   f. I wouldn't have gone to the movies, if I ______ study. (*have to*)

6. Use the correct form of the verb in parentheses as shown in the examples.

   Examples: I will study tonight if I *have* time. (*have*)

   If I *had* a million dollars, I would travel around the world. (*have*)

   If I *had had* a million dollars, I would have traveled around the world. (*have*)

   a. If I ______ time, I will run some errands for you. (*have*)

b. If I ______ faster, I would have time for breakfast. (*get dressed*)

c. If I ______ you didn't have training, I wouldn't have hired you. (*know*)

d. If you ______ home, you can do your laundry. (*stay*)

e. If you ______ home, you could wash your hair. (*stay*)

f. If you ______ home, you could have studied. (*stay*)

7. Using the adverbial clause in parentheses, give a complete answer to each question. Follow the example. Be sure to use the correct pronoun.

Example: Will you study tonight? (*if I have time*)
I will study tonight if I have time.

a. Will you go to the banquet with John? (*if I am introduced to him*)

b. Would you have stayed in bed? (*if the doctor had told me to*)

c. Will you marry me? (*if you have money*)

d. Could you have visited all the museums? (*if I had had time*)

e. Wouldn't he have seen you? (*if I hadn't shouted to him*)

f. Would you have had time for breakfast? (*if I hadn't slept so late*)

WORD LIST

acceptable	bone	easily	lump-sum
agreeable	carefully	even	museum
alarm	cash	key	training

Verb Forms

enroll	lose, lost (*p. and p. part.*)
give in	shout
hurry up	sell, sold (*p. and p. part.*)
introduce	sprain
look back (on)	wave

Expressions

come to think of it
do the laundry
get lost
lose (one's) way

Supplementary Word List

(Conversation and Reading Practice)

excuse fault

UNIT 7 ASKING ABOUT LIKES AND DISLIKES

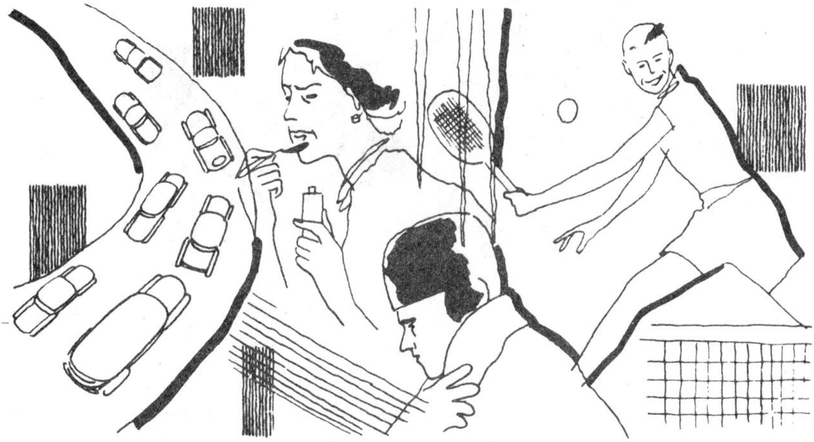

691 **What is it you don't like about winter weather?**
692 **I don't like it when the weather gets real cold.**
693 **I can't stand summer weather.**
694 **The thing I don't like about driving is all the traffic on the road.**
695 **He doesn't like the idea of going to bed early.**
696 **I like to play tennis, but I'm not a very good player.**
697 **I don't like spinach even though I know it's good for me.**
698 **I'm afraid you're being too particular about your food.**
699 **He always finds fault with everything.**
700 **She doesn't like anything I do or say.**
701 **You have wonderful taste in clothes.**
702 **What's your favorite pastime?**
703 **What did you like best about the movie?**
704 **I didn't like the taste of the medicine, but I took it anyway.**
705 **Why do you dislike the medicine so much?**

UNIT 7 ASKING ABOUT LIKES AND DISLIKES

691. 겨울 날씨에서 당신이 싫어하는 건 어떤것입니까?
692. 나는, 날씨가 아주 추워질 때 겨울이 싫습니다.
693 나는 여름 날씨는 견딜 수 없읍니다.
694. 내가 운전을 좋아하지 않는 건, 도로가 복잡하고 혼잡하기 때문입니다.
695. 그는 일찍 잠자리에 든다는 생각을 좋아하지 않읍니다.
696. 나는 정구를 좋아합니다만, 훌륭한 선수까지는 못 됩니다.
697. 시금치가 내게 좋다는 걸 알지만 나는 어쩐지 시금치를 좋아하지 않읍니다.
698. 나는 당신이 음식물에 너무 까다로운게 아닌가 싶읍니다.
699. 그는 언제나 모든 것의 흠을 잡읍니다.
700. 그녀는 내가 행하거나 말하는 것이면 무엇이든지 좋아하지 않읍니다.
701. 당신에게는 의복에 대한 놀랄만한 심미안이 있읍니다.
702. 당신이 좋아하는 오락은 무엇입니까?
703. 그 영화에서 가장 좋았던 것은 무엇입니까?
704. 나는 그 약의 맛을 좋아하진 않지만 어쨌든 그 약을 먹었읍니다.
705. 왜 당신은 그 약을 그다지도 싫어합니까?

*** 새로 나온 단어와 어귀 ***

get cold「추워지다」 **real**「진짜의, 정말의」 **can't stand～**「～을 참을 수 없다」 **traffic**「교통, 교통량」 **play tennis**「정구를 하다」 **player**「선수」 **spinach**「시금치」 **be good for me**「내 건강에 좋다」 **be particular about～**「～에 대해서 까다롭다」 **find fault with～**「～에 대해서 흠을 잡다」 **anything I do or say**「내가 행하거나 말하는 것이면 무엇이나」 **taste**「심미안, 맛」 **favorite**「좋아하는」 **pastime**「오락」 **medicine**「약」 **take medicine**「약을 먹다」 **dislike**「싫어하다」

문 법

691. **What is it you don't like～?** : What is it다음에 that가 생략되어 있다. that you don't like (네가 싫어하는 것은)+What is it? (무엇이냐?)의 결합형이다.

What is it (that) you particularly dislike?
(네가 특히 싫어하는 것은 무엇이냐?)

What is it (that) you like so much?
(네가 그다지도 좋아하는 것은 무엇이냐?)

694. **The thing I don't like about driving is all the traffic on the road.** : I don't like～는 the thing에 걸려서 the thing I don't like about driving 의 뜻은「내가 운전에 대해서 좋아하지 않는 것」

The thing *I don't like about flying* is all the other planes in the air.
(내가 비행에 대해서 좋아하지 않는 것은 하늘의 모든 다른 비행기 때문이다)

The thing I don't *like about photography* is all the expense.
(내가 사진술에 대해서 좋아하지 않는 것은 모든 비용 때문이다)

695. **He doesn't like the idea of going to bed early.** : the idea of going to ～는「잠자리에 일찍 든다는 생각」으로 번역한다. 이와 같이 of를 해석 안 할 때의, of는「동격의 of」라 칭한다.

I don't like *the idea of getting up early.*
(나는 일찍 일어난다는 생각도 싫다)

He doesn't like *the idea of sleeping eigh hours every night.*
(그는 매일 8 시간 잔다는 생각조차 싫어한다)

698. **I'm afraid you're being too particular～** : I'm afraid～는 I think와 같이 이「…라 생각된다」라든가「…일 것 같아 보인다」든가 하는 뜻이지만, I think와는 달리, (유감스럽지만)…일 것 같다」는 등에 쓰인다. 이를테면 I'm afraid he will die. (유감스럽지만(혹은 안됐지만) 그는 죽을 것 같다)와 같은 경우 쓰인다.

I'm afraid you're being too critical about your food.
(유감스럽지만 너는 음식에 대해서 너무 흠만 잡는다)

I'm afraid I cannot help you.
(유감스럽지만 당신을 도울 수는 없을 것 같습니다)

700. **She doesn't like anything I do or say.** : anything I do or say는「내가 행하거나 말하는 것이면 무엇이나」의 뜻으로 whatever I do or say라 말할 수도 있다.

He always finds fault with *anything I do or say.*
(그는 내가 행하거나 말하는 것은 무엇이든지 흠만 잡는다)

INTONATION

691 What is it you don't like about winter weather?

692 I don't like it when the weather gets real cold.

693 I can't stand summer weather.

694 The thing I don't like about driving is all the traffic on the road.

695 He doesn't like the idea of going to bed early.

696 I like to play tennis, but I'm not a very good player.

697 I don't like spinach even though I know it's good for me.

698 I'm afraid you're being too particular about your food.

699 He always finds fault with everything.

700 She doesn't like anything I do or say.

701 You have wonderful taste in clothes.

702 What's your favorite pastime?

703 What did you like best about the movie?

704 I didn't like the taste of the medicine, but I took it anyway.

705 Why do you dislike the medicine so much?

VERB STUDY

1. can't stand, couldn't stand (something or somebody)

a. I can't stand summer weather.
b. If you can't stand summer weather, why don't you go north?
c. She can't stand the winter, and she is miserable in summer.
d. She couldn't stand me, and I couldn't stand her.

2. play

a. I like to play tennis, but I'm not a very good player.
b. He played baseball all afternoon yesterday.
c. I have a friend who plays chess.
d. Have you ever played tennis with Mr. Cooper?
e. We're playing bridge right now. We'll be finished in an hour.

3. find fault (with)

a. He always finds fault with everything.
b. Did he find fault with anything you said?
c. He found fault with everything I did.
d. I've never found fault with anything you've ever done.

4. dislike

a. Why do you dislike the medicine so much?
b. You don't dislike John, do you?
c. He doesn't really dislike you, does he?
d. I don't know why I dislike spinach.

5. like (best or best of all)

a. What did you like best about the movie?
b. Of all the movies you saw last year, which did you like best?
c. Did you like your language teacher best of all?
d. What did he like best about the restaurant?

6. object (to)

a. Why do you object to cleaning the house?
b. He always objects to taking his medicine.
c. The lawyer objected to the decision.
d. I've never objected to winter weather.

VERB STUDY

1. **can't stand, couldn't stand (something or somebody)**
 (참을 수가 없다, 참을수가 없었다)
 a. 나는 여름 날씨는 참을 수가 없다.
 b. 여름 날씨를 견딜 수 없으면, 북쪽으로 가지 그래?
 c. 그녀는 겨울은 견딜 수가 없고 여름에는 비참해 진다.
 d. 그녀는 나를 견딜 수 없었고 나는 그녀가 견딜 수 없었다.
2. **play (놀이를 하다)**
 a. 나는 정구를 좋아하지만 훌륭한 선수는 못된다.
 b. 그는 어제, 오후 내내 야구를 했다.
 c. 나는 장기를 두는 친구가 있다.
 d. 쿠우퍼 씨와 정구해 본 경험이 있읍니까?
 c. 우리는 지금 부릿지를 하고 있는 중입니다. 한 시간이면 끝날 것입니다.
3. **find fault (with) (…의 흠을 잡다)**
 a. 그는 항상 모든 것의 흠을 잡는다.
 b. 그는 네 말을 흠 잡던가?
 c. 그는 내가 하는 것이면 무엇이든 흠 잡았다.
 d. 나는 네가 한 일에 대해 결코 흠을 잡은 적이 없다.
4. **dislike (싫어하다)**
 a. 왜 당신은 그다지도 약을 싫어합니까?
 b. 당신은 죤을 싫어하지 않지요, 그렇지요?
 c. 그는 당신을 정말 싫어하지는 않지요?
 d. 나는 내가 시금치를 싫어하는 이유를 모르겠다.
5. **like (best or best of all) (가장 좋아하다)**
 a. 영화에서 가장 좋았던 것은 무엇입니까?
 b. 작년에 본 모든 영화 중에서 가장 좋았던 것은 어느 것입니까?
 c. 모든 선생님 중에서 어학 선생님을 가장 좋아하셨읍니까?
 d. 그가 그 식당에서 가장 좋아했던 것은 무엇입니까?

6. **object (to) (～에 반대하다, 싫어하다)**
 a. 너는 왜 집안 청소에 반대 하느냐?
 b. 그는 항상 약먹기를 싫어한다.
 c. 그 변호사는 그 판결에 불복했다.
 d. 나는 겨울 날씨를 결코 싫어 한적 없다.

*** 새로 나온 단어와 어귀 ***

miserable「비참한」
chess「체스, 장기」 **bridge**「브릿지, 카드 놀이의 일종」
of all the movies you saw last year「작년 본 모든 영화중에」
decision「결정, 판결」

SUBSTITUTION DRILLS

1. What is it you | don't like
particularly dislike
especially don't like
hate
like so much
find so attractive | about winter weather?

2. I don't like it when the weather gets | real
very
really
unusually
uncomfortably
terribly
miserably | cold.

3. I | can't stand
can't take
especially dislike
bitterly hate
simply can't take | summer weather.

4. The thing I don't like about | driving

flying

photography
walking | is all the | traffic on
the road
other planes
in the air
expense
exercise
you get | .

5. He doesn't like the idea of

going to bed early
getting up early
sleeping eight hours every night
working long hours
getting married too young

.

6. I like to play

tennis
ping-pong
bridge
golf
card games
chess
checkers

, but I'm not a very good player.

7. I don't like spinach even though I know

it's good for me
it makes me strong
it makes me healthy
I have to eat it

.

8 I'm afraid you're being too

particular
fussy
difficult
cautious
critical

about your food.

9. He always

finds fault with
sees something wrong with
sees the negative side of
objects to
is critical of

everything.

10. She doesn't

like
pay any attention to
ever appreciate
give any importance to

anything I do or say.

11. You have	wonderful excellent exceptionally good amazingly good unbelievably good remarkably good marvelous	taste in clothes.

12. What's your favorite	pastime game hobby kind of animal musical instrument baseball team kind of entertainment	?

13. What did you like best about the	movie novel last TV program you saw book you've just finished reading play you've just seen	?

14. I didn't like the	taste looks smell	of the medicine, but I took it anyway.

15. Why do you dislike	the medicine taking your medicine hard work cleaning house housekeeping doing the laundry	so much?

SUBSTITUTION DRILLS

1.
좋아하지 않는
특별히 싫어하는
특별히 좋아하지 않는
싫어하는
그토록 좋아하는
그토록 매력적이라고 보는

2.
아주
매우
진짜
유별나게
불 유쾌하게
지독하게
비참하게

3.
견딜 수 없다
좋아하지 않는다
특별히 싫어하다
지독하게 싫어하다
좋아할 수가 없다

4.
드라이브
비 행
사 진
걷 기

도로가 혼잡해서이다
타 비행기가 공중에 있는 때문이다
비싸다
운동이 너무 심하다

5.
일찍 잔다
일찍 일어난다
매일밤 8 시간 잔다
장시간 일한다
아주 어려서 결혼한다

6.
정구
탁구
브릿지
골프
카아드놀이
장기
체커

7.
내게 좋다
튼튼하게 만든다
건강하게 만든다
먹어야만 한다

우리는
우리는 있을 것이다
우리는 있었을 것이다

8.
까다로운
꼼꼼한
까다로운
조심하는
흠을 잡는

9.
흠을 잡는다
잘못된 것을 보다
좋지 않은 면을 보다
에 반대하다
을 비평하다

10.
좋아하다
주시하다
고마워하다
중요시하다

11.
놀랄만한
우수한
비상하게 훌륭한
놀랍게 훌륭한
믿을 수 없을 만큼 좋은
뛰어나게 좋은
놀랄만한

12.
오락
게임
취미
놀불
악기
야구팀
여흥

13.
영화
소설
네가 마지막 본 TV쇼
방금 다 읽은 책
방금 본 연극

14.
맛
외양
냄새

15.
약
약을 먹다
힘든 일
집 청소
집 보기
세탁하기

READING

Likes and Dislikes

There was a very interesting story in this morning's newspaper about a man who had just received an inheritance of a million dollars. The newspaper account was quite detailed. It said the man behaves very strangely. What others like, he dislikes, and what most people enjoy, he doesn't care for.

For example, most people enjoy summer weather when they can wear lightweight clothes. No one else would think of wearing a long coat and a hat on a hot day, but he does. He says he can't stand the sun, but he'll take long walks in the rain without a raincoat or an umbrella. He's extremely particular about selecting the correct tie to wear with his suit, but it doesn't bother him if his shirt is dirty or his suit isn't pressed.

He always sees the negative side of everything. He finds fault with the best movie of the year, but stays awake until two a.m. watching very old movies on television. Even his taste in food is peculiar. He drinks warm water and cold tea, eats raw eggs and can't stand fresh fruit.

Last week his uncle died and left him the million dollars. Perhaps the uncle was rather odd, too. Or maybe he knew about his nephew's strange preferences—one of them, anyway—and decided to try to cure him.

In his will, the old man insisted that the nephew spend half the inheritance within the next five years. If he didn't, the money would be given to a university.

Everyone is anxious to know what the nephew will do. You see, he likes to buy things, but he hates to spend money.

Questions

1. What are some of the strange preferences of the man in the story?
2. What happened last week?
3. What did the uncle insist on in his will?
4. Why do you suppose the uncle wrote his will in this way?
5. Do you think the nephew will spend half the money in the next five years?
6. What would you buy if you had to spend half a million dollars in five years?

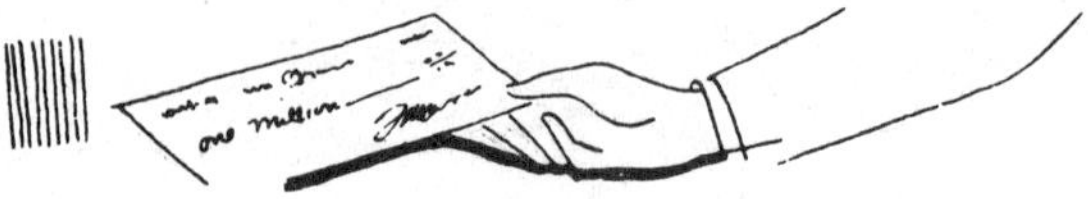

READING

(좋고 싫은 것)

오늘 아침 신문에, 백만달러의 유산을 물려받은 한 남자에 관한 아주 재미있는 기사가 실렸읍니다. 그 신문기사는 무척 자세했읍니다. 그 남자의 행동은 무척 괴상하다는 것이었읍니다. 남이 좋아하는 것을, 그는 싫어하고 모든 사람이 즐기는 것을 그는 거들떠 보지도 않는다는 것입니다.

예를 들면, 대부분의 사람들은 가벼운 옷을 입을수 있는 여름 날씨를 좋아하는 것입니다. 아무도 더운 날씨에 긴 코오트를 입거나 모자를 쓸 생각을 하지 않읍니다. 그러나 실제로 그는 그러합니다. 그는 햇볕을 견딜 수 없다는 것입니다. 그런가 하면 또 비가 올 때는 비옷이나 우산도 없이 마냥 걷읍니다. 또한 그는 그의 옷에 맞춰서 맬 적당한 넥타이를 고르는 데도 꽤나 까다롭읍니다. 하지만 그의 샤쓰가 더럽건 옷을 안다렸건 그런 것은 상관하지 않읍니다.

그는 항상 만사의 부정적인 면만 봅니다. 그는 그 해에 가장 우수한 영화마저 흠을 잡으면서, 텔레비젼에서 하는 옛날 영화를 보느라고 새벽 2시까지 잠을 안자기도 합니다. 음식에 대한 기호도 괴상망칙하여 따뜻한 물과, 찬 냉차를 마시며, 달걀을 날로 먹고 신선한 과일을 못먹읍니다.

지난 주에 그의 아저씨가 죽어, 그에게 백만달러를 남겨 주었읍니다. 아마도 아저씨 역시 괴상한 사람이었을 것입니다. 아니면 그 조카의 이상한 면에 대해서 — 어쨌든 그중 한가지만이라도 — 알고 있었을 지도 모릅니다. 그래서 그를 치료하려고 애썼을지도 모릅니다. 유서에서, 노인은 앞으로 5년 이내에 그 유산의 절반을 써야 한다고 써 있읍니다. 만약 그렇지 않다면, 그 돈을 대학에 희사할지도 모른다는 것입니다. 모든 사람은 그 조카가 무엇을 할 것인지 알고 싶어 하고 있읍니다. 아시다시피 그는 물건 사는 것은 좋아하지만 돈을 쓰는 것은 질색이니 말입니다.

＊ 새로 나온 단어와 어귀 ＊

inheritance「유산」 **million**「백만」 **newspaper account**「신문기사」 **detailed**「자세한」 **What others like, he dislikes**=He dislikes what others like **What most people enjoy, he doesn't care for**=he doesn't care for what most people enjoy **raincoat**「비옷」 **umbrella**「우산」 **negative**「부정적인」 **stay awake**「잠깨어 있다」 **raw egg**「달걀 날것」 **odd**「괴상한」 **preference**「편견, 편애」 **cure**「치료하다」 **insist**「주장하다」 **be anxious to～**「～하고 싶어하다」

CONVERSATION

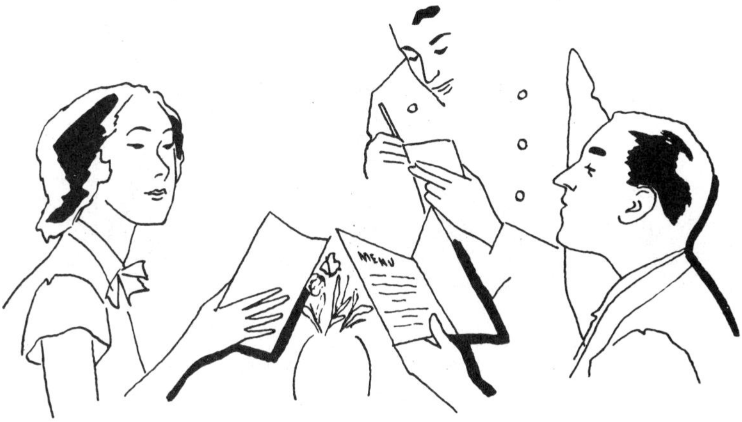

Likes and Dislikes

WAITER: May I take your order now?

DONALD: Yes, I think we're ready to order. Elizabeth, what would you like to have?

ELIZABETH: I haven't made up my mind yet. You order first, Donald.

DONALD: All right. I'll start with chicken soup. Then I want a steak, medium rare. I'll have a baked potato, green beans, and a tossed salad. I'll order dessert later.

WAITER: Yes, sir. And you, miss. What would you like to have?

ELIZABETH: I can't decide. I don't see anything I really like.

WAITER: There are over thirty dishes to select from, miss.

DONALD: There ought to be something you like, Elizabeth.

ELIZABETH: Well, I guess so. But I only see food that I don't like. I don't care for chicken and I can't stand fish. Do you have any oysters?

WAITER: No, miss. I'm afraid not. How about some other seafood?

ELIZABETH: Oysters are the only seafood I like; I dislike the rest.

DONALD: I wish I could think of something for you.

WAITER: May I suggest cream of tomato soup, steak with mushroom gravy, asparagus, and buttered cauliflower. For dessert—strawberry pie with ice cream?

ELIZABETH: No, that isn't my idea of a good meal. I'll have a hamburger. That's my favorite dish. I have it every day.

CONVERSATION

(좋고 싫은 것)

Waiter : 지금 주문을 받을까요?

Donald : 예, 주문받으세요. 엘리자베드, 무엇을 드시겠어요?

Elizabeth : 아직 결정하지 못했는데요. 당신 먼저 주문하세요. 도날드.

Donald : 그러죠. 난 우선 치킨수우프하고 그 담엔 스테익을 설 익혀 주시오. 구운 감자와 강남콩과 비빔 샐러드를 들겠읍니다. 디저어트는 나중에 주문하겠읍니다.

Waiter : 예, 그러십쇼, 그런데, 아가씨 당신께선 무엇을 드시겠읍니까?

Elizabeth : 결정할 수 없군요 . 정말 좋아하는 것이 무엇인지 모르겠어요.

Waiter : 선택할 것이 서른 가지가 넘는데요. 아가씨.

Donald : 엘리자베드, 당신이 좋아하는 것이 있겠죠, 설마.

Elizabeth : 그러게요. 그런데 좋아하지 않는 음식만 눈에 띄는군요. 나는 병아리는 싫고, 생선은 못 먹고요. 굴이 있읍니까?

Waiter : 없는데요. 아가씨, 아마 없을 거예요. 다른 해산물은 어떻읍니까?

Elizabeth : 굴이 제가 좋아하는 유일한 해산물입니다. 그 나머지는 다 싫어요

Donald : 당신이 무엇을 좋아 할지 알수 있어야지.

Waiter : 토마트 수우프에 버섯국물 친 스테이크나 아스파라가스가 어떨까요? 디저어트로는 아이스 크림을 곁들인 딸기파이로 하고요.

Elizabeth : 아녜요. 그것은 내 생각으로는 훌륭한 음식이 아닙니다. 나는 햄버거를 들겠어요. 그게 내가 좋아하는 요리입니다. 나는 매일 그걸 먹지요.

*** 새로 나온 단어와 어귀 ***

oyster「굴」 **seafood**「해산물」 **mushroom**「버섯」 **asparagus**「아스파라거스」 **cauliflower** 「꽃양배추」 **hamburger**「햄버그 스테이크용의 잘게 다진 고기」

PARTICIPATION DRILLS

Drill 1

STUDENT A	STUDENT B
What is it you *don't like*(1) about *driving?*(2)	The thing I *don't like*(1) is *all the traffic.*(3)

(1)	(2)	(3)
don't like	driving	all the traffic
particularly dislike	photography	the expense
especially don't like	winter weather	the miserable cold
hate	flying	the long delays
dislike	tennis	the exercise
hate	the medicine	the taste

Drill 2

STUDENT A	STUDENT B
Do you like to play *tennis?*	Yes, but I'm not a very good player.

tennis
ping-pong
golf
bridge
chess
checkers
card games

EXERCISES

Modals

1. Use "can" to express ability or opportunity.

Examples: I am able to paint.
I can paint.

I was able to study last year.
I could study last year.

a. I have a friend who is able to play chess.

b. He had the time and was able to play baseball all afternoon yesterday.

c. He is taking lessons and is able to play bridge now.

d. I didn't have to study, so I was able to watch TV last night.

e. I am not able to play a musical instrument.

f. I didn't have the money, so I wasn't able to go to the movies last night.

2. Use "should" with the verb, to express advisability or obligation.

Examples: I have an exam, so I ought to study.
I have an exam, so I should study.

I have to study, so I ought to stay home tonight.
I have to study, so I should stay home tonight.

a. I work long hours, so I ought to go to bed early.

b. Coffee keeps me awake, so I ought not to drink it.

c. I don't like spinach, but I ought to eat it.

d. I was tired today. I ought not to have gone to bed so late last night.

e. I ought to have finished that book last night, but I didn't.

f I ought to have taken the plane, but I don't like flying.

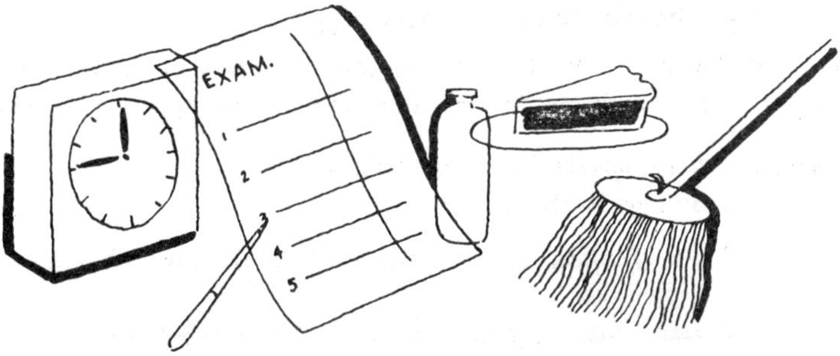

3. **Use "must" with the verb, to express necessity.**

Example: My exam begins at 9:00, and I have to be on time.
My exam begins at 9:00, and I must be on time.

a. I don't like the looks of that medicine, but I have to take it.

b. I am very fussy about food, but I have to eat.

c. I dislike housekeeping, but I have to clean house.

d. I don't like the idea of getting up early, but I have to go to the airport.

e. My apartment is uncomfortably cold, so I have to turn on the heat.

4. **Substitute the informal expression "I've got to", to express necessity in each of the sentences in Exercise 3.**

Example: My exam begins at 9 a.m., and I must be on time.
My exam begins at 9 a.m., and I've got to be on time.

5. **Change each of the sentences in Exercise 3 to past time. Use "had to" to denote necessity in the past.**

Example: My exam begins at 9 a.m., and I have to be on time.
My exam began at 9 a.m., and I had to be on time.

6. **Use "may" with the verb to express permission. Use "may" or "might" with the verb to express possibility.**

Substitute "may" + base form, "might" + base form, or "might have" + past participle for the italicized words in each sentence.

Examples: I *have permission to go* to the movies.
I *may go* to the movies.

I *am thinking about studying* English, but I haven't decided yet.
I *may study* English, but I haven't decided yet. *or*
I *might study* English, but I haven't decided yet.

I *thought about studying* English last year, but I decided not to.
I *might have studied* English last year, but I decided not to.

a. I like pets and I *have permission to have* an animal in my apartment.

b. We *thought about going* south last winter, but it was too expensive.

c. Since I am old enough, I *have permission to get married.*

d. We *are talking about going* to the movies, but we don't know if we can.

e. Since I don't like driving, I *am thinking about not taking* my car.

f. Because I dislike walking, I *am thinking about buying* a car.

7. **Answer the following questions with a complete answer.**

Example: I have to go to class tomorrow. What *must* I do?
You must go to class tomorrow.

a. Mary plays tennis well. What *can* she do?

b. Spinach makes you strong. What *should* you eat?

c. I dislike the taste of medicine, but what *must* I take?

d. He didn't like going to bed early, but what *should* he *have* done?

e. I don't know how to play bridge. What *can't* I do?

f. I couldn't stand cold weather, so I thought of moving to a warmer place last year. What *might* I have done last year?

g. She is 21 years old and she is not too young to get married. What *may* she do?

h. The library permits me to borrow books. What *may* I do?

i. He read the novel, so he doesn't think he wants to see the movie What *might* he not see?

j. I dislike doing the laundry, but I need clean clothes. What *must* I do?

8. **Answer the following questions using short answers as shown in the examples.**

Examples: Did I have to go to class?
Yes, *you had to.*

Must I go to class?
Yes, *you must.*

Might he have gone to the movies?
Yes, *he might have.*

a. Might it get miserably cold in winter? Yes, ______.

b. Are you able to play chess? Yes, ______.

c. Couldn't you play golf yesterday? No, ______.

d. Must you work long hours? Yes, ______.

e. Should you have taken the plane to save time? Yes, ______.

f. Should you be so critical about your food? No, ______.

g. Did you have to take the medicine? Yes, ______.

h. Might I have watched television last night? Yes, ______.

WORD LIST

amazingly
animal
bitterly
bridge
card
cautious
checkers
chess
critical
entertainment
especially
expense
fussy
golf
hobby
housekeeping
instrument
miserably
musical
negative
particular
particularly
pastime
photography
ping-pong
player
real
remarkably
simply
smell
taste
team
tennis
terribly
though
traffic
unbelievably
uncomfortably
unusually

Verb Forms

appreciate
despise
dislike
hate
object (to)

Expressions

can't stand
can't take
clean house
do the laundry
find attractive
find fault (with)
get cold
give importance (to)
have taste (in)
pay attention (to)
take medicine

Supplementary Word List
(Conversation and Reading Practice)

hamburger
inheritance
million
oyster
preference
seafood
umbrella
will

UNIT 8 GIVING ADVICE AND OPINIONS

706 If you want my advice, I don't think you should go.
707 I suggest that you tear up the letter and start over again.
708 It's only a suggestion, and you can do what you please.
709 Let me give you a little fatherly advice.
710 If you don't like it, I wish you would say so.
711 Please don't take offense. I only wanted to tell you what I think.
712 In my opinion, the house isn't worth the price they're asking.
713 My feeling is that you ought to stay home tonight.
714 It's none of my business, but I think you ought to work harder.
715 In general, my reaction is favorable.
716 If you don't take my advice, you'll be sorry.
717 I've always tried not to interfere in your affairs.
718 I'm old enough to make up my own mind.
719 Thanks for the advice, but this is something I have to figure out myself.
720 He won't pay attention to anybody. You're just wasting your breath.

UNIT 8 GIVING ADVICE AND OPINIONS

706. 원하신다면 충고하겠는데, 내충고는 당신이 가지 말아야 한다는 겁니다.

707. 당신이 그 편지를 찢어버리고 다시 쓰기를 제안합니다.

708. 그건 제안에 지나지 않는 것이니까, 당신 좋을대로 해도 좋읍니다.

709. 내가 아버지처럼 충고를 좀 하겠다.

710. 그게 싫으면 그렇다고 말해주기기 바랍니다.

711. 화는 내지 마세요. 생각나는대로 당신에게 이야기하고 싶었을 뿐이니까요.

712. 내 생각에는 그 집이 부르는값은 나가지 않을 것 같군요.

713. 내가 느끼기에는 당신이 오늘밤 집에 있어야 할것 같읍니다.

714. 그건 내가 상관할바아니겠지만, 당신이 보다 더 열심히 일해야 하리라 생각합니다.

715. 대체로 나의 반응은 찬성입니다.

716. 당신이 내 충고를 받아들이지 않으면 후회하게될겁니다.

717. 나는 언제나 당신의 일에 간섭하지 않으려고 노력해 왔읍니다.

718. 나는 내 스스로 결정하기에 충분히 나이를 먹었읍니다.

719. 충고는 감사하지만 이것은 내 스스로 해결해야 할 문제 입니다.

720. 그는 누구의 말에도 거들떠보지 않읍니다. 당신은 쓸데없이 지껄이고 있을 뿐입니다.

＊ 새로 나온 단어와 어귀 ＊

advice「충고」 **suggest**「제안하다」 **tear up**「찢다」 **suggetion**「제안」 **what you please**「네가 하고 싶어하는 것」 **fatherly**「아버지다운, 아버지로서의」 **take offense**「화를 내다」 **in my opinion**「내 생각에는」 **be worth~**「~만큼의 가치가 있다」 **the price they're asking**「그들이 요청하는 값」 **none of my business**「내가 상관할 바 아니다」 **in general**「일반적으로, 대체로」 **reaction**「반응」 **favorable**「유리한, 찬성인」 **interfere in**「간섭하다」 **old enough to~**「~하기에 충분히 나이를 먹은」 **make up my mind**「결심하다」 **figure out**「해결하다」 **pay attention to**「주의를 기울이다」 **waste one's breath**「쓸데없이 지껄이다」

문 법

706. If you want my advice, ~ : If you want my advice 는 If you are interested in my advice 나 If you care for my adivce 로 나타낼 수도 있다.

707. I suggest that you tear up the letter~ : suggest는「제안하다, 건의하다」의 뜻으로 that~절을 받는다.「…할 것을 제안한다」의 뜻.

708. ~and you can do what you please. : What you please 는「당신 하고싶은 대로의」의 뜻으로 what you want to라 할 수도 있다.

712. ~the house isn't worth the price they're asking. : be worth 는 뒤에「명사」를 받아서「…만큼 가치가 있다」의 뜻이다. they're asking 은 앞의 the price에 걸려서「그들이 요구하는(부르는) 값」이라 번역이 된다.

A bird in the hand is *worth two*(birds) in the bush.

(손안의 새 한마리는 수풀의 두마리의 값어치 있다.)

The book is *worth reading.*

(그 책은 읽을만한 값어치가 있다)

713. My feeling is that you ought to stay ~ :「글자 그대로의 뜻은「나의 느낌은 that~ 이하이다」의 뜻이지만「나는 …라 느낀다, …라 생각한다」로 번역한다.

The problem is that I have no money.

(문제는 내가 돈이 없다는 것이다)

The fact is that he is not honest.

(사실, 그는 정직하지가 않다)

714. It's none of my business~ : It's none of my business 는「나와는 상관없다, 내가 간섭할 일이 아니다」라는 뜻으로 It's none of your business 라 하면「상관말아」의 뜻이다.

717. I've always tried not to interfere~ : try not to~는「~하지 않으려고 애쓰다」, do not try to~는「~하려고 애쓰지 않다」의 뜻.

I *tried not to meet her.*

(나는 그녀를 만나지 않으려고 애썼다)

I *did not try to* meet her.

(나는 그녀를 만나려고 애쓰지 않았다)

718. I'm old enough to make up my own mind. :「be+형용사+enough to~」는「~할만치 충분히 …하다」의 뜻.

He is *rich enough to* buy a car.

(그는 차를 살만치 충분히 부자이다)

She is *old enough to* get married.

(그녀는 결혼할 만치 충분히 나이가 들었다)

INTONATION

706 If you want my advice, I don't think you should go.

707 I suggest that you tear up the letter and start over again.

708 It's only a suggestion, and you can do what you please.

709 Let me give you a little fatherly advice.

710 If you don't like it, I wish you would say so.

711 Please don't take offense. I only wanted to tell you what I think

712 In my opinion, the house isn't worth the price they're asking.

713 My feeling is that you ought to stay home tonight.

714 It's none of my business, but I think you ought to work harder.

715 In general, my reaction is favorable.

716 If you don't take my advice, you'll be sorry.

717 I've always tried not to interfere in your affairs.

718 I'm old enough to make up my own mind.

719 Thanks for the advice, but this is something I have to figure out myself.

720 He won't pay attention to anybody. You're just wasting your breath

VERB STUDY

1. suggest

a. She suggests that we go out for dinner tonight.
b. Who suggested that we go to the movies?
c. I didn't want to suggest it, but it's a good idea.

2. tear up

a. I suggest you tear up the letter.
b. I listened to your suggestion and tore up the letter.
c. If I hadn't torn up the letter, you could have read it.

3. start over

a. I suggest that you tear up the letter and start over again.
b. We tore up the letter and started over again.
c. They're starting over again today. Maybe they'll do it right this time.

4. take (offense)

a. Please don't take offense. I only wanted to tell you what I think.
b. She takes offense easily, so watch what you say.
c. I've never taken offense at anything you've said.

5. interfere (in, with)

a. I've tried not to interfere in your affairs.
b. Are you interfering in my affairs?
c. We didn't want to interfere with your work.
d. She never interferes with my work.

6. figure out

a. This is something I have to figure out myself.
b. We figured it out ourselves. We didn't need help.
c. I'm figuring out how much money I have in the bank.

7. pay attention (to)

a. He won't pay attention to anybody.
b. She pays attention to him, but she never pays attention to me.
c. We paid attention to everything he said.
d. I'm paying close attention to what you say.

8. waste (one's breath)

a. You're just wasting your breath. He isn't paying attention to you
b. He was wasting his breath on her. She wasn't listening to him
c. I've been wasting my breath all these years. You never listen to me.

VERB STUDY

1. **suggest** (제안하다, 암시하여 알리다, 건의하다)
   a. 그녀는 우리에게 오늘 저녁 나가서 저녁식사를 하자고 제안합니다.
   b. 우리 보고 극장에 가자고 누가 제의했읍니까?
   c. 나는 그런 제안을 하고 싶지 않았읍니다. 그러나 그것은 참 좋은 생각이었읍니다.
2. **tear up** (찢어 버리다)
   a. 나는 당신이 저 편지를 찢어 버릴 것을 제안합니다.
   b. 나는 당신의 제안에 유의해서 그 편지를 찢었읍니다.
   c. 내가 그 편지를 찢지 않았더라면, 당신은 그 편지를 읽을 수 있었을 것입니다.
3. **start over** (다시 시작하다)
   a. 나는 당신이 저 편지를 찢어 버리고 다스 쓰기를 제안합니다.
   b. 우리는 편지를 찢어 버리고 다시 시작했읍니다.
   c. 그들은 오늘 다시 시작하고 있읍니다. 이번에는 아마 옳바로 할 것입니다.
4. **take (offense)** (화내다)
   a. 화는 내지 말아 주십시요. 나는 생각하는 바를 당신에게 말하고 싶었을 뿐입니다.
   b. 그녀는 화를 잘 냅니다. 그러니 당신은 말 조심해야 합니다.
   c. 나는 당신의 어떤 말에도 화낸 일이 없읍니다.
5. **interfere (in, with)** (간섭하다, 방해하다)
   a. 나는 당신의 일에 간섭하지 않으려고 노력해 왔읍니다.
   b. 당신은 나의 일에 간섭하려는 것 입니까?
   c. 우리는 당신 일에 방해하지 않으려 했읍니다.
   d. 그녀는 나의 일에 방해하지 않읍니다.
6. **figure out** (이해하다, 해결하다, 계산하다)
   a. 이것은 내 자신이 해결해야만 할 문제입니다.
   b. 우리는 그것을 스스로 해결했읍니다. 우리는 도움이 필요없었읍니다.
   c. 나는 은행에 예금한 돈이 얼마나 되는가 계산하고 있읍니다.
7. **pay attention (to)** (유의하다, 주의를 기울이다)
   a. 그는 누구의 말에도 귀를 기울이려 하지 않읍니다.
   b. 그녀는 그에게 주의를 기울입니다. 그러나 나에겐 관심이 없읍니다.
   c. 우리는 그의 모든 말에 관심을 두었읍니다.
   d. 나는 당신의 말에 유의하고 있읍니다.
8. **waste (one's breath)** (쓸데없이 지껄이다)
   a. 당신은 공연히 지껄이는 것입니다. 그는 당신 말에 전연 유의하지 않고 있어요.
   b. 그는 그녀에 관해서 쓸데없이 지껄이고 있읍니다. 그녀는 그의 말에 귀를 기울이고 있지 않읍니다.
   c. 나는 근년에 쓸데없이 지껄여 왔읍니다. 당신들은 내 말을 듣지 않고 있읍니다.

＊ 새로 나온 단어와 어귀 ＊

tore＝tear의 과거 **torn**＝tear의 과거분사. **watch**「조심하다, 주의하니」
pay close attention to～「～에 자세히 주의를 기울이다」

SUBSTITUTION DRILLS

1. If [you want / you're interested in / you care for] my advice, I don't think you should go.
   - you want
   - you're interested in
   - you care for

2. I suggest that you tear up the letter and [...].
   - start over again
   - begin again
   - start from the beginning again
   - do it all over again

3. It's only a suggestion, and you can do what you [...].
   - please
   - want to

4. Let me give you a little [...] advice.
   - fatherly
   - friendly
   - simple
   - motherly

5. If you don't [...], I wish you would say so.
   - like it
   - agree with me
   - appreciate my helping you

6. Please don't [...]. I only wanted to tell you what I think.
   - take offense
   - get upset
   - get mad
   - be offended
   - take it that way

7. [...], the house isn't worth the price they're asking.
   - In my opinion
   - Unless I'm wrong
   - Unless I'm mistaken
   - Unless I miss my guess
   - As I see it
   - As far as I can tell
   - As far as I'm concerned

8. My feeling is that you [...] stay home tonight.
   - ought to
   - would be well advised to
   - should
   - had better

It's none of my business
It's not my affair
I have nothing to do with it
I don't have any say in the matter
It's not my responsibility

, but I think you ought to work harder.

10. In general, my reaction is
favorable
negative
not entirely negative
not very favorable
that we ought to wait and see
that we should proceed cautiously
.

11. If you don't take my advice, you'll
be sorry
regret it later
find out for yourself
.

12. I've always tried not to interfere in your
affairs
business
private affairs
problems
.

13. I'm
old
big
grown up
mature
smart
intelligent
 enough to make up my own mind.

14. Thanks for the advice, but this is something I have to
figure out myself
work out myself
do on my own
decide alone
solve by myself
.

15. He won't pay any attention to anybody. You're just wasting your
breath
money
time
energy

SUBSTITUTION DRILLS

1.
원하다
에 관심이 있다
바란다

2.
다시 하다
다시 시작 하다
처음부터 다시 하다
전부 다시 하다

3.
좋을대로
원하는 대로

4.
아버지로서
친구로서
단순한
어머니로서

5.
좋아하다
동의하다
나의 도움에 감사하다

6.
화내다
당황하다
흥분하다
화내다
그런 식으로 하다

7.
나의 견해로는
내가 틀리지 않는한
〃 〃 〃
내가 잘못 생각하지 않는한
내 생각으로는
내가 말할 수 있는한
내가 관련된 한

8.
반드시 ~해야 한다
충고하고 싶다
그래야 한다
있는 것이 더 좋을 것 같다

9.
나와 관계 없다
내 일이 아니다
그것은 어찌할 수 없다
그 문제에 대해 말할 수 없다
그것은 내 책임이 아니다

10.
찬성이다
반대다
완전히 반대는 아니다
별로 찬성하지 않는다
기다리고 두고 봐야겠다
조심스럽게 일을 진척시키다

11.
후회할거요
나중에 후회할거요
스스로 알게 될거요

12.
문제
일
개인일
문제

13.
나이가 들다
컸다
자랐다
성숙하다
완전히 발달하다
영리하다
지식이 많다

14.
스스로 해결하다
내 자신이 해야하다
혼자 결정하다
혼자 해결하다
내 자신이 해결하다

15.
노고
돈
시간
정력

READING

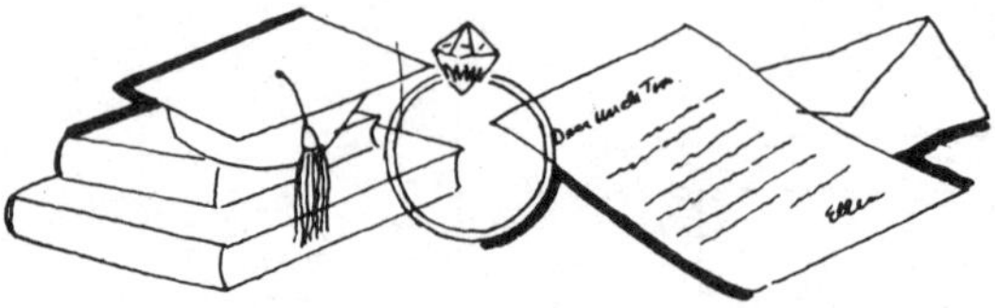

Giving Advice and Opinions

Dear Ellen,

I just received your letter and I want to let you know my opinion of your plans for the future. I hope you won't take offense, but will accept what I say here as some fatherly advice.

I was quite surprised when I read in your letter that you had decided not to finish your studies at the university. I realize that Peter wants you to marry him this summer. But with only one more year to go, you would be well advised to finish. A year is really a short time, and later you will be glad you postponed getting married.

As you know, my reaction to Peter was extremely favorable when I met him. He's an exceptionally fine young man and should be a good husband. But I suggest you complete your education first.

You are twenty-one, a grown-up young lady old enough to make up your own mind. This is something you'll have to work out yourself. As your uncle, I have always tried not to interfere in your affairs and I don't intend to begin now. But, my dear niece, please do consider my words very carefully before you decide. Whatever you do, though, Ellen, you know I only want one thing for you, and that is your happiness.

Affectionately,
Uncle Tim

Questions

1. What was Ellen's uncle surprised about?
2. How much longer did Ellen have to study to complete her education at the university?
3. What was Ellen's uncle's opinion of Peter?
4. What did he advise Ellen to do?
5. What was the one thing that Ellen's uncle wanted for her?
6. Do you think Ellen should wait or marry Peter this summer?

READING

(충고와 의견의 제시)

사랑하는 엘렌.

너의 편지를 받고, 네 장래의 계획에 대한 내 생각을 알려 주고 싶다. 네가 화를 내지 않고, 내 말을 아버지의 충고라고 생각하고 받아들여 주었으면 한다.

나는 네가 대학공부를 마치지 않겠다는 결심을 했다는 편지를 읽고 정말 놀랬다. 피터가 금년 여름, 네가 결혼해 주길 원하고 있다는 것도 나는 알고 있다. 그러나 일년만 더 기다려서, 대학을 졸업하라는 충고에 따르면 좋을 것이다. 일년이란 참 짧은 기간이다. 나중에 너는 결혼을 연기한 것을 다행으로 생각할 것이다.

네가 알다시피 내가 피터를 만났을 때 나는 그에 대해 퍽 호의적이었다. 그는 특히 훌륭한 청년으로서 좋은 남편이 될게다. 그러나 나는 네가 우선 교육을 마치기를 제안한다.

네 나이 스물 한 살의 성숙한 숙녀이니 자신의 문제를 스스로 결정 할 수 있는 연령이다. 이것은 네 스스로가 해결해야 될 문제이다. 네 삼촌으로써 나는 지금까지 네 문제에 대해 간섭하지 않으려 노력해 왔고, 앞으로도 그럴 것이다. 그러나 나의 사랑하는 조카야. 네가 그 문제를 결정짓기 전에 삼촌의 말을 깊이 생각해 주길 바란다.

그러나 네가 무슨 일을 하건 삼촌은 너의 행복을 기원할 뿐이란 걸 잊지 말아다오.

아저씨 짐.

＊ 새로 나온 단어와 어귀 ＊

plans for the future「장래 계획」 **with only one more year to go**「일년만 더 있으면」 **be well advised to~**「~하라는 충고를 받아들이는 편이 좋을 것이다」 **as you know**「네가 알다시피」 **complete**=finish **as your uncle**「네 아저씨로서」

CONVERSATION

Giving Advice and Opinions

GEORGE: Jack, would you please read this letter of application I've just written? I'd like to have your opinion.

JACK: I'd be glad to tell you what I think.

GEORGE: If you don't think it's any good, please say so. I really want to get this job.

JACK: It looks fine to me. But I have one suggestion.

GEORGE: Good! I'm interested in your advice.

JACK: If I were you I'd change the beginning. You should write about your education first.

GEORGE: Good idea, Jack. What do you think about the second part?

JACK: Now that you've asked me, I think it's too short. You should include much more information about your work experience.

GEORGE: You're right. I'll change it. How do you feel about the last part of the letter?

JACK: Very good. But, unless I miss my guess, you should say something about your family, too.

GEORGE: I agree. I appreciate your helping me, Jack. Do you think the end is all right?

JACK: Oh, yes, George. But personally I believe a business letter should end with "Very truly yours", not "Sincerely".

GEORGE: I guess I'd better tear up the letter and start over again.

JACK: Oh, don't do that, George! Just make the few changes I suggested, and your letter will be perfect!

CONVERSATION

(충고와 의견의 제시)

George : 잭, 내가 방금 쓴 이 지원서를 읽어보겠니? 네 의견을 듣고싶어.
Jack : 내 의견을 기꺼이 얘기 해 줄께.
George : 내 생각에 좋지 않다고 생각되면 그렇게 얘기해. 난 정말로 이 자리를 얻고 싶으니까.
Jack : 내겐 그것이 괜찮아 보이는데 그렇지만, 한 가지 제안이 있어.
George : 좋아! 너의 충고에 나는 관심이 있어.
Jack : 만일 내가 너라면, 서두를 바꾸겠어. 먼저 네 교육문제에 대해 우선 써야 해.
George : 좋은 생각이야 잭, 그 다음 부분은 어떻게 생각하니?
Jack : 네가 물으니까 말인데 그것은 너무 짧다고 생각해. 너는 너의 경력에 대해 더 많은 사항을 써야 할 거야.
George : 그렇겠군. 다시 써야겠는데. 그 맨 마지막 부분은 어떻게 생각해?
Jack : 잘 됐어, 그러나 내 생각이 틀리지 않는다면, 너는 가족사항에 관해서도 좀 써야 할거야.
George : 그래 동감이야. 네 도움을 감사 한다. 잭, 끝은 됐다고 생각해?
Jack : 그럼, 죠오지. 그러나 내 개인적 의견으로는 공용서신은 "Sincerely"가 아니고 "Very truly yours"로 끝을 맺어야 할 것이라고 생각해.
George : 그 서신을 찢어 버리고 아주 처음부터 시작하는게 좋겠다고 생각되는군.
Jack : 오, 죠오지 그럴건 없어! 내가 제안한 부분만 몇 군데 바꾸면 그 서신은 아주 완전해 질꺼야!

＊ 새로 나온 단어와 어귀 ＊

letter of application「신청서, 지원서」 **now that～**「～이니까」 **include**「포함하다, ～도 써 넣어야 한다」 **work experience**「경력」 **appreciate** 「감사하다」 **business letter**「공용 서신」

PARTICIPATION DRILLS

Drill 1

STUDENT A

What do you think about *this letter?*

this letter
this plan
this advice
this house
this affair

STUDENT B

Of course, *it's none of my business,* but I really don't like it.

it's none of my business
it's not my affair
it's not my responsibility
I have nothing to do with it
it's not my problem

Drill 2

STUDENT A

May I suggest that we *go out to dinner?*

go out to dinner
write her a letter
figure it out together
tear up the letter
start over

STUDENT B

That's a good idea. Let's *go out to dinner.*

EXERCISES

Other Important Verb Patterns

1. Combine the two sentences below to form one complete sentence as shown in the examples.

   Examples: I permitted him. He studied English.
   I permitted him to study English.
   I let him. He studied English.
   I let him study English.

   a. I ordered him. He tore up the letter.

   b. I had him. He tore up the letter.

   c. I permitted him. He thought for himself.

   d. I let him. He thought for himself.

   e. I urged him. He worked harder.

   f. I made him. He worked harder.

   g. I asked him. He drove carefully.

   h. I watched him. He drove carefully.

   i. I didn't want him. He got upset.

   j. I didn't see him. He got upset.

   k. I advised him. He listened to me.

   l. I made him. He listened to me.

2. Complete the sentences using the correct form of the verb in parentheses. Follow the examples.

   Examples: I finished *studying* early. (*study*)
   I expect to *study* tonight. (*study*)

   a. I insist on ______ my own mind. (*make up*)

   b. I have to ______ my own mind. (*make up*)

   c. He kept on ______ in my affairs. (*interfere*)

   d. He tried to ______ in my affairs. (*interfere*)

   e. He enjoys ______ advice to everyone. (*give*)

f. He wants to ______ advice to everyone. (*give*)

g. He considered ______ before making his decision. (*wait*)

h. He planned to ______. (*wait and see*)

i. He avoided ______ his opinion. (*give*)

j. He didn't intend to ______ his opinion. (*give*)

3. Answer each of the following questions with short "yes" and "no" answers as shown in the example.

Example: Do you intend to study English?
Yes, I intend to. No, I don't intend to.

a. Do you expect to work harder?

b. Should you work harder?

c. Do you intend to take my advice?

d. Will you take my advice?

e. Do you want to do it all over again?

f. Must you do it all over again?

g. Do you plan to listen to my opinion?

h. Will you listen to my opinion?

4. Complete the following sentences by inserting the correct preposition from the list.

up	in	down
at	out	across
with	to	on
over	for	

Example: Are you interested *in* my advice?

a. Don't get mad ______ me. I only wanted to help.

b. I must figure ______ the problem by myself.

c. I suggest you tear ______ the letter and begin again.

d. Please don't interfere ______ my affairs.

e. If you don't agree ______ me, I wish you would say so.

f. If you don't listen ______ me, you'll regret it later.

g. Take my advice and start the letter ______.

h. If you care ______ my opinion, I don't think you should go.

i. I'm depending ______ you to help me.

j. Please come in and sit ______.

k. What point are you trying to get ______?

5. **Change each of the following sentences from the passive form of the verb ("be" + participle) to the active form. Follow the examples.**

Examples: My class will be taught by Mr. Jones. *Mr. Jones will teach my class.*

My advice was taken. (*by him*) *He took my advice.*

a. Your help won't be appreciated. (*by him*)

b. Will my suggestion be accepted? (*by you*)

c. I hope you weren't offended. (*by me*)

d. The problem must be solved. (*by me*)

e. Time is being wasted. (*by you*)

f. Their money was wasted. (*by them*)

g. The speech will be given by Mr. Jones.

h. The question was answered by the student.

i. The letter was torn up by Helen.

j. The decision was made by the lawyer.

6. **Change each of the following from the active form of the verb to the passive form ("be" + participle). Follow the examples.**

Examples: You must attend school. *School must be attended.*

I followed your suggestion. *Your suggestion was followed.*

a. I must make up my own mind.

b. You should tear up the letter.

c. He shouldn't offend you.

d. You must take your father's advice.

e. I will solve the problem.

f. I took your advice.

g. He accepted my suggestion.

h. They appreciated your help.

i. He made up his mind.

j. We couldn't solve the problem.

WORD LIST

alone
beginning
breath
cautiously
energy
entirely
fatherly
favorable
intelligent
matter
mature
motherly
responsibility
simple
smart
suggestion
unless

Verb Forms

care (for)
figure out
interfere (in)
please
proceed
regret
solve
start over
tear up, tore up (*p.*), torn up (*p. part.*)
waste
work out

Expressions

as far as I can tell
be concerned
be offended
be well advised
be worth
get mad
get upset
have (any) say in
have (nothing) to do with
in general
miss (one's) guess
none of (one's) business
on (one's) own
take advice
take it
take offense
wait and see
waste (one's) breath

Supplementary Word List
(Conversation and Reading Practice)

education
happiness
Very truly yours

UNIT 9 ASKING FAVORS OF OTHER PEOPLE

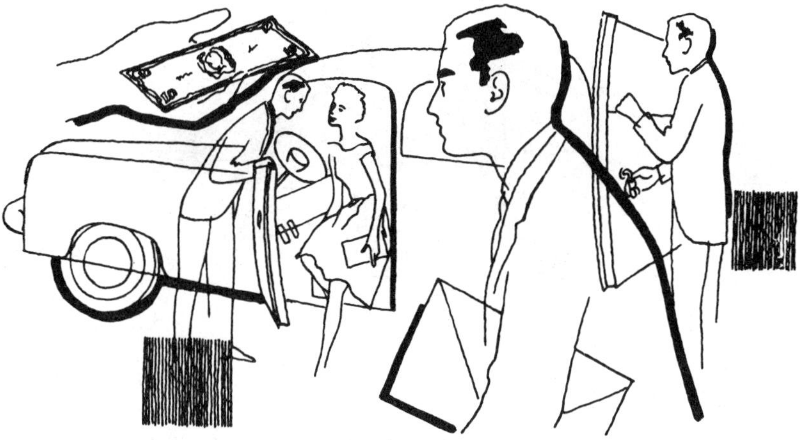

721 **Would you please hold the door open for me?**
722 **You're very kind to take the trouble to help me.**
723 **I wish I could repay you somehow for your kindness.**
724 **I'm afraid it was a bother for you to do this.**
725 **It wasn't any bother. I was glad to do it.**
726 **There's just one last favor I need to ask of you.**
727 **I'd be happy to help you in any way I can.**
728 **Would you mind giving me a push? My car has stalled.**
729 **Would you be so kind as to open this window for me? It's stuck.**
730 **If there's anything else I can do, please let me know.**
731 **This is the last time I'll ever ask you to do anything for me.**
732 **I certainly didn't intend to cause you so much inconvenience.**
733 **He'll always be indebted to you for what you've done.**
734 **Could you lend me ten dollars? I left my wallet at home.**
735 **I'd appreciate it if you would turn out the lights. I'm sleepy.**

UNIT 9 ASKING FAVORS OF OTHER PEOPLE

721. 날 위해서 문 좀 열어 두어 주시겠읍니까?
722. 저를 돕기 위해 수고해 주시니, 정말 친절하신 분이군요.
723. 어떻게 해서라도 당신의 친절에 보답하고 싶읍니다.
724. 이 일을 하는게 당신에게 폐가 되지 않았을까 염려됩니다.
725. 괴롭기는요. 오히려 기뻤읍니다.
726. 당신에게 청할 필요가 있는 마지막 부탁이 꼭 하나 있읍니다.
727. 어떻게든 할 수만 있다면 기꺼이 도와 드리겠읍니다.
728. 차 좀 밀어 주시겠어요? 제 차가 발동이 끊어져서요.
729. 창문 좀 열어 주시겠읍니까? 방안이 답답하군요.
730. 제가 할 수 있는 일이 있다면, 말씀해 주십시요.
731. 이건 저를 위해서 당신에게 드리는 저의 마지막 부탁입니다.
732. 당신에게 그런 불편을 끼쳐 드릴려고 한 건 정말 아니었읍니다.
733. 그는 늘 당신이 베푼 일에 감사하고 있을 겁니다.
734. 10달러만 꿔 주겠오? 지갑을 집에 두고 왔군요.
735. 불 좀 꺼 주셨으면 감사하겠읍니다. 졸립군요.

*** 새로 나온 단어와 어귀 ***

hold～open「～을 계속 열어 두다」 **take the trouble**「수고하다」 **repay～for…**「…에 대해서 ～에게 보답을 하다」 **bother**「성가신 일」 **favor**「돌봐줌, 은혜, 친절, 부탁」 **ask of～**「～에게 청하다」 **in any way I can**「내가 할 수 있는 어느 방식으로든, 가능하다면 어떤 방법으로든」 **give a push**「밀어주다」 **stall**「발동이 끊어지다」 **stuck**「답답한」 **cause**「일으키다, 야기하다」 **inconvenience**「불편」 **be indebted to～**「～에게 감사하다」 **wallet**「돈 지갑」 **turn out**「(불을)끄다」 **sleepy**「졸리운」

문 법

721. **Would you please hold the door open for me?** : Would you please ~는 Will you~보다 훨씬 더 겸손한 표현방법으로서 남에게 무언가 부탁할 때 쓰인다.
hold the door open 「문을 열어 놓아 두다」의 반대의 표현은 hold the door closed 「문을 닫아 두다」이다.

722. **You're very kind to take the trouble to help me.** : You're very kind to~ 「~하므로 당신은 친절한 분이다」의 뜻. take the trouble to~는 「수고스럽게 ~하다」의 뜻.

You are very nice to help me.
(나를 도와 주시니 당신은 참 훌륭하신 분이군요)
You are very thoughtful to take my advice.
(저의 충고를 받아들여 주시니 당신은 무척 신중하신 분이군요)

726. **There's just one last favor I need to ask of you.** : ask one last favor of you 「당신에게 마지막 부탁을 하다」에서 one last favor가 앞으로 나아간 것이다.

There's just *one last favor* I'd like to ask of you.
(당신에게 청하고 싶은 마지막 부탁이 하나 있읍니다)
There's just *one last favor* I must ask of you.
(당신에게 청하지 않으면 안 될 부탁이 마지막으로 하나 있읍니다)

728. **Would you mind giving me a push?** : Would you mind~ing?에 대한 대답은 yes로 하면 「싫다」는 뜻이 되므로 이때 만큼은 Not at all, Certainly not, Of course, not. 등으로 답해야 한다.

729. **Would you be so kind as to open~?** : 「친절하게 문 좀 열어 주시겠읍니까?」와 같은 표현 중의 하나로서 Will you please~? Would you please ~? Would you be so good as to~와 같은 표현이다.

Would you be so kind as to help me up?
(친절히 저를 도와서 태워 주시겠읍니까?)
Would you be so good as to call the doctor?
(친절히 의사를 좀 불러 주시겠읍니까?)

733. **He'll always be indebted to you for what you've done.** : be indebted to~ for… 「…에 대해서 ~에게 감사하다」의 뜻으로 be grateful to~ for…; be thankful to~ for…도 같다.

I'll always be indebted to you for your advice.
(당신의 충고에 대해서 나는 언제까지나 감사할 것입니다)

INTONATION

721 Would you please hold the door open for me?

722 You're very kind to take the trouble to help me.

723 I wish I could repay you somehow for your kindness.

724 I'm afraid it was a bother for you to do this.

725 It wasn't any bother. I was glad to do it.

726 There's just one last favor I need to ask of you.

727 I'd be happy to help you in any way I can.

728 Would you mind giving me a push? My car has stalled.

729 Would you be so kind as to open this window for me? It's stuck.

730 If there's anything else I can do, please let me know.

731 This is the last time I'll ever ask you to do anything for me.

732 I certainly didn't intend to cause you so much inconvenience.

733 He'll always be indebted to you for what you've done.

734 Could you lend me ten dollars? I left my wallet at home.

735 I'd appreciate it if you would turn out the lights. I'm sleepy.

VERB STUDY

1. hold (something) open

a. Would you please hold the door open for me?
b. He held the door open for me because my arms were full.
c. We've held the job open for him for two weeks now.

2. repay

a. I wish I could repay you somehow for your kindness.
b. He hasn't repaid the money I loaned him.
c. We repaid him for his kindness by taking him to dinner.
d. I can't repay you for what you've done.
e. He always repays the money he owes.

3. push

a. Would you mind giving me a push? My car has stalled.
b. He pushed his books off the table.
c. Push the door open, will you?
d. I'm pushing as hard as I can, but the car won't move.

4. stall

a. My car stalled yesterday.
b. It stalled last week, too.
c. It stalls all the time. I think I have engine trouble.
d. Are you stalling for time? Don't you want to go with me?

5. open

a. Would you be so kind as to open this window?
b. She opens the window in the morning and closes it at night.
c. I just opened the door and came in.
d. Please open the door and come in.

6. intend (to)

a. I didn't intend to start an argument.
b. She intends to go to the movies tonight.
c. We've never intended to inconvenience you.
d. They intended to get here last night, but they had a flat tire on the way.

7. lend

a. Could you lend me ten dollars?
b. I've already lent you more than fifty dollars.
c. She lends me money once in a while.
d. Why did you lend him so much money?
e. Would you lend me that book until next week?

VERB STUDY

1. **hold (something) open** (…을 열어 놓아 두다)
   a. 저를 위해 문 좀 열어 놓아 두시겠읍니까?
   b. 그는 내 양손에 짐이 있어서, 문을 열어 놓아 두었다.
   c. 우린 2주일 동안이나 그를 위해 일자리를 비워 놓아 두고있다.
2. **repay** (…을 갚다, 보상하다)
   a. 어떻게 해서라도 너의 친절에 보답할 수 있으면 좋겠는데.
   b. 그는 내가 빌려준 돈을 갚지 않았다.
   c. 우리는 그를 식사에 초대함으로써 친절에 보답했다.
   d. 네가 해 준 것에 대해서 보답을 할 수 없다.
   e. 그는 항상 꾸어 간 돈은 갚는다.
3. **push** (밀다)
   a. 저 좀 밀어 주겠읍니까? 내 차가 엔진이 멎어서요.
   b. 그는 테이블에서 책을 치웠다.
   c. 문 좀 밀어 열지 그래.
   d. 힘껏 밀고 있지만, 차는 움직이려 하지 않는다.
4. **stall** (지연시키다, 발동이 꺼지다)
   a. 어제 내 차는 발동이 꺼졌다.
   b. 지난 주 에도 차가 발동이 멎었다.
   c. 차가 늘 발동이 멎는데, 엔진에 고장이 있는것 같다.
   d. 왜 꾸물대지? 나와 함께 가기 싫어?
5. **open** (열다)
   a. 창문 좀 열어 주겠니?
   b. 그녀는 아침에 창문을 열고 밤에 닫는다.
   c. 난 문을 열고 들어왔다.
   d. 문을 열고 들어 오세요.
6. **intend (to)** (마음먹다, …할 의도가 있다)
   a. 나는 논쟁을 시작하려는 의사는 없다.
   b. 오늘 밤 그녀는 극장에 갈 작정이다.
   c. 우린 네게 폐를 끼치려는 것은 아니었다.
   d. 그들은 어젯밤 이곳에 도착할 작정이었으나, 도중에 타이어 빵구가 났다.
7. **lend** (빌려주다)
   a. 10달러만 꿔 줄래?
   b. 난 네게 벌써 50달러 이상 빌려 주었는데
   c. 그녀는 가끔 내게 돈을 빌려준다.
   d. 왜 넌 그에게 그렇게 많은 돈을 꿔줬지?
   e. 다음 주까지 그 책 좀 빌려 주겠니?

＊ 새로 나온 단어와 어귀 ＊

loan「대부하다, 빌려주다」 **owe**「빚지고 있다」
push ~ off the table「식탁에서 ~를 밀어 치우다」 **engine trouble**「엔진 고장」 **on the way**「도중에」 **once in a while**「가끔, 때때로」

SUBSTITUTION DRILLS

1. Would you please	hold the door open leave the door unlocked keep the fire burning have dinner ready have these clothes washed	for me?
2. You're very	kind nice thoughtful considerate sweet understanding	to take the trouble to help me.
3. I wish I could	repay reward show my gratitude to pay thank	you somehow for your kindness.
4. I'm afraid it was	a bother for bothersome for a burden on an inconvenience to an imposition on	you to do this.
5. It wasn't	any bother any trouble a bit of trouble any bother at all at all difficult anything at all	. I was glad to do it.

6. There's just one last favor

I need to	ask of you.
I feel I need to	
I'd like to	
I must	
I feel I must	
I ought to	
I just have to	

7. I'd be happy to help you in any way I

can
possibly can
might be able to
am able to
could

8. Would you mind

giving me a push	? My	car has stalled
opening the door		arms are full
helping me up		ankle is sprained
calling the doctor		head is bleeding
loaning me some money		wallet is gone

9. Would you be so kind as to open this window for me?

It's

stuck
jammed
tightly closed
stuck somehow
locked

10. If there's anything else I can do, please

let me know
don't hesitate to let me know
call on me
tell me
send me a memorandum

11. This is the last time I'll ever ask you

| to do anything for me |
| to do me a favor |
| to do a favor for me |
| for favors |
| to bother to help me |
| for anything |

.

12. I certainly didn't intend to

| cause you so much inconvenience |
| bother you so much |
| interfere in your affairs |
| upset your plans |
| worry you with my problems |
| get you so involved in my problems |

.

13. He'll always be

| indebted |
| grateful |
| thankful |

to you for what you've done.

14. Could you lend me ten dollars? I

| left my wallet at home |
| don't have any money with me |
| seem to have left my wallet at home |
| don't get paid until tomorrow |
| seem to be broke |

.

15. I'd appreciate it if you would

| turn out the light |
| try to be quiet |
| not be so noisy |
| excuse me now |
| not talk so loudly |

. I'm sleepy.

SUBSTITUTION DRILLS

1.
문을 열어 놔 두다
문을 잠그지 말고 두다
불을 피워 두다
저녁을 준비해 주다
옷을 빨아 주다

2.
친절한
좋은
생각깊은
신중한
상냥한
이해심이 많은

3.
보답하다
보상하다
감사를 표시하다
지불하다
감사하다

4.
수고를 끼치다
수고를 좀 끼치다
수고를 하다
불편하다
부담이 되다

5.
괴로움
고생
약간의 고생
전혀 고생이 아닌
아무것도 아닌

6.
해야 하는
하고픈
하고저하는
해야만 하는
해야 한다고 생각하는
해야만 되는
그래야만 되는

7.
할 수 있는
가능하다면
할 수 있다면
내가 할 수 있다면
할 수 있다면

8.

밀어주어	시동이 꺼었다
문을 열어	양팔에 짐이 있다
나를 도와	발목을 삐었다
의사를 불러	머리에서 피가 난다
돈좀 꿔	지갑이 없어 졌다

9.
늘러붙다
빡빡하다
너무 꽉 다쳤다
어떻게 좀 들러붙다
잠겼다

10.
알려다오
주저말고 말해다오
전화해 다오
이야기해 다오
메모를 보내다오

11.
내게 무언가 해 달라고
부탁하려고
부탁의 페를 끼치려고
도와 달라고
나에게 수고해 달라고
무엇을 좀 해 달라고

12.
불편을 주는
괴롭히려는
네 일에 간섭하려는
계획을 바꾸려는
내 문제로 너를 성가시게 하려는
내일에 너를 관여 시키려는

13.
은혜를 입은
감사해 하는
고마워 하는

14.
지갑을 집에 두고 왔다
내게 돈이 없다
집에 지갑을 두고 온 것 같다
내일까지 돈을 못탄다
무일푼 인것 같다

15.
불을 끄다
조용히 하다
시끄럽게 굴지 않는다
날 이해해 준다
시끄럽게 떠들지 않는다

READING

Asking Favors of Other People

There are two men in important positions in my office—Mr. Thompson and Mr. White. Everyone enjoys working with Mr. Thompson, but no one likes Mr. White.

Mr. Thompson is always thoughtful and considerate. When he wants something done, he'll ask, "Would you mind getting this information for me, please?" Mr. White is just the opposite. He usually shouts across the room, "Get me this memorandum, and hurry up."

Mr. White surprised us this morning, though. At first we thought he must be sick. He was kind and agreeable. "Miss Erickson," he asked, "if it isn't too much trouble for you, could you please make these telephone calls for me?" June Erickson was astonished. Right after that, Mr. White said, "Miss Reed, would you be so kind as to open the window? It's quite warm in here." Then he talked to me. "I'd appreciate it very much if you'd mail these letters for me."

We couldn't imagine why he was behaving so strangely. Should we offer him aspirins? Or had Mr. White changed his personality?

The situation was soon cleared up. "Ladies," Mr. Thompson said, "I've been told that the president of the company will be here soon. He's very interested in the welfare of his employees and will have some questions to ask you about your working conditions here."

Questions

1. What kind of positions do Mr. Thompson and Mr. White have?
2. Why does everyone like Mr. Thompson?
3. What does Mr. White usually do when he wants something?
4. How did Mr. White behave this morning?
5. What did everyone think?
6. What did Mr. Thompson say to clear up the situation?
7. Which man would you rather work for—Mr. Thompson or Mr. White? Why?

READING

(타인에 대한 부탁)

나의 사무실엔 중요한 직책을 맡고 있는 두 사람—톰프슨 씨와 화이트 씨가 있읍니다. 누구나 톰프슨 씨와 함께 일하기를 즐거워 하지만 아무도 화이트 씨를 좋아 하지는 않읍니다.

톰프슨 씨는 항상 생각이 깊고 신중합니다. 그는 무언가 해 주기를 바랄 때에는 "이 자료를 좀 알아다 주시겠어요?"하고 공손하게 요청합니다. 그렇지만 화이트 씨는 그와 정반대입니다. 그는 늘 방 넘어로 냅다 소리를 질러 "메모좀 내게 갖다 줘, 빨리"하고 말합니다.

그런데 오늘 아침 화이트 씨는 우리들을 놀라게 했읍니다. 처음에 우린 그가 어디가 아픈것이 틀림없다고 생각했으니까요. 어쩐지 그는 친절하고, 상냥했던 겁니다. "미쓰 에릭슨, 수고스럽겠지만 전화 좀 해 주겠어요?"하고 부탁했읍니다. 에릭슨 양은 놀랬읍니다. 그리고 조금 후엔 화이트 씨는 "미쓰 리드, 창문 좀 열어줘요, 이 방에선 무척 덥군"하고 말하고 또 나에게는 "이 편지 좀 부쳐 주면 고맙겠는데"하고 말했읍니다.

우린 왜 그가 그처럼 이상한 행동을 하는지 알 수 없었읍니다. 그에게 아스피린이라도 주어야 할까? 아니면 그가 성격이 바꾸어지기라도 한 것일까?

사태는 곧 분명해 졌읍니다. "여직원 여러분, 사장님이 곧 이곳에 오신다는 전갈을 받았읍니다. 사장님은 사원들의 복지 문제에 관심이 크셔서 여러분들의 근로 조건에 대해서 여러 가지로 물을 것입니다"하고 톰프슨 씨가 말한 것입니다.

✱ 새로 나온 단어와 어귀 ✱

considerate「신중한」 **he wants something done**「무언가를 다른 사람이 해 주기를 바랄 때」 **opposite**「정 반대」 **personality**「인격, 개성」 **clear up**「(의심이) 풀리다」 **welfare**「안녕, 복지」

CONVERSATION

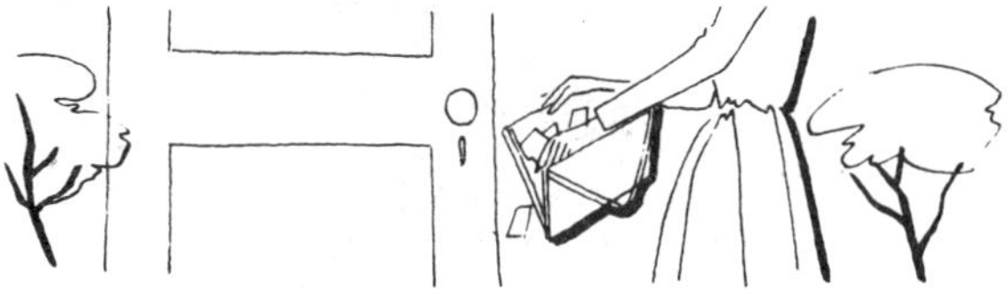

Asking Favors of Other People

Dialog 1

MARJORIE: Would you help me for a minute, please?
DAN: Of course. What do you want me to do?
MARJORIE: Could you hold these packages while I look for the key to the door?
DAN: I'd be glad to. What's in these packages? They're extremely heavy.
MARJORIE: Just the things we need for the picnic tomorrow.
DAN: Well, hurry up and open the door. I told you these things were heavy.
MARJORIE: I can't find the key. *You* must have it.
DAN: You're right, but how can I get the key while I'm holding all these packages?

Dialog 2

BOB: Would you please do me a favor, Ben?
BEN: It depends on what it is.
BOB: Could you loan me five dollars until Tuesday?
BEN: I suppose so—if you're sure you can pay me on Tuesday.
BOB: Of course. There's something else, too, Ben. Would you mind lending me your car tonight?
BEN: Well, I guess not. I have to study anyway, so I won't be using it.
BOB: Wonderful! I have one last favor to ask you. I'd appreciate it if I could borrow your blue suit tonight.
BEN: What's the matter with your suit?
BOB: It's in the cleaners. I'm taking Genevieve to the movies tonight, and I want to look good.
BEN: Genevieve? But she's my girl.
BOB: Oh, I nearly forgot. Could I borrow Genevieve, too?

CONVERSATION
(타인에 대한 부탁)

대 화1

Marjorie : 잠깐 도와 주겠니?

Dan : 물론. 뭔데?

Marjorie : 내가 열쇠를 찾는 동안, 이 짐 좀 붙들어 줄 수 있겠어?

Dan : 그러지. 이 짐 속에 뭐가 있지? 굉장히 무거운 걸.

Marjorie : 내일 피크닉 갈 때 필요한 거야.

Dan : 음, 어서 문 열어. 짐이 무겁다고 했잖아.

Marjorie : 열쇠가 없는데. 네가 가지고 있는 것 아냐?

Dan : 그렇구나, 하지만 짐을 들고서 어떻게 열쇠를 꺼내지?

대 화2

Bob : 부탁 하나 들어 주겠니, 벤?

Ben : 뭔지 알아야지.

Bob : 화요일에 줄테니, 5 달러만 꿔 줄래?

Ben : 글쎄 — 네가 화요일 까지 갚기만 한다 면야.

Bob : 물론. 한 가지 또 있는데, 벤. 오늘 밤 차 좀 빌려 줄래?

Ben : 글쎄, 안 될 것 없지. 나야 공부해야 되니까, 차는 안 써.

Bob : 정말 고맙군. 그런데 마지막 부탁이 있어서. 오늘 밤 파란 샤쓰 좀 빌려 주었으면.

Ben : 옷은 무얼하게?

Bob : 내 옷이 세탁소에 있거든. 제네비브를 오늘 밤 영화관에 데리고 가는데. 좀 멋있게 보이고 싶어서.

Ben : 뭐! 제네비브? 그 여잔 내가 사귀는 여자야.

Bob : 아, 깜박 잊었군. 그 여자도 아주 빌리자꾸나.

*** 새로 나온 단어와 어귀 ***

the key to the door 「그 도아의 열쇠」 **the things we need** 「우리가 필요로 하는 것」 **Would you please do me a favor?** 「부탁좀 드릴까요?」 **depend on what it is** 「그 부탁이 무엇인가에 달려 있다」

PARTICIPATION DRILLS

Drill 1

STUDENT A	STUDENT B
Would you please *hold the door open for me?*	Of course, I'd be glad to *hold the door open for you.*

hold the door open for me
open the window
lend me some money
have dinner ready
wash my clothes

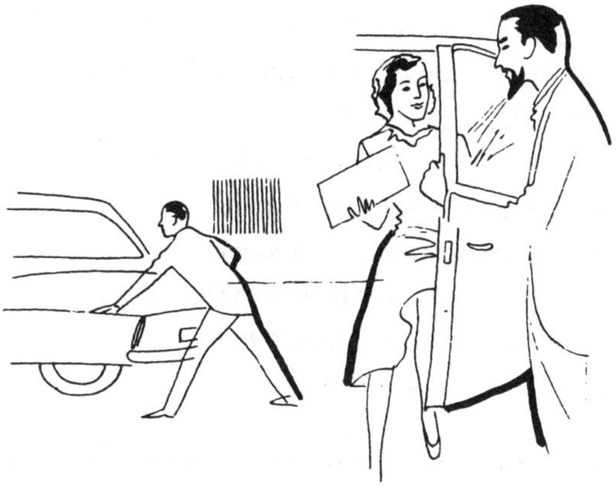

Drill 2

STUDENT A	STUDENT B
Would you mind *giving me a push?*	Not at all. If I can do anything else, please *let me know.*

giving me a push	let me know
opening the door	tell me
calling the doctor	don't hesitate to ask me
loaning me some money	call on me
turning out the lights	ask me
loaning me that book	don't hesitate to tell me
changing my tire	let me know

EXERCISES

Verbs and Modifiers of Verbs (3)

1. **Place the adverb in parentheses in the correct position in the following sentences.**

Examples: I study for exams.(*usually*)
I *usually* study for exams.
Have you been interested in that subject? (*always*)
Have you *always* been interested in that subject?
I am late to class.(*seldom*)
I am *seldom* late to class.

a. He'll be grateful to you. (*always*)
b. Have I worried you with my problems? (*often*)
c. I seem to be broke. (*usually*)
d. Have you left your wallet at home? (*ever*)
e. He is happy to help you. (*generally*)
f. I've asked you for favors. (*seldom*)
g. I get you involved in my affairs. (*frequently*)
h. Am I a burden on you? (*sometimes*)
You are a bother. (*never*)

2. **Complete the following sentences by inserting the appropriate modifier from the list. Follow the examples.**

still	already
anymore	yet

Examples: I've *already* read that book.
I haven't read that book *yet*.
I *still* haven't read that book.
I don't want to read that book *anymore*.

a. I haven't thanked you for your kindness ______.

b. You've ______ thanked me many times.

c. But I ______ haven't thanked you enough.

d. That's all right. You don't have to thank me ______.

e. Has he shown his appreciation ______?

f. Yes, he's ______ shown his gratitude.

g. Does he ______ worry you with his problems?

h. No, he doesn't bother me ______.

3. **Complete the following sentences by placing the modifiers given in parentheses in correct positions in the sentence. Follow the examples.**

Examples: We studied our notes (*carefully, for the exam*)
We *carefully* studied our notes *for the exam.*
I want to learn English (*definitely, next year*).
I *definitely* want to learn English *next year.*

a. My friend helped me out. (*thoughtfully, yesterday*)
b. I'll push your car. (*gladly, to the gas station*)
c. My brother sent me some money. (*generously, in the mail*)
d. This is the last time I'll ask you. (*ever, for favors*)
e. I won't get paid. (*definitely, until tomorrow*)
f. I didn't intend to worry you. (*certainly, with my problems*)
g. Would you open the door for me? (*kindly, now*)
h. Thank you. (*for helping me, yesterday, very much*)

4. **Using the adverbial clause in parentheses, give a complete answer to each question. Follow the examples. Use contractions wherever possible.**

Examples: Why are you studying? (*because I have an exam*)
I'm studying because I have an exam.
How long will you study? (*until I finish the book*)
I'll study until I finish the book.
When will you go to bed? (*after I finish studying*)
I'll go to bed after I finish studying.

a. When did he ask you for money? (*when he came to work*)
b. Why did he ask you for money? (*because he left his wallet at home*)
c. Why didn't you help him? (*because I was broke*)
d. How long have you been worried? (*since I lost my job*)
e. Why didn't you ask me for help? (*because I didn't want to bother you*)

f. How long will you look for a job? (*until I find one*)

g. When will you call on me again? (*after I find a job*)

h. Where can you meet me? (*wherever it is convenient for you*)

i. How long has he been asking you for favors? (*since I've known him*)

j. Why won't you listen to his problems? (*because I don't want to get involved in his affairs*)

WORD LIST

a bit of
bother
bothersome
burden
considerate
full
grateful
gratitude
imposition
inconvenience
kindness
loudly
memorandum
open
push
somehow
sprained
sweet
thankful
thoughtful
tightly
understanding
wallet

Verb Forms

cause
hold, held (*p. and p. part.*)
loan
repay, repaid (*p. and p. part.*)
reward
stall
unlock
upset, upset (*p. and p. part.*)

Expressions

at all
be broke
be indebted (to)
be jammed
be stuck
get involved
get paid
keep the fire burning
take the trouble (to)

Supplementary Word List
(Conversation and Reading Practice)

company
personality
president
welfare

UNIT 10 MAKING PREPARATIONS TO TRAVEL

736 **I didn't realize the time had passed so quickly.**

737 **I've got a lot of things to do before I can leave.**

738 **For one thing, I've got to drop by the bank to get some money.**

739 **It'll take almost all my savings to buy the ticket.**

740 **Oh, I just remembered something! I have to apply for a passport.**

741 **I almost forgot to have the phone disconnected.**

742 **It's a good thing you reminded me to take my heavy coat.**

743 **I never would have thought of it if you hadn't mentioned it.**

744 **I'll see you off at the airport.**

745 **They're calling your flight now. You barely have time to make it.**

746 **You'd better run or you're going to be left behind.**

747 **Don't forget to cable to let us know you arrived safely.**

748 **I'm sure I've forgotten something, but it's too late now.**

749 **Do you have anything to declare for customs?**

750 **You don't have to pay any duty on personal belongings.**

UNIT 10 MAKING PREPARATIONS TO TRAVEL

736. 시간이 그렇게 빨리 지나간 줄 몰랐읍니다.
737. 나는 떠나기 전에 해야 할 일이 많읍니다.
738. 먼저 나는 돈을 찾으러 은행에 들러야 합니다.
739. 표를 사는데 내 저축금이 거의 다 들 것입니다.
740. 아, 생각났네! 나는 여권을 신청해야 합니다.
741. 나는 전화를 끊는다는 걸 깜박 잊었읍니다.
742. 당신이 내게 나의 무거운 코우트를 가져가라고 일러주신 것은 잘 하셨어요.
743. 당신이 말해 주지 않았으면, 난 그것을 생각도 못했을 거예요.
744. 공항에, 당신을 전송 나가겠어요.
745. 당신이 타고 갈 비행기를 호명하는군요. 시간에 댈려면 남은 시간이 거의 없었어요.
746. 뛰어가는 게 좋을 겁니다. 그렇지 않으면 뒤에 처질 겁니다.
747. 잊지 말고, 당신의 안착을 우리에게 전보로 알려 주세요.
748. 무언가 잊고 있는게 확실한데, 그렇지만 너무 늦었어요.
749. 관세품으로 신고해야 할 물건이 있읍니까?
750. 개인 소지품에는 관세를 지불할 필요가 없읍니다.

*** 새로 나온 단어와 어귀 ***

for one thing「첫째는, 하나는, 우선」 **drop by~**「~에 들리다」 **savings**「저축한 돈」 **apply for**「신청하다」 **passport**「여권」 **mention**「언급하다, 말하다」 **see off**「전송하다」 **flight**「비행기」 **make it**「시간에 대다, 잘 해내다」 **barely**「겨우, 간신히」 **be left behind**「뒤에 처지다」 **cable**「전보를 치다」 **declare**「(세관에서) 신고하다」 **customs**「관세, 세관」 **duty**「관세」 **belongings**「소지품」

문 법

738. **For one thing, I've got to drop by the bank～** : for one thing 「첫째는」의 뜻. for another (thing)이 「둘째는, 다음으로는」. have got 는 have 의 뜻. 따라서 have got to는 have to=must와 같다.

739. **It'll take almost all my savings to buy the ticket.** : It takes… to～는 「～하기에는 …이 필요하다(…을 요한다)」의 뜻.

It'll take almost all my salary *to buy* the ticket.
(그 표를 사려면 내 봉급이 거의 전부 필요하다)

It'll take almost all my money *to buy* the ticket.
(그 표를 사려면 내 돈이 거의 전부 필요하다)

It'll take almost all my hard-earned money *to buy* the ticket.
(그 표를 사려면 힘들게 번 내 돈 거의 전부가 필요하다)

742. **It's a good thing you reminded me to take～** : It's a good thing～은 「…은 잘한 일이다」의 뜻으로 ～다음에 나오는 문장을 가리킨다. remind me to～는 「나에게 ～하도록 일깨워 주다, 상기시키다」의 뜻.

746. **You'd better run or you're going to be left behind.** had better～는 「～하는 편이 좋다」의 뜻이며, or는 「그렇지 않으면」의 뜻.

You'd better run or you're going to miss your flight.
(달리는 것이 좋다, 그렇지 않으면 비행기를 놓칠 것이다)

You'd better study hard or you're going to fail.
(열심히 공부하는 것이 좋다, 그렇지 않으면, 낙제 할 거다)

747. **Don't forget to cable to let us know～** : Don't forget to～는 「잊지 않고 ～하라의 뜻.

Don't forget to drop by the bank.
(잊지 말고 은행에 들르세요)

Don't forget to see him off at the airport.
(잊지 말고 공항에 나가서 그를 전송하세요)

Don't forget to have the phone disconnected.
(잊지 말고 전화를 끊으세요)

750. **You don't have to pay any duty～** : don't have to～는 「～할 필요가 없다」는 뜻.

You *don't have to* pay me the ten dollars you owe me.
(나에게 빚지고 있는 10달러를 갚을 필요가 없읍니다)

You *don't have to* see me off at the airport.
(공항에 나와 저를 전송할 필요는 없읍니다)

INTONATION

736 I didn't realize the time had passed so quickly.

737 I've got a lot of things to do before I can leave.

738 For one thing, I've got to drop by the bank to get some money.

739 It'll take almost all my savings to buy the ticket.

740 Oh, I just remembered something! I have to apply for a passport.

741 I almost forgot to have the phone disconnected.

742 It's a good thing you reminded me to take my heavy coat.

743 I never would have thought of it if you hadn't mentioned it.

744 I'll see you off at the airport.

745 They're calling your flight now. You barely have time to make it.

746 You'd better run or you're going to be left behind.

747 Don't forget to cable to let us know you arrived safely.

748 I'm sure I've forgotten something, but it's too late now.

749 Do you have anything to declare for customs?

750 You don't have to pay any duty on personal belongings.

VERB STUDY

1. **apply (for)**
   - *a.* I have to apply for a passport.
   - *b.* I applied for my visa three weeks ago.
   - *c.* What are you applying for? I'm applying for a job.
2. **disconnect**
   - *a.* I almost forgot to have the phone disconnected.
   - *b.* They disconnected the water and the gas.
   - *c.* Why are you disconnecting the phone?
3. **remind, mention**
   - *a.* It's a good thing you reminded me to take my heavy coat.
   - *b.* She reminded me of my sister.
   - *c.* That reminds me. I have to go see my doctor.
   - *d.* I never would have thought of it if you hadn't mentioned it.
   - *e.* Don't mention it. I was glad to do it.
4. **arrive, see (somebody) off**
   - *a.* Don't forget to cable to let us know you arrived safely.
   - *b.* She arrives today on the 6:25 train.
   - *c.* I'm arriving in San Francisco tomorrow at 9:30 a.m.
   - *d.* I'll see you off at the airport.
   - *e.* We saw our friends off at the railroad station last night.
5. **cable**
   - *a.* Don't forget to cable me when you arrive.
   - *b.* I cabled my mother last night. It cost ten dollars.
   - *c.* She cables me once a week to let me know how she is.
   - *d.* I'm cabling my wife now. I'm telling her where I am.
6. **declare**
   - *a.* Do you have anything to declare for customs?
   - *b.* We declared that we weren't going with them.
   - *c.* We declared our love for each other.
   - *d.* We've never declared our personal belongings for customs.
7. **pay, pay back**
   - *a.* You don't have to pay any duty on personal belongings.
   - *b.* He paid me the ten dollars he owed me.
   - *c.* We're paying him for the new house today.
   - *d.* I've never paid you back the ten dollars I owe you.
   - *e.* I'll lend you some money if you'll pay it back soon.

VERB STUDY

1. **apply for** (신청하다, 지원하다)
   a. 나는 여권을 신청해야만 합니다.
   b. 나는 3주일 전에 나의 비자를 신청했다.
   c. 당신은 무엇을 신청하고 있읍니까? 나는 직장에 응모하고 있읍니다.
2. **disconnect** ([전화를] 끊다)
   a. 나는 전화 끊는 것을 거의 잊을뻔 했다.
   b. 그들은 수도와 개스를 끊었다.
   c. 너는 왜 전화를 끊으려고 하느냐?
3. **remind, mention** (상기시키다, 말하다)
   a. 당신은 내게 나의 무거운 코우트를 가져가라고 일러주었으니 잘했소.
   b. 그녀를 보니 내 누이 생각이 났다.
   c. 그러고 보니 생각나는군. 나는 병원에 가봐야 겠다.
   d. 당신이 그 얘길하지 않았으면 나는 그것을 생각 못했을 것이다.
   e. 천만에요. 나는 그일을 하게되어 기뻤읍니다.
4. **arrive, see (somebody) off** (도착하다, 전송하다)
   a. 잊지 말고 당신의 안착을 우리에게 전보로 알려 주세요.
   b. 그녀는 오늘 6시 25분차로 도착 할 것이다.
   c. 나는 내일 오전 9시30분 샌프란시스코에 도착할 것이다.
   d. 나는 공항에서 당신을 전송 하겠읍니다.
   e. 우리는 어젯밤 기차역에서 친구들을 전송했다.
5. **cable** (전보 치다)
   a. 도착하거든 꼭 전보치세요.
   b. 나는 어젯밤 어머님께 전보쳤다. 전보는 10달러 들었다.
   c. 그녀는 내게 한 주일에 한 번 그녀의 안부를 전하는 전보를 친다.
   d. 그는 지금 나의 부인에게 전보치고 있다. 나는 나의 소재를 그녀에게 전한다.
6. **declare** ([세관에]신고하다, 선언하다)
   a. 세관 과세 물품을 휴대 하신 것 있읍니까?
   b. 우리는 그들과 동행하지 않을 것을 선언했다.
   c. 우리는 서로의 사랑을 선서했다.
   d. 우리는 개인 소지품을 세관에 신고하지 않았다.
7. **pay, pay back** (지불하다, 갚다)
   a. 당신은 개인 소지품에 대해 관세를 지불할 필요가 없읍니다.
   b. 그는 내게 빚진 10달러를 지불했다.
   c. 우리는 오늘 새 집 값을 지불할 것이다.
   d. 나는 네게 빚진 10달러를 갚지 않았다.
   e. 네가 곧 돌려주겠다면 돈을 좀 빌려주지.

*** 새로 나온 단어와 어귀 ***

visa「사증(査證), 비자」 **remind～of…**「～에게 …을 생각나게하다」 **Don't mention it.**「천만에요」

SUBSTITUTION DRILLS

1. I | didn't realize / had no idea / simply couldn't believe / couldn't believe | the time had passed so quickly.

2. I've got a lot of things | to do / to be done / that have to be done / left to do | before I can leave.

3. For one thing, I've got to drop by the bank to | get some money / cash a check / close my checking account / get some traveler's checks |.

4. It'll take almost all my | savings / salary / money / hard-earned money | to buy the ticket.

5. Oh, I just remembered something! I have to | apply for a passport / get a visa / go and get some inoculations / leave my forwarding address |

6. I almost forgot to have the | phone disconnected / milk delivery stopped / furniture covered up / postman stop delivering my mail / dog taken to the kennels |.

7. | It's a good thing / Luckily, / Fortunately, / By some good fortune, / It's lucky for me | you reminded me to take my heavy coat.

8. | I never would have thought of it / It wouldn't have occurred to me / I would have forgotten it / It would have slipped my mind / It would have escaped me | if you hadn't mentioned it.

9. I'll | see you off / say good-bye to you / tell you good-bye / kiss you good-bye | at the airport.

10. They're calling your flight now. You | barely / hardly / just / just barely / may just | have time to make it.

11. You'd better run or you're going to | be left behind / miss your flight / miss your train connection |.

12. Don't forget to | cable / send a cable / send a telegram / write | to let us know you arrived safely.

13. I'm sure I've forgotten something, but | it's too late now / it's a little late now / I shouldn't worry about it now / I mustn't think about it now |

14. Do you have | anything / any articles / any goods / any prohibited articles | to declare for customs?

15. You don't have to pay any duty on | personal belongings / things for your own use / your personal articles / used cameras / used clothing / birds and pets |.

SUBSTITUTION DRILLS

1. 인식하지 못했다
생각이 없었다
믿을 수가 었다
" " "

2. 할 일
해야 할 일
끝내야 할 일
남겨논 일

3. 돈을 찾다
수표를 현금으로 바꾸다
당좌예금을 모두 찾다
여행자 수표를 끊다

4. 저금
봉급
돈
열심이 번 돈

5. 여권신청을 하다
비자를 받다
예방주사를 맏다
여행지 주소를 남겨놓다

6. 전화를 끊다
우유배달을 끊다
가구를 덮어 놓다
우체부에게 편지배달을 중지하라고 하다
개를 훈련소에 데리고 가다

7. 좋은 일이다
다행이
다행이
다행이
나에게 운이었다

8. 그것을 생각하지 못할뻔하다
그것이 떠오르지 못할 뻔하다
그것을 잊어 버릴뻔 하다
그냥 넘겨 버릴뻔 하다
생각나지 않을뻔 하다

9. 전송
작별인사
잘 가시라고 하다
작별키스

10. 간신히
"
"
"
"

11. 처지다
놓치다
기차 연결을 놓치다

12. 전보하다
전보치다
"
편지쓰다

13. 너무늦다
약간늦다
걱정해선 안된다
그건생각해선 안된다

14. 물건
물품
물건
금지품

15. 개인 소지품
개인 용품
개인 물건
쓰던 카메라
입던 의복
새나 애완 동물

READING

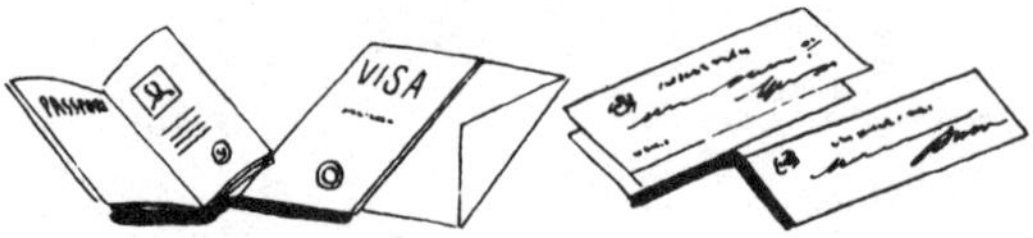

Making Preparations To Travel

Everyone told me to make my travel preparations early, but I thought I had plenty of time. I had no idea how much there was to do and I waited too long before I began getting ready.

First, I had to apply for a passport and visa because I was going to visit a foreign country. I had to get several inoculations at the doctor's office. Then I needed to drop by the bank and get some traveler's checks.

At the same time, there were many things to be taken care of at home. I had the phone disconnected and the dog taken to the kennels, but I almost forgot to have the milk and newspaper deliveries stopped. The postman had to remind me to leave my forwarding address at the post office. I know it would have slipped my mind if he hadn't mentioned it.

The day I was supposed to leave, I realized I still hadn't received my passport and visa. I simply couldn't believe the time had passed so quickly. I was really afraid I would be left behind.

Fortunately, the mail was delivered early and my passport arrived. By the time I got to the airport, they were already calling my flight. I just barely had time to make it. As soon as I sat down inside the plane, I remembered that I hadn't taken my camera, but it was too late to worry about that. I would have to buy another one if I wanted to take pictures.

I did have a wonderful time during this trip, but the next time I plan to travel, I'm going to be sure to start preparing early enough to avoid all the last-minute problems.

Questions

1. Why did I wait so long to begin getting ready for my trip?
2. What did I need because I was going to visit a foreign country?
3. What were the things I had to take care of at home?
4. Why was I afraid I would be left behind?
5. What did I forget to take?
6. Why is it a good idea to begin making travel plans early?

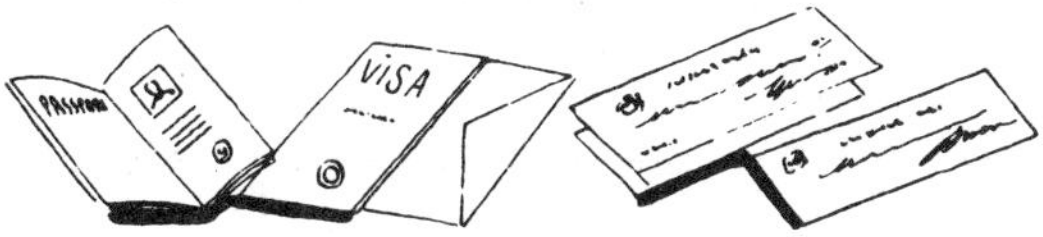

READING

(여행준비에 대한 대화)

여행 준비는 일찍 해 두라고, 모든 사람들이 내게 말해 주었지만 나는 시간이 많이 남았거니 하고 생각하고 있었읍니다. 할 일이 그렇게 많으리라고는 생각지 못하고 한참 지난 후에야 준비를 시작했읍니다.

우선 나는 외국을 방문하려고 하니까 여권과 비자를 신청해야 했읍니다. 나는 병원에 가서 여러가지 예방 접종을 맞아야 되었읍니다. 그리고 나서 은행에 들러 여행자 수표를 끊어야 할 필요가 있었읍니다.

동시에 집에서도 처리해야 할 일이 많이 있었읍니다. 나는 전화를 끊고 개를 개 훈련소에 데려다 주게 했읍니다. 그러나 나는 우유나 신문 배달을 중지시킨다는 걸 잊을 뻔 했읍니다. 우체부가 내게 나의 여행지 주소를 우체국에 남겨 놓고 가라고 일러 주어야 했읍니다. 만일 그 우체부가 그 얘기를 일러주지 않았으면 나는 잊을 뻔 했으리라고 생각합니다.

내가 떠나기로 된 날에야 나는 내가 아직도 여권과 비자를 받지 못했다는 걸 알았읍니다. 나는 도대체 시간이 그렇게 빨리 지나갈까 믿을 수가 없을 정도 였읍니다. 나는 정말 비행기를 못 타고 처지는 게 아닌가 염려되었읍니다.

다행히 우편물이 일찍 배달되어서 나의 여권이 도착되었읍니다. 내가 공항에 닿았을때, 내가 탈 비행기의 호명을 이미 하고 있었읍니다. 나는 시간에 댈 여유가 거의 없었읍니다. 내가 비행기 안에 자리를 잡자마자 나는 카메라를 가져오지 않은 것이 생각났읍니다만 이미 그런 걱정을 하기에는 시간이 너무 늦었읍니다. 사진을 찍으려면 사진기를 하나 더 사지 않으면 안 될 것입니다.

나는 여행도중 멋있는 시간을 보냈읍니다만 다음에 내가 여행계획을 세울 때는 일찍 준비를 해서 최종 순간의 그런 모든 곤란을 피하도록 할 것입니다.

＊ 새로 나온 단어와 어귀 ＊

I had no idea「나는 알지 못했다」 **I waited too long before～**「나는 한참 후에야 ～하게 되었다」 **inoculation**「예방접종」 **traveler's check**「여행자 수표」 **kennel**「개 훈련소」 **delivery**「배달」 **forwarding address**「여행지 주소」 **slip my mind**「잊다」 **deliver**「배달하다」 **last-minute**「최종 순간의」

CONVERSATION

Making Preparations To Travel

Dialog 1

MRS. JONES: I'm sure I'm forgetting something, steward, but I don't know what it is.

STEWARD: Do you have your passport, Mrs. Jones?

MRS. JONES: Yes, I have it right here. And I have the boat tickets. What else could it be?

STEWARD: You have all your suitcases, don't you?

MRS. JONES: I believe so. Let's see. One . . . two . . . three . . . four . . . five. Yes, they're all here.

STEWARD: Well, it seems to me you have everything you'll need, Mrs. Jones.

MRS. JONES: No, I don't. Something is missing, but I can't think what it could be.

STEWARD: Don't worry about it now. The ship is about to leave. By the way, where is Mr. Jones?

MRS. JONES: Mr. Jones? Oh! Now I know what it is! I forgot my husband!

Dialog 2

CLERK: May I help you, sir?

JIM: Yes, please. I want to buy a personal gift for my brother. He's taking a trip to South America.

CLERK: Is he going by ship or by plane?

JIM: He's flying. My gift will have to be something light in weight. What can you suggest?

CLERK: What about this wallet? It's made of very fine leather.

JIM: My sister already gave him one. I'd like something unusual.

CLERK: Here is a gift for the man who has everything.

JIM: Oh, a folding toothbrush. That's a wonderful idea. I'll take it.

CONVERSATION

(여행준비에 대한 대화)

대 화1.

Mrs.Jones : 이봐요. 웨이터 뭔가 내가 잊은것이 있는것 같은데.

Steward : 죠운즈 부인, 여권은 갖고 계신가요?

Mrs.Jones : 예, 그건 여기 갖고 있어요. 배표도 갖고 있는데. 도대체 그 이외엔 뭘까요?

Steward : 여행 가방은 모두 갖고 계시죠?

Mrs.Jones : 그럴거예요. 가만있자, 하나…, 둘…, 셋… 넷… 다섯. 모두 있는데요.

Steward : 그렇다면 부인께 필요한 건 모두 있는것 같습니다. 죠운즈 부인.

Mrs.Jones : 아녜요, 그렇지 않아요. 뭔가 잊은 것이 있는데, 도무지 언지 생각이 안나요.

Steward : 자, 그점에 대해선 걱정하지 마십시요. 배가 곧 출발할겁니다. 그런데 죠운즈 씨는 어디 계십니까?

Mrs.Jones : 죠운즈 씨요? 아! 이제 알겠어요! 남편을 잊고 있었어요.

대 화2.

Clerk : 도와 드릴까요, 선생님?

Jim : 예, 부탁합니다. 동생에게 줄 선물을 하나 사고 싶은데요. 그는 남아메리카로 여행을 떠날려고 합니다.

Clerk : 선편인가요, 비행기편인가요?

Jim : 비행기편입니다. 무게가 가벼운 선물이라야 하겠는데요. 뭐 좋은 것이 있겠읍니까?

Clerk : 이 지갑은 어떻읍니까? 고급 가죽 제품입니다.

Jim : 그건 벌써 내 누이가 선물했읍니다. 좀 특이한 거라면 좋겠는데요.

Clerk : 모든 것이 다 있는 분 한테는 이 선물이 괜찮읍니다.

Jim : 아 접는 치솔이군요. 그거 좋은 생각입니다. 그걸로 하지요.

*** 새로 나온 단어와 어귀 ***

steward=waiter **by the way**「그건 그렇고」 **folding**「접는」 **toothbrush**「치솔」

PARTICIPATION DRILLS

STUDENT A	STUDENT B
Have you *applied for a visa?*	I'm glad you reminded me. I keep forgetting to *do it*.
applied for a visa	do it
had the phone disconnected	have it done
bought a ticket	stop by the railroad station
left your forwarding address	go to the post office
called your sister	call her up
cashed a check	stop by the bank
covered the furniture	cover it up
seen the doctor	make an appointment
read that book	go to the library

EXERCISES

Question Patterns

1. **Student A changes the following statements to questions having a "yes - no" answer. Student B gives a short answer. Be sure to use the correct pronouns. Follow the examples.**

Examples: I'm going to study English next year.

Student A: *Are you going to study English next year?*
Student B: *Yes, I am.*

I'll need an English book for my class.

Student A: *Will you need an English book for your class?*
Student B: *Yes, I will.*

a. I have a lot of things to do before I leave on my trip.
b. I closed my checking account.
c. I should get some traveler's checks.
d. I might get some inoculations.
e. I must apply for a passport.
f. I'll leave my forwarding address at the post office.
g. I prefer to have the postman stop delivering my mail.
h. I could have the phone disconnected.
i. I'd rather say good-bye at the airport.
j. I'm going to send a cable as soon as I arrive.

2. **Student A changes each of the following statements into questions by attaching a tag question.**
Student B answers the questions.
Follow the examples.

Examples: You're studying English now.

Student A: *You're studying English now, aren't you?*
Student B: *Yes, I am.*

It won't be too difficult.

Student A: *It won't be too difficult, will it?*
Student B: *No, it won't.*

a. You have to drop by the bank to get some money.
b. It didn't take all your savings to buy the ticket.
c. You'll cover up the furniture.

d You won't forget to have the milk delivery stopped

e. You can take the dog to the kennels.

f. You couldn't miss your train connection.

g. You are taking your camera.

h. You weren't going to take your bird.

3. **Using the question words given, form questions which will ask for information contained in the statement. Be sure to use the correct pronouns. Follow the examples.**

Examples: I studied English at school last year.

Who: *Who studied English at school last year?*

When: *When did you study English at school?*

What: *What did you study at school last year?*

Where: *Where did you study English last year?*

a. I have to cash a check before I can leave.
What:
When:

b My ticket was paid for with my savings.
How:
What:

c. I'm going outside the country by plane.
How:
Where:

d. I have to take a taxi because I'm late.
Why:
What:

e. My friend will kiss me good-bye at the airport.
Who:
Where:

f. The customs office will examine my things to look for prohibited articles.
Which:
Why:

g. A traveler doesn't have to pay duty on personal articles.
What:
Who:

h. I'll send a cable as soon as I arrive.
What:
When:

4. Change the following statements into questions asking for the italicized item of information. Use the appropriate question word. Be sure to use the correct pronouns. Follow the examples.

Examples: It takes *a long time* to learn English fluently.
How long does it take to learn English fluently?
I travel to school *by bus.*
How do you travel to school?
I go to school *to learn English.*
Why do you go to school?
I need an *English* book.
What kind of book do you need?

a. I had to get a passport *because I was leaving the country.*
b. I'll be gone *for three months.*
c. I'm leaving for South America *tomorrow.*
d. I'm traveling *by plane.*
e. It's *five miles* to the airport from my house.
f. I'll need *a lot of* time for my trip.
g. I'll need a *smallpox* inoculation.
h. *My family* will come with me.

5. Form a new question using the phrase in parentheses. Be sure to use the correct word order. Follow the example.

Example: When will you study English? (*Do you know*)
Do you know when you will study English?

a. What kind of visa do you need? (*Can you find out*)
b. What should you declare for customs? (*Do you know*)
c. When did you apply for a passport? (*Do you remember*)
d. When will you send a telegram? (*Did you tell your family*)
e. How long will the flight take? (*Did you ask*)
f. Where should I leave my forwarding address? (*Will you please tell me*)

WORD LIST

article
barely
belongings
bird
cable
check
checking account
connection
customs
delivery
duty
flight
fortune
forwarding address
goods
hard-earned
hardly
inoculation
kennel
luckily
lucky
oh
passport
prohibited
safely
salary
traveler's check
use
visa

Verb Forms

cable
cash
cover up
declare
drop by
escape
kiss
leave behind
mention
pass
see off

Expressions

for one thing
slip (one's) mind

Supplementary Word List
(Conversation and Reading Practice)

folding toothbrush
steward
unusual

WORD INDEX

TO BOOK 5

The following is a listing of words introduced in Book Five. Each word in the listing is accompanied by the sentence in which the word was introduced in the text. The number shown in parentheses indicates the unit in which the sentence appeared.

A

a bit of	It wasn't a bit of trouble.	(9)
acceptable	Everything would have been acceptable if you hadn't said that.	(6)
account	I wish you would give me a more detailed account of your trip.	(1)
account	For one thing, I've got to drop by the bank to close my checking account.	(10)
agreeable	Everything would have been agreeable if you hadn't said that.	(6)
agreement	I must know your opinion. Are you in agreement with me?	(4)
aid	We may be able to aid you in some way.	(5)
air conditioning	That house is for sale. It has air conditioning.	(2)
alarm	If you had set your alarm, you would have had time for breakfast.	(6)
alike	Our views are not so much alike after all.	(4)
all right	I'm going to wear my blue suit. Is that all right?	(3)
alone	Thanks for the advice, but this is something I have to decide alone.	(8)
alternatives	What alternatives do I have?	(4)
amazing	An amazing thing happened to me this morning.	(1)
amazingly	You have amazingly good taste in clothes.	(7)
ambulance	I was crossing the street and was almost hit by an ambulance.	(1)
animal	What's your favorite kind of animal?	(7)
antiques	We have a few kitchen things and some antiques.	(2)
anymore	This dress doesn't fit me anymore.	(3)
apart	Our views are not so far apart after all.	(4)
appeal (to)	This dress doesn't appeal to me anymore.	(3)
appearance	I'm worried about the appearance of the floor.	(2)
appreciate	She doesn't ever appreciate anything I do or say.	(7)
approach	You approach it in a different way than I do.	(4)
aqua	I'm going to wear my aqua skirt.	(3)
architect	My son wants to be an architect when he grows up.	(5)
argument	Please forgive me. I didn't mean to start an argument.	(4)
articles	Do you have any articles to declare for customs?	(10)
assist	We may be able to assist you in some way.	(5)
astronaut	My son wants to be an astronaut when he grows up.	(5)

attend	If you were to attend the banquet, what would you wear?	(5)
attention	She doesn't pay any attention to anything I do or say.	(7)
attic	This is an interesting floor plan. Please show me the attic.	(2)
automatic	We have a few kitchen things and an automatic washing machine.	(2)
avoid	Fortunately, I jumped back in time to avoid being hit.	(1)

B

back	Does the back door have a lock on it?	(2)
bag	If I went with you, I'd have to take an overnight bag.	(5)
banquet	If you were to attend the banquet, what would you wear?	(5)
barber	I hope I remember to ask the barber not to cut my hair too short.	(5)
barbershop	If I have time tomorrow, I think I'll go to the barbershop.	(5)
barely	They're calling your flight now. You barely have time to make it.	(10)
bargain	This split-level house is for rent. It's a bargain.	(2)
bathing suit	I guess I've outgrown this bathing suit.	(3)
bathrobe	I guess I've outgrown my bathrobe.	(3)
beauty parlor	If I have time tomorrow, I think I'll go to the beauty parlor.	(5)
be back	If I went with you, I'd have to be back by six o'clock.	(5)
become	We never imagined that John would become a doctor.	(1)
bedroom	We've got to get a bed and a dresser for the bedroom.	(2)
beginning	I suggest that you tear up the letter and start from the beginning again.	(8)
behave	We used to behave strangely when we were that age.	(1)
belief	You have your belief, and I have mine.	(4)
belongings	You don't have to pay any duty on personal belongings.	(10)
below	You'd better wear gloves. It's below zero today.	(3)
beneath	After a while, we found a shady place beneath some oak trees.	(1)
be off (for)	If I get my work finished in time, I'll be off for New York Monday.	(5)
beside	If you want a wastebasket, look beside the desk.	(2)
birds	You don't have to pay any duty on birds and pets.	(10)
bitterly	I bitterly hate summer weather.	(7)
blouse	I'm going to wear my skirt and blouse.	(3)
blowout	On the way back home,we had a blowout.	(1)
bones	If you hadn't slipped and fallen, there wouldn't be any broken bones.	(6)
boots	I guess I've outgrown these boots.	(3)
borrow	If I buy that car, I'll have to borrow some money.	(5)
bother	I'm afraid it was a bother for you to do this.	(9)
bothersome	I'm afraid it was bothersome for you to do this.	(9)
breakdown	On the way back home, we had a breakdown.	(1)

breath	He won't pay attention to anybody—you're just wasting your breath.	(8)
bridge	I like to play bridge, but I'm not a very good player.	(7)
bright	He seems to have a lot of bright ideas.	(4)
broke	Could you lend me ten dollars? I seem to be broke.	(9)
brook	We prepared a picnic lunch and drove down by the brook.	(1)
buckle	I can't buckle this belt.	(3)
burden	I'm afraid it was a burden on you to do this.	(9)
burning	Would you please keep the fire burning for me?	(9)
business	It's none of my business, but I think you ought to work harder.	(8)
button	I can't fasten this collar button.	(3)

C

cabin	We're looking for a cabin to rent for the summer.	(2)
cable	Don't forget to send a cable to let us know you arrived safely.	(10)
cable	Don't forget to cable to let us know you arrived safely.	(10)
canal	We prepared a picnic lunch and drove down by the canal.	(1)
card	I like to play card games, but I'm not a very good player.	(7)
care (for)	If you care for my advice, I don't think you should go.	(8)
carefully	Thinking it over carefully, I wish we hadn't given in so easily.	(6)
carpeted	They've already carpeted the floors.	(2)
cash	If he had only had enough money, he would have paid cash for the car.	(6)
cash	For one thing, I've got to drop by the bank to cash a check.	(10)
cause	I certainly didn't intend to cause you so much inconvenience.	(9)
cautious	I'm afraid you're being too cautious about your food.	(7)
cautiously	In general, my reaction is that we should proceed cautiously.	(8)
central	That house is for sale. It has central heating.	(2)
ceremony	If you were to attend the ceremony, what would you wear?	(5)
check	For one thing, I've got to drop by the bank to cash a check.	(10)
checkers	I like to play checkers, but I'm not a very good player.	(7)
checking	For one thing, I've got to drop by the bank to close my checking account.	(10)
chess	I like to play chess, but I'm not a very good player.	(7)
childish	I won't argue with you,but I think you're being childish.	(4)
Christmas	There's a chance he won't be able to be home for Christmas.	(5)

Christmastime	There's a chance he won't be able to make it home at Christmastime.	(5)
circumstances	I can't recall the exact circumstances.	(1)
cleaned	You ought to have that coat cleaned and pressed.	(3)
cleaners	I have two suits to send to the cleaners.	(3)
clever	He seems to have a lot of clever ideas.	(4)
close	Our views are not so close together after all.	(4)
club	If it doesn't rain tomorrow, I think I'll attend the club meeting.	(5)
collar	I can't fasten this collar button.	(3)
colonial	This colonial style house is for rent.	(2)
conceive (of)	You conceive of it in a different way than I do.	(4)
concerned	As far as I'm concerned, the house isn't worth the price they're asking.	(8)
condition	The house needs painting. It's in bad condition.	(2)
conflict	Please forgive me. I didn't mean to start a conflict.	(4)
conflicting	We have conflicting views on this.	(4)
connection	You'd better run or you're going to miss your connection.	(10)
conservative	That's a conservative point of view.	(4)
considerate	You're very considerate to take the trouble to help me.	(9)
conveniences	That house is for sale. It has all the modern conveniences.	(2)
cottage	We're looking for a cottage to rent for the summer.	(2)
covered up	I almost forgot to have the furniture covered up.	(10)
creek	We prepared a picnic lunch and drove down by the creek.	(1)
critical	I'm afraid you're being too critical about your food.	(7)
crossing	I was crossing the street and was almost hit by a car.	(1)
curtains	We have drapes for the living room, but we need kitchen curtains.	(2)
customs	Do you have anything to declare for customs?	(10)
cutting	The roof has leaks in it, and the grass needs cutting.	(2)

D

dance	If you were to attend the formal dance, what would you wear?	(5)
danger	Fortunately, I realized the danger in time to avoid being hit.	(1)
debate	Please forgive me. I didn't mean to start a debate.	(4)
debating	I don't see any point in debating the question any further.	(4)
declare	Do you have anything to declare for customs?	(10)
delivery	I almost forgot to have the milk delivery stopped.	(10)
den	This is an interesting floor plan. Please show me the den.	(2)
depart	If I get my work finished in time, I'll depart for New York Monday.	(5)
depends (on)	There's a possibility we'll go, but it all depends on the weather.	(5)

description	I wish you would give me a more detailed description of your trip.	(1)
deserves	Everyone deserves the right to his own opinion.	(4)
detailed	I wish you would give me a more detailed description of your trip.	(1)
details	Let me tell you all the details.	(1)
disagree (with)	I must know your opinion. Do you disagree with me?	(4)
discussing	I don't see any point in discussing the question any further.	(4)
discussion	Please forgive me. I didn't mean to start a long discussion.	(4)
dislike	Why do you dislike the medicine so much?	(7)
double	That house is for sale. It has a double garage.	(2)
drapes	We have drapes for the living room, but we need kitchen curtains.	(2)
drawer	If you want a paper clip, look inside the drawer of the desk.	(2)
dreamed	We never dreamed that John would become a doctor.	(1)
dresser	We've got to get a bed and a dresser for the bedroom.	(2)
drop by	For one thing, I've got to drop by the bank to get some money.	(10)
duplex	This duplex apartment is for rent.	(2)
duty	You don't have to pay any duty on personal belongings.	(10)

E

easily	Looking back on it, I wish we hadn't given in so easily.	(6)
efficiency	This efficiency apartment is for rent.	(2)
electricity	They've already turned on the electricity.	(2)
electronic	My son wants to be an electronic engineer when he grows up.	(5)
elm	After a while, we found a shady place near some elm trees.	(1)
energy	He won't pay any attention to anybody. You're just wasting your energy.	(8)
engine	On the way back home,we had some engine trouble.	(1)
enrolled	Even if we could have enrolled in a class, we might not have wanted to.	(6)
entertainment	What's your favorite kind of entertainment?	(7)
entirely	In general, my reaction is not entirely negative.	(8)
entitled	Everyone is entitled to his own opinion.	(4)
errands	If it doesn't rain tomorrow, I think I'll run some errands.	(5)
escaped	It would have escaped me if you hadn't mentioned it.	(10)
especially	What is it you especially don't like about winter weather?	(7)
even	Even if we could have taken a vacation, we might not have wanted to.	(6)

evening dress	Why don't you get dressed now? Put on your evening dress.	(3)
ever	Speaking of trips, did I ever tell you about the experience I had?	(1)
everything	There are always two sides to everything.	(4)
exhausted	It was after dark when we got back, and we were all exhausted.	(1)
expense	The thing I don't like about photography is all the expense.	(7)
experience	It was a terrible experience, and I won't forget it.	(1)

F

fair	Are you being fair? Have you listened to both sides of the question?	(4)
fasten	I can't fasten this collar button.	(3)
fatherly	Let me give you a little fatherly advice.	(8)
fault	He always finds fault with everything.	(7)
favorable	In general, my reaction is favorable.	(8)
feeling	It was a terrible feeling, and I won't forget it.	(1)
fight	Please forgive me. I didn't mean to start a fight.	(4)
figure out	Thanks for the advice, but this is something I have to figure out myself.	(8)
fire	Would you please keep the fire burning for me?	(9)
fire engine	I was crossing the street and was almost hit by a fire engine.	(1)
fireplace	That house is for sale. It has a nice fireplace.	(2)
flat	On the way back home, we had a flat tire.	(1)
flight	They're calling your flight now.	(10)
floor plan	This is an interesting floor plan.	(2)
flower beds	The roof has leaks in it, and the flower beds have to be weeded.	(2)
for	I must know your opinion. Are you for or against me?	(4)
forgive	Please forgive me. I didn't mean to start an argument.	(4)
formal	If you were to attend the formal dance, what would you wear?	(5)
fortune	By some good fortune you reminded me to take my heavy coat.	(10)
fortunately	Fortunately, I jumped back in time to avoid being hit.	(1)
forwarding	Oh, I just remembered something! I have to leave my forwarding address.	(10)
front	The roof has leaks in it, and the front steps need to be fixed.	(2)
full	Would you mind opening the door? My arms are full.	(9)
fun	We used to have a lot of fun when we were that age.	(1)
furnished	Are you trying to find a furnished house?	(2)
further	I don't see any point in discussing the question any further.	(4)
fussy	I'm afraid you're being too fussy about your food.	(7)

G

garage	That house is for sale. It has a double garage.	(2)
general	In general, my reaction is favorable.	(8)
genius	I never realized that someday I would be married to a genius.	(1)
get across	What point are you trying to get across?	(4)
given in	Looking back on it, I wish we hadn't given in so easily.	(6)
glorious	Yesterday was such a glorious day we decided to go for a drive.	(1)
gloves	You'd better wear gloves. It's below zero today.	(3)
golf	I like to play golf, but I'm not a very good player.	(7)
goods	Do you have any goods to declare for customs?	(10)
go off (on)	One of these days, I'd like to go off on a vacation.	(5)
got back	It was after dark when we got back, and we were all tired.	(1)
grass	The roof has leaks in it, and the grass needs cutting.	(2)
grateful	He'll always be grateful to you for what you've done.	(9)
gratitude	I wish I could show my gratitude to you somehow for your kindness.	(9)
guess	Unless I miss my guess, the house isn't worth the price they're asking.	(8)

H

haircut	If I have time tomorrow, I think I'll get a haircut.	(5)
hallway	This is an interesting floor plan. Please show me the hallway.	(2)
hang	We have drapes, but we need pictures to hang on the walls.	(2)
happened	A strange thing happened to me this morning.	(1)
hard-earned	It'll take almost all my hard-earned money to buy the ticket.	(10)
hardly	They're calling your flight now. You hardly have time to make it.	(10)
hate	What is it you hate about winter weather?	(7)
head (for)	If I get my work finished in time, I'll head for New York Monday.	(5)
heating	That house is for sale. It has central heating.	(2)
help	We may be able to give help to you in some way.	(5)
help out	We may be able to help you out in some way.	(5)
highway	My son wants to be a highway engineer when he grows up.	(5)
hit	I was crossing the street and was almost hit by a car.	(1)
hobby	What's your favorite hobby?	(7)
hold	Would you please hold the door open for me?	(9)
housekeeping	Why do you dislike housekeeping so much?	(7)
hurried up	If you had hurried up, you would have had time for breakfast.	(6)

I		
importance	She doesn't give any importance to anything I do or say.	(7)
imposition	I'm afraid it was an imposition on you to do this.	(9)
impractical	I won't argue with you, but I think you're being impractical.	(4)
inconvenience	I certainly didn't intend to cause you so much inconvenience.	(9)
indebted	He'll always be indebted to you for what you've done.	(9)
inexpensive	Are you trying to find an inexpensive house?	(2)
inoculations	Oh, I just remembered something! I have to go and get some inoculations.	(10)
installed	They've already installed the telephone.	(2)
instrument	What's your favorite musical instrument?	(7)
intelligent	I'm intelligent enough to make up my own mind.	(8)
interfere (in)	I've always tried not to interfere in your affairs.	(8)
interior	They've already completed the interior.	(2)
involved	I certainly didn't intend to get you so involved in my problems.	(9)
introduced	Would he have seen you if you hadn't introduced yourself to him?	(6)
ironed	I've got to get this shirt washed and ironed.	(3)
J		
jammed	Would you be so kind as to open this window for me? It's jammed.	(9)
jokes	We used to tell a lot of jokes when we were that age.	(1)
jumped back	Fortunately, I jumped back in time to avoid being hit.	(1)
K		
kennels	I almost forgot to have the dog taken to the kennels.	(10)
key	Had I known you didn't have a key, I wouldn't have locked the door.	(6)
kindness	I wish I could repay you somehow for your kindness.	(9)
kiss	I'll kiss you good-bye at the airport.	(10)
L		
lake	We prepared a picnic lunch and drove down by the lake.	(1)
laundry	This is an interesting floor plan. Please show me the laundry room.	(2)
leaks	The roof has leaks in it, and the front steps need to be fixed.	(2)
leave	There's a chance he won't be able to get leave in December.	(5)
left behind	You'd better run or you're going to be left behind.	(10)
lend	If I buy that car, I'll have to get somebody to lend me money.	(5)

less	I must know your opinion. Do you more or less agree with me?	(4)
let down	You ought to have that coat let down in the sleeves.	(3)
liberal	That's a liberal point of view.	(4)
lightweight	You'd better wear a lightweight suit. It's hot today.	(3)
linen	If you want a towel, look in the linen closet.	(2)
linens	I've got to get these linens washed and ironed.	(3)
loaning	Would you mind loaning me some money?	(9)
lock	Does the back door have a lock on it?	(2)
looking back (on)	Looking back on it, I wish we hadn't given in so easily.	(6)
looks	I'm worried about the looks of the woodwork.	(2)
lost	If I had asked for directions, I wouldn't have gotten lost.	(6)
loudly	I'd appreciate it if you would not talk so loudly.	(9)
luckily	Luckily you reminded me to take my heavy coat.	(10)
lucky	It's lucky for me you reminded me to take my heavy coat.	(10)
lump-sum	If he had only had enough money, he would have made a lump-sum payment.	(6)

M

mad	Please don't get mad.	(8)
magnificent	Yesterday was such a magnificent day we decided to go for a drive.	(1)
makes	I don't like spinach even though I know it makes me strong.	(7)
market	If it doesn't rain tomorrow, I think I'll go to the market.	(5)
matter	I don't have any say in the matter, but I think you ought to work harder.	(8)
mature	I'm mature enough to make up my own mind.	(8)
mean to	Please forgive me. I didn't mean to start an argument.	(4)
memorandum	If there's anything else I can do, please send me a memorandum.	(9)
mentioned	I never would have thought of it if you hadn't mentioned it.	(10)
mirror	We've got to get a mirror and a rug for the bathroom.	(2)
miserably	I don't like it when the weather gets miserably cold.	(7)
modern	That house is for sale. It has all the modern conveniences.	(2)
monthly	If I buy that car, I'll have to make monthly payments.	(5)
motherly	Let me give you a little motherly advice.	(8)
motor	On the way back home, we had motor trouble.	(1)
motorcycle	I was crossing the street and was almost hit by a motorcycle.	(1)
museums	If I had had time, I would have visited all the museums.	(6)
musical	What's your favorite musical instrument?	(7)

N

narrow-minded	I won't argue with you, but I think you're being narrow-minded.	(4)
need	We have drapes for the living room, but we need kitchen curtains.	(2)
negative	He always sees the negative side of everything.	(7)
notice	I didn't notice you were wearing your new hat.	(3)

O

oak	After a while, we found a shady place beneath some oak trees.	(1)
objects (to)	He always objects to everything.	(7)
occur	It didn't occur to me that you were wearing your new hat.	(3)
odd	An odd thing happened to me this morning.	(1)
offended	Please don't be offended.	(8)
offense	Please don't take offense.	(8)
oh	Oh, I just remembered something! I have to apply for a passport.	(10)
open	Would you please hold the door open for me?	(9)
opponent	The debate was fair. Each opponent had a chance to speak.	(4)
opportunity	As soon as I have an opportunity, I'm going to change jobs.	(5)
opposing	We have opposing views on this.	(4)
opposite	We have opposite views on this.	(4)
outgrown	I guess I've outgrown this pair of trousers.	(3)
overnight	If I went with you, I'd have to take an overnight bag.	(5)

P

paid	Could you lend me ten dollars? I don't get paid until tomorrow.	(9)
paint	We have drapes, but we need paint to paint the house with.	(2)
painting	The house needs painting.	(2)
paper clip	If you want a paper clip, look inside the drawer of the desk.	(2)
particular	I'm afraid you're being too particular about your food.	(7)
particularly	What is it you particularly dislike about winter weather?	(7)
passed	I didn't realize the time had passed so quickly.	(10)
passport	Oh, I just remembered something! I have to apply for a passport.	(10)
pastime	What's your favorite pastime?	(7)
payments	If I buy that car, I'll have to make monthly payments.	(5)
peculiar	A peculiar thing happened to me this morning.	(1)
period	What style furniture do you have? Is it period furniture?	(2)

permission	If I went with you, I'd have to get my father's permission.	(5)
photography	The thing I don't like about photography is all the expense.	(7)
physicist	My son wants to be a physicist when he grows up.	(5)
picnic	We prepared a picnic lunch and drove down by the river.	(1)
ping-pong	I like to play ping-pong, but I'm not a very good player.	(7)
player	I like to play tennis, but I'm not a very good player.	(7)
please	It's only a suggestion, and you can do what you please.	(8)
plumbing	They've already put in the plumbing.	(2)
point	You have your point of view and I have mine.	(4)
policeman	My son wants to be a policeman when he grows up.	(5)
poplar	After a while, we found a shady place under some poplar trees.	(1)
porch	Does the front porch have a street number on it?	(2)
present	The debate was fair. Each opponent had a chance to present his argument.	(4)
pressed	You ought to have that coat cleaned and pressed.	(3)
proceed	In general, my reaction is that we should proceed cautiously.	(8)
prohibited	Do you have any prohibited articles to declare for customs?	(10)
prove	What point are you trying to prove?	(4)
push	Would you mind giving me a push?	(9)
put across	What point are you trying to put across?	(4)
put in	They've already put in the plumbing.	(2)

Q

quarrel	Please forgive me. I didn't mean to start a quarrel.	(4)

R

radical	That's a radical point of view.	(4)
rainy	You'd better wear a raincoat. It's rainy today.	(3)
rattan	What style furniture do you have? Is it rattan?	(2)
reacted	Fortunately, I reacted in time to avoid being hit.	(1)
reaction	What would be your reaction if I told you I couldn't go with you?	(5)
real	I don't like it when the weather gets real cold.	(7)
realized	I never realized that someday I would be living in New York.	(1)
reception	If you were to attend the reception, what would you wear?	(5)
reconcile	We should be able to reconcile our differences.	(4)
reconstruct	I can't reconstruct the exact circumstances.	(1)
redwood	After a while, we found a shady place by some redwood trees.	(1)
refrigerator	We've got to get a refrigerator for the kitchen.	(2)
regret	If you don't take my advice, you'll regret it later.	(8)

remarkably	You have remarkably good taste in clothes.	(7)
remodeling	The house needs remodeling.	(2)
rent	We're looking for a house to rent for the summer.	(2)
repaired	The roof has leaks in it, and the side door ought to be repaired.	(2)
repay	I wish I could repay you somehow for your kindness.	(9)
report	I wish you would give me a more detailed report of your trip.	(1)
report	I can't report the exact circumstances.	(1)
resolve	We should be able to resolve our differences.	(4)
responsibility	It's not my responsibility, but I think you ought to work harder.	(8)
revolution	Please forgive me. I didn't mean to start a revolution.	(4)
reward	I wish I could reward you somehow for your kindness.	(9)
rid of	One of these days, I'd like to get rid of my old car.	(5)
right	Everyone has a right to his own opinion.	(4)
riot	Please forgive me. I didn't mean to start a riot.	(4)
river	We prepared a picnic lunch and drove down by the river.	(1)
roof	The roof has leaks in it, and the front steps need to be fixed.	(2)
room	We're looking for a room to rent for the summer.	(2)
run	If it doesn't rain tomorrow, I think I'll run some errands.	(5)

S

safely	Don't forget to cable to let us know you arrived safely.	(10)
salary	It'll take almost all my salary to buy the ticket.	(10)
savings	If I buy that car, I'll have to use all my savings.	(5)
say	I don't have any say in the matter, but I think you ought to work harder.	(8)
scissors	If you want scissors, look over on the table.	(2)
scrub	I'm worried about the looks of the woodwork. I need to scrub it.	(2)
see off	I'll see you off at the airport.	(10)
selfish	That's a selfish point of view.	(4)
set	If I have time tomorrow, I think I'll get my hair set.	(5)
set	We have a few kitchen things and a dining room set.	(2)
settle	We should be able to settle our differences.	(4)
shady	After a while, we found a shady place under some poplar trees.	(1)
shampoo	If I have time tomorrow, I think I'll shampoo my hair.	(5)
sheets	If you want some sheets, look down in the laundry room.	(2)
shock	It was a terrible shock and I won't forget it.	(1)
shoelaces	I can't tie these shoelaces.	(3)
shoestrings	I can't tie these shoestrings.	(3)
shouted	Would he have seen you if you hadn't shouted to him?	(6)
simple	Let me give you a little simple advice.	(8)

simply	I simply can't take summer weather.	(7)
sink	We've got to get a sink and a stove for the kitchen.	(2)
skirt	I'm going to wear my aqua skirt.	(3)
slacks	I have a pair of slacks to send to the cleaners.	(3)
sleeves	You ought to have that coat taken up in the sleeves.	(3)
sliding	Does the garage have a sliding door on it?	(2)
slipped	It would have slipped my mind if you hadn't mentioned it.	(10)
slippers	I guess I've outgrown my old house slippers.	(3)
smart	I'm smart enough to make up my own mind.	(8)
smell	I didn't like the smell of the medicine, but I took it anyway.	(7)
sofa	We've got to get a sofa and a chair for the living room.	(2)
sold	Had I known you didn't have money, I wouldn't have sold you the car.	(6)
solve	Thanks for the advice, but this is something I have to solve by myself.	(8)
someday	I never realized that someday I would be living in New York.	(1)
somehow	I wish I could repay you somehow for your kindness.	(9)
split-level	This split-level house is for rent.	(2)
sports car	I was crossing the street and was almost hit by a sports car.	(1)
sprained	Would you mind helping me up? My ankle is sprained.	(9)
sprained	If you hadn't slipped and fallen, you wouldn't have sprained your ankle.	(6)
stairway	This is an interesting floor plan. Please show me the stairway.	(2)
stalled	Would you mind giving me a push? My car has stalled.	(9)
stand	I can't stand summer weather.	(7)
stand	We've got to get a telephone stand for the hallway.	(2)
start over	I suggest that you tear up the letter and start over again.	(8)
steps	The roof has leaks in it, and the front steps need to be fixed.	(2)
stove	We've got to get a sink and a stove for the kitchen.	(2)
strangely	We used to behave strangely when we were that age.	(1)
stubborn	I won't argue with you,but I think you're being stubborn.	(4)
stuck	Would you be so kind as to open this window for me? It's stuck.	(9)
style	What style furniture do you have?	(2)
such	Yesterday was such a beautiful day we decided to go for a drive.	(1)
suggest	I suggest that you wear something warm. It's cold today.	(3)
suggestion	It's only a suggestion, and you can do what you please.	(8)
suspected	We never suspected that John would become a doctor.	(1)
sweet	You're very sweet to take the trouble to help me.	(9)
swimming trunks	I guess I've outgrown these swimming trunks.	(3)

T

tablecloths	I've got to get these tablecloths washed and ironed.	(3)
tailored	You ought to have that coat tailored to fit you.	(3)
tails	Why don't you get dressed now? Put on your white tie and tails.	(3)
taken up	You ought to have that coat taken up in the sleeves.	(3)
taste	You have wonderful taste in clothes.	(7)
taste	I didn't like the taste of the medicine, but I took it anyway.	(7)
team	What's your favorite baseball team?	(7)
tear up	I suggest that you tear up the letter and start over again.	(8)
tell	As far as I can tell, the house isn't worth the price they're asking.	(8)
tennis	I like to play tennis, but I'm not a very good player.	(7)
terribly	I don't like it when the weather gets terribly cold.	(7)
thankful	He'll always be thankful to you for what you've done.	(9)
though	I don't like spinach even though I know it's good for me.	(7)
thoughtful	You're very thoughtful to take the trouble to help me.	(9)
tie	I can't tie these shoestrings.	(3)
tightly	Would you be so kind as to open this window for me? It's tightly closed.	(9)
tire	On the way back home we had a flat tire.	(1)
tonic	I hope I remember to ask the barber not to put tonic on my hair.	(5)
towel	If you want a towel, look in the linen closet.	(2)
trade in	One of these days I'd like to trade my old car in.	(5)
traditional	What style furniture do you have? Is it traditional?	(2)
traffic	The thing I don't like about driving is all the traffic on the road.	(7)
training	Had I known you didn't have training, I wouldn't have hired you.	(6)
traveler's	For one thing, I've got to drop by the bank to get some traveler's checks.	(10)
trousers	I guess I've outgrown this pair of trousers.	(3)
trunk	If you want a trunk, look up in the attic.	(2)
tuxedo	I'm going to wear my tuxedo.	(3)

U

unbelievably	You have unbelievably good taste in clothes.	(7)
unbutton	I can't unbutton this shirt.	(3)
uncomfortably	I don't like it when the weather gets uncomfortably cold.	(7)
under	After a while, we found a shady place under some poplar trees.	(1)
understanding	You're very understanding to take the trouble to help me.	(9)
underwear	I have some underwear to send to the laundry.	(3)
undressed	My brother came in, undressed, and went to bed.	(3)

unfair	I won't argue with you, but I think you're being unfair.	(4)
unfurnished	Are you trying to find an unfurnished house?	(2)
unless	Unless I'm wrong, the house isn't worth the price they're asking.	(8)
unlocked	Would you please leave the door unlocked for me?	(9)
unusually	I don't like it when the weather gets unusually cold.	(7)
upset	I certainly didn't intend to upset your plans.	(9)
use	You don't have to pay any duty on things for your own use.	(10)
used	These shoes are worn out. They've been used for a long time.	(3)

V

vacation	One of these days, I'd like to take a vacation.	(5)
view	You view it in a different way than I do.	(4)
viewpoint	You have your viewpoint, and I have mine.	(4)
visa	Oh, I just remembered something! I have to get a visa.	(10)
visualize	You visualize it in a different way than I do.	(4)

W

wallet	Could you lend me ten dollars? I left my wallet at home.	(9)
washing machine	We have a few kitchen things and an automatic washing machine.	(2)
wastebasket	If you want a wastebasket, look beside the desk.	(2)
wasting	He won't pay attention to anybody. You're just wasting your breath.	(8)
waved	Would he have seen you if you hadn't waved to him?	(6)
wax	I'm worried about the appearance of the floor. I need to wax it.	(2)
weeded	The roof has leaks in it, and the flower beds have to be weeded.	(2)
well advised	My feeling is that you would be well advised to stay home tonight.	(8)
whole	Let me tell you the whole story.	(1)
widely	We have widely different views on this.	(4)
woodwork	I'm worried about the looks of the woodwork.	(2)
work out	Thanks for the advice, but this is something I have to work out myself.	(8)
worn out	It was after dark when we got back, and we were all worn out.	(1)
worth	In my opinion, the house isn't worth the price they're asking.	(8)
wrinkled	All my suits are wrinkled. I don't have anything to wear.	(3)

Y

yard	That house is for sale. It has a big back yard.	(2)

KEY
TO EXERCISES

UNIT 1

Page 10

1. *a.* Yesterday, *b.* lunch, *c.* peculiar thing, *d.* I, *e.* blowout, *f.* accident, *g.* We, *h.* shady place

2. *a.* Others, *b.* Several, *c.* one, *d.* another, *e.* That, *f.* That, *g.* those, *h.* these

3. *a.* Yes, reacting quickly to a blowout could avoid an accident.
   b. Yes, having an automobile accident was a terrible experience.
   c. Yes, flying a plane is difficult.
   d. Yes, having a picnic near the river was a wonderful experience.
   e. Yes, exchanging stories about foreign countries was interesting.
   f. No, crossing the street against the light was not a good joke.

4. *a.* v, *b.* x, *c.* z, *d.* w, *e.* y, *f.* u

5. *a.* It is expensive to take a trip.
   b. It is important to remember the exact circumstances of an accident.
   c. It is wonderful to picnic near a lake.
   d. It is a lot of fun to tell jokes.
   e. It is not easy to forget a terrible experience.
   f. There was a big oak tree near the canal.
   g. There were several accounts of the accident given to the police.

UNIT 2

Page 22

1. *a.* a, *b.* (no article), *c.* an, *d.* a, *e.* a, *f.* a, the, *g.* (no article), the, *h.* the, the, *i.* (no article), *j.* a, an

2. *a.* Many, *b.* a lot of, *c.* a few, *d.* a few, *e.* a little, *f.* much

3. *a.* Some, *b.* any, *c.* some, *d.* some, *e.* any, *f.* any (some) (*both are correct for questions*), *g.* any

4. *a.* bigger, *b.* simpler, *c.* worse, *d.* smaller, *e.* easier, *f.* better, *g.* more expensive, *h.* more convenient

5. *a.* biggest, *b.* oldest, *c.* worst, *d.* best, *e.* nicest, *f.* most modern

UNIT 3

Page 34

1. *a.* A *lightweight suit* is comfortable on a hot day.
   b. I send *dirty clothes* to the laundry.
   c. It's cloudy so you'd better put on a *raincoat* today.
   d. This *wrinkled suit* will have to be pressed.
   e. My *aqua skirt* is the same color as my blouse.
   f. If you're going to clean the basement, you'd better wear your *work clothes.*
   g. I can't fasten this *collar button.* Will you help me?
   h. Those *swimming trunks* are too small.
   i. I didn't realize I had outgrown my *bathing suit.*

2. *a.* The tailor who is on Main Street cleaned and pressed my coat.
   b. The men who came to the party wore dress clothes.
   c. My husband, who likes to be comfortable, wears slippers and a bathrobe in the house.
   d. The man who forgot his jacket is chilly.

3. *a.* The tailor who cleaned and pressed my coat is on Main Street.
   b. The men who wore dress clothes came to the party.
   c. My husband, who wears slippers and a bathrobe in the house likes to be comfortable.
   d. The man who is chilly forgot his jacket.

4. *a.* These shoes, which are worn-out, lasted for a long time.
   b. This dress, which doesn't fit me anymore, doesn't look good.
   c. These sleeves, which are too short, have to be let down.
   d. This dress,which is too long, has to be taken up.

5. *a.* These shoes, which lasted for a long time, are worn-out.
   b. This dress, which doesn't look good, doesn't fit me anymore.
   c. These sleeves, which have to be let down, are too short.
   d. This dress, which has to be taken up, is too long.

6. *a.* My children's shoes are too small. They need larger ones.
   b. My brother's dress suit is out of style. He borrowed mine.
   c. The girl's dress was worn out. She needed a new one.
   d. The woman's hat was new. She showed it to all her friends.
   e. The man's clothes were dirty. He took them to the cleaners.

7. *a.* which, *b.* who, *c.* which, *d.* whose, *e.* who

UNIT 4

Page 46

1. *a.* viewpoints, *b.* agreement, *c.* conservative's, *d.* side, *e.* argument, *f.* conflict

2. *a.* theirs, *b.* mine, *c.* ours, *d.* his, *e.* yours, *f.* hers, *g.* our, *h.* their, *i.* her, *j.* my, *k.* your

3. *a.* I learned what John's point of view is.
   b. I don't understand why they are arguing.
   c. I can't say how many answers there are to this question.
   d. Please explain what point you are trying to prove.
   e. I would like to know what the discussion is all about.
   f. I can't imagine how long this conflict has been going on.
   g. Please tell me who the speaker is.
   h. I've found out why he is so narrow-minded.
   i. I don't know what a radical is.
   j. Please repeat what the speaker said about revolution.

4. *a.* He explained his point of view to me.
   b. I'm going to ask him for some practical arguments.
   c. I asked my opponent for his opinion.
   d. The teacher told us about the revolution in ideas.
   e. I talked over our differences with him.
   f. He tried to put his peculiar viewpoint across to me.
   g. The conservative student debated the question with the liberal.
   h. The teacher gave him alternative answers to the question.
   i. The speaker couldn't give us answers to our questions.
   j. I asked my opponent for proof of his strange statements.

UNIT 5

Page 57

1. *a.* tomorrow, *b.* last night, *c.* every year, *d.* one of these days, *e.* some day, *f.* every month, *g.* in the near future, *h.* the day before yesterday, *i.* every year

2. *a.* Highway engineers built this road last year.
   b. An architect will design my house next year.
   c. I go shopping every Saturday.
   d. Did you buy a new car a year ago?

e. I will get somebody to lend me money tomorrow.
f. The teacher will help the student out with his problem next week.
g. I tried to get my father's permission to travel yesterday.
h. Could you get rid of your old car last year?

3. *a.* last week, *b.* many times, *c.* already, *d.* last summer, *e.* since 1960, *f.* last month, *g.* last night, *h.* never

4. *a.* I have already gone to the market.
b. The barber cut my hair too short last Saturday.
c. The physicist has studied physics since 1957.
d. I took an overnight bag when I went to San Francisco last weekend.
e. He found it impossible to change jobs a year ago.
f. The young girl has never attended (never attended) a wedding reception.
g. The businessmen have held (held) an annual banquet for many years.
h. I tried to trade my old car in, but nobody wanted it.
i. I have never been to the beauty parlor.
j. I went shopping last night.

5. *a.* I need a haircut because I haven't been to the barber recently.
b. I've already had my vacation.
c. I haven't changed jobs for years.
d. He just left for San Francisco.
e. I haven't ever borrowed any money.
f. I've never made monthly payments.
g. I haven't taken a trip around the world yet.
h. I haven't been home for Christmas since 1960.
i. I haven't been to New York for a long time.
j. I've been to Washington many times.

UNIT 6

Page 70

1. *a.* had visited
b. had gone
c. had slept
d. had gotten lost
e. had bought
f. had enrolled

2. *a.* had already started
b. had borrowed
c. had lost
d. had never met
e. had seen

3. *a.* is
   b. has
   c. lose
   d. asks
   e. use

4. *a.* was (were) (*both are acceptable*)
   b. had
   c. lost
   d. asked
   e. used
   f. had to

5. *a.* had been
   b. had had
   c. had lost
   d. had asked
   e. had used
   f. had had to

6. *a.* have
   b. got dressed
   c. had known
   d. stay
   e. stayed
   f. had stayed

7. *a.* I will go to the banquet with John if I am introduced to him.
   b. I would have stayed in bed if the doctor had told me to.
   c. I will marry you if you have money.
   d. I could have visited all the museums if I had had time.
   e. He wouldn't have seen me if I hadn't shouted to him.
   f. I would have had time for breakfast if I hadn't slept so late.

UNIT 7

Page 82

1. *a.* I have a friend who can play chess.
   b. He had the time and could play baseball all afternoon yesterday.
   c. He is taking lessons and can play bridge now.
   d. I didn't have to study, so I could watch T V last night.
   e. I can't play a musical instrument.
   f. I didn't have the money, so I couldn't go to the movies last night.

2. *a.* I work long hours, so I should go to bed early.
   b. Coffee keeps me awake, so I shouldn't drink it.
   c. I don't like spinach, but I should eat it.
   d. I was tired today. I shouldn't have gone to bed so late last night.
   e. I should have finished that book last night, but I didn't.
   f. I should have taken the plane, but I don't like flying.

3. *a.* I don't like the looks of that medicine, but I must take it.
   b. I am very fussy about food, but I must eat.
   c. I dislike housekeeping, but I must clean house.
   d. I don't like the idea of getting up early, but I must go to the airport.
   e. My apartment is uncomfortably cold, so I must turn on the heat.

4. *a.* I don't like the looks of that medicine, but I've got to take it.
   b. I am very fussy about food, but I've got to eat.
   c. I dislike housekeeping, but I've got to clean house.
   d. I don't like the idea of getting up early, but I've got to go to the airport.
   e. My apartment is uncomfortably cold, so I've got to turn on the heat.

5. *a.* I didn't like the looks of that medicine, but I had to take it.
   b. I was very fussy about food, but I had to eat.
   c. I disliked housekeeping, but I had to clean house.
   d. I didn't like the idea of getting up early, but I had to go to the airport.
   e. My apartment was uncomfortably cold, so I had to turn on the heat.

6. *a.* I like pets and I may have an animal in my apartment.
   b. We might have gone south last winter, but it was too expensive.
   c. Since I am old enough, I may get married.
   d. We might (may) go to the movies, but we don't know if we can.
   e. Since I don't like driving, I might (may) not take my car.
   f. Because I dislike walking, I might (may) buy a car.

7. *a.* She can play tennis well.
   b. I should eat spinach.
   c. You must take medicine.
   d. He should have gone to bed early.
   e. You can't play bridge.
   f. You might have moved to a warmer place.
   g. She may get married.
   h. You may borrow books.
   i. He might not see the movie.
   j. You must do the laundry.

8. *a.* Yes, it might.
   b. Yes, I am able to.
   c. No, I couldn't.
   d. Yes, I must.
   e. Yes, I should have.
   f. No, I shouldn't.
   g. Yes, I had to.
   h. Yes, you might have.

UNIT 8

Page 95

1. *a.* I ordered him to tear up the letter.
   b. I had him tear up the letter.
   c. I permitted him to think for himself.
   d. I let him think for himself.
   e. I urged him to work harder.
   f. I made him work harder.
   g. I asked him to drive carefully.
   h. I watched him drive carefully.
   i. I didn't want him to get upset.
   j. I didn't see him get upset.
   k. I advised him to listen to me.
   l. I made him listen to me.

2. *a.* making up
   b. make up
   c. interfering
   d. interfere
   e. giving
   f. give
   g. waiting
   h. wait and see
   i. giving
   j. give

3. *a.* Yes, I expect to. No, I don't expect to.
   b. Yes, I should. No, I shouldn't.
   c. Yes, I intend to. No, I don't intend to.
   d. Yes, I will. No, I won't.
   e. Yes, I want to. No, I don't want to.
   f. Yes, I must. No, I mustn't.
   g. Yes, I plan to. No, I don't plan to.
   h. Yes, I will. No, I won't.

4. *a.* at, *b.* out, *c.* up, *d.* in, *e.* with, *f.* to, *g.* over,
   h. for, *i.* on, *j.* down, *k.* across

5. *a.* He won't appreciate your help.
   b. Will you accept my suggestion?
   c. I hope I didn't offend you.
   d. I must solve the problem.

e. You are wasting time.
f. They wasted their money.
g. Mr. Jones will give the speech.
h. The student answered the question.
i. Helen tore up the letter.
j. The lawyer made the decision.

6. *a.* My own mind must be made up.
b. The letter should be torn up.
c. You shouldn't be offended.
d. Your father's advice must be taken.
e. The problem will be solved.
f. Your advice was taken.
g. My suggestion was accepted.
h. Your help was appreciated.
i. His mind was made up.
j. The problem couldn't be solved.

UNIT 9

Page 108

1. *a.* He'll always be grateful to you.
b. Have I often worried you with my problems?
c. I usually seem to be broke.
d. Have you ever left your wallet at home?
e. He is generally happy to help you.
f. I've seldom asked you for favors.
g. I frequently get you involved in my affairs.
h. Am I sometimes a burden on you?
i. You are never a bother.

2. *a.* I haven't thanked you for your kindness *yet.*
b. You've *already* thanked me many times.
c. But I *still* haven't thanked you enough.
d. That's all right. You don't have to thank me *anymore.*
e. Has he shown his appreciation *yet?*
f. Yes, he's *already* shown his gratitude.
g. Does he *still* worry you with his problems?
h. No, he doesn't bother me *anymore* .

3. *a.* My friend thoughtfully helped me out yesterday.
b. I'll gladly push your car to the gas station.

c. My brother generously sent me some money in the mail.
d. This is the last time I'll ever ask you for favors.
e. I definitely won't get paid until tomorrow.
f. I certainly didn't intend to worry you with my problems.
g. Would you kindly open the door for me now?
h. Thank you very much for helping me yesterday.

4. *a.* He asked me for money when he came to work.
b. He asked me for money because he left his wallet at home.
c. I didn't help him because I was broke.
d. I've been worried since I lost my job.
e. I didn't ask you for help because I didn't want to bother you.
f. I'll look for a job until I find one.
g. I'll call on you again after I find a job.
h. I can meet you wherever it's convenient for you.
i. He's been asking me for favors since I've known him.
j. I won't listen to his problems because I don't want to get involved in his affairs.

UNIT 10

Page 119

1. *a.* Student A: Do you have a lot of things to do before you leave on your trip?
Student B: Yes, I do.
b. Student A: Did you close your checking account?
Student B: Yes, I did.
c. Student A: Should you get some traveler's checks?
Student B: Yes, I should.
d. Student A: Might you get some inoculations?
Student B: Yes, I might.
e. Student A: Must you apply for a passport?
Student B: Yes, I must.
f. Student A: Will you leave your forwarding address at the post office?
Student B: Yes, I will.
g. Student A: Do you prefer to have the postman stop delivering your mail?
Student B: Yes, I do.
h. Student A: Could you have the phone disconnected?
Student B: Yes, I could.

i. Student A: Would you rather say good-bye at the airport?
Student B: Yes, I would.

j. Student A: Are you going to send a cable as soon as you arrive?
Student B: Yes, I am.

2. *a.* Student A: You have to drop by the bank to get some money, don't you?
Student B: Yes, I do.

b. Student A: It didn't take all your savings to buy the tickets, did it?
Student B: No, it didn't.

c. Student A: You'll cover up the furniture, won't you?
Student B: Yes, I will.

d. Student A: You won't forget to have the milk delivery stopped, will you?
Student B: No, I won't.

e. Student A: You can take the dog to the kennels, can't you?
Student B: Yes, I can.

f. Student A: You couldn't miss your train connection, could you?
Student B: No, I couldn't.

g. Student A: You are taking your camera, aren't you?
Student B: Yes, I am.

h. Student A: You weren't going to take your bird, were you?
Student B: No, I wasn't.

3. *a.* What do you have to cash before you can leave?
When do you have to cash a check?

b. How was your ticket paid for?
What was paid for with your savings?

c. How are you going outside the country?
Where are you going by plane?

d. Why do you have to take a taxi?
What do you have to take because you're late?

e. Who will kiss you good-bye at the airport?
Where will your friend kiss you good-bye?

f. Which office will examine your things to look for prohibited articles?
Why will the customs office examine your things?

g. What doesn't a traveler have to pay duty on?
Who doesn't have to pay duty on personal articles?

h. What will you send as soon as you arrive?
When will you send a cable?

4. *a.* Why did you have to get a passport?
   b. How long will you be gone?
   c. When are you leaving for South America?
   d. How are you traveling?
   e. How far is it to the airport from your house?
   f. How much time will you need for your trip?
   g. What kind of inoculation will you need?
   h. Who will come with you?

5. *a.* Can you find out what kind of visa you need?
   b. Do you know what you should declare for customs?
   c. Do you remember when you applied for a passport?
   d. Did you tell your family when you will send a telegram?
   e. Did you ask how long the flight will take?
   f. Will you please tell me where I should leave my forwarding address?

ENGLISH 900

WORKBOOK FIVE

prepared by

ENGLISH LANGUAGE SERVICES, INC.

The Macmillan Company
Collier – Macmillan Limited, London
Collier – Macmillan Canada, Ltd.

INTRODUCTION

This workbook is one of a series of six prepared for students of English as a second language. The six workbooks contain drill and review material covering all the basic patterns of English.

The workbooks are self-teaching. The student knows immediately whether his answer to each question is right or wrong. He works by himself, with little or no outside assistance, and he can proceed rapidly through material he knows and more slowly through material which is difficult for him. The material in each book is divided into ten units.

These workbooks have been designed to be used independently by students of English, but they can also be used as supplements to the six textbooks in the same series, or with any other series of textbooks.

DIRECTIONS

Read item 1 below. Write in your answer. If you select "am", you are directed to item 6, as the arrow below shows. Here you are told that your answer to item 1 is right. So you go ahead and try item 6. From item 6 go to the number that appears next to the answer you have selected, and so on.

1. I ____________ John Smith.
   am 6 *is* 10 *are* 8

2.

3.

4.

5.

6. **Right! Go to next question.**

   She ____________ Helen Brown.
   am 5 *is* 9 *are* 7

7.

8.

9. **Right! Go to next question.**

Read item 1 again. If you select "is" as the answer, you are directed to item 10 (see below). Now see what happens. Here you are told that your answer is wrong. Item 10 contains some study sentences to help you correct your mistake, and another question. Read item 10 and write in your answer to this question. Go to the number that appears next to the answer you have selected. Again you will be told whether your answer is right or wrong.

1. I ____________ John Smith.
   am 6 *is* 10 *are* 8

2.

3.

4.

5.

6.

7.

8.

9.

10. **Wrong. Study this.**

    She is Helen Brown.
    She is Mrs. Brown.

    ____________ is Mrs. Green.
    she 15 *you* 4

11.

12.

13.

14.

15. **Right! Go to next question.**

Now go ahead and begin the first question in Unit One.

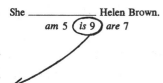

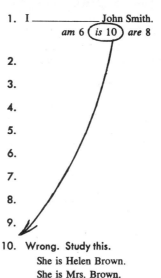

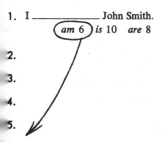

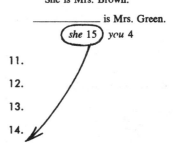

머 리 말

본 workbook은 영어를 제2 외국어로하는 학도를 위해서 만들어진 것으로 전부 6권으로 되어 있다. 6권의 workbook에는 각각 영어의 기본 문형에 관한 연습문제(drill)와 복습문제(review)가 들어 있다.

본 workbook은 자습용으로서, 독자는 자신의 해답이 정답인지 오답인지 곧 알 수 있도록 되어 있으며, 선생의 도움이 없어도, 잘 아는 문제라면 빠르게, 좀 힘든 문제라면 천천히라도 할 수는 있을 것이다. 각권은 각기 10개의 Unit로 나누어져 있다.

본 workbook은 독립적으로 이용되도록 만들어진 것이지만, 같은 자매서인 English 900나 또 다른 textbook와 같이 사용해도 무방할 것이다.

본 workbook 이용 방법

아래의 1번을 보고 답을 맞춰보라. 만일 "am"을 골랐으면 아래의 화살표가 가리키듯이 몇개의 항을 건너 뛰어 6번을 보게 되어 있다. 그러면 6번에는, 1번에 대한 너의 답이 정답(Right!)이라 쓰여있다. 그러면 이번에는 6번의 답을 맞추어 보자. 6번에서도 역시 네가 선택한 답의 옆에 씌어 있는 숫자를 따라 가서 너의 답이 옳았는지 틀렸는지 알아보게 되어있다.

1. I____________John Smith.
   am 6　*is* 10　*are* 8
2.
3.
4.
5.
6. **Right! Go to next question.**
   She____________Helen Brown.
   am 5　*is* 9　*are* 7
7.
8.
9. **Right! Go to next question.**

1번을 다시 보자. 만일 "is"를 골랐다면 "is"옆의 숫자 10을 따라 10번을 보아야 한다. 자 어떻게 되었을까? 10번에는 너의답이 틀렸다(Wrong)고 씌여 있다. 뿐만 아니라 10번에는 역시 너의 잘못을 정정해 주는 예문과 또 다른 Sentence가 또 씌여 있을 것이다. 그러면 이번에는 10번을 읽고 답을 맞춰보자. 그리고 네가 선택한 답 옆의 숫자를 따라가 보면, 또다시 네가 옳았는지 틀렸는지 여부를 알수 있게 되어 있다.

1. I____________John Smith.
   am 6　*is* 10　*are* 8
2.
3.
4.
5.
6.
7.
8.
9.
10. **Wrong. Study this.**
    She is Helen Brown.
    She is Mrs. Brown.
    __________is Mrs. Green.
    she 15　*you* 4
11.
12.
13.
14.
15. **Right! Go to next question.**

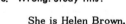

자 그러면 Unit One의 제일 첫문제 부터 풀어보자.

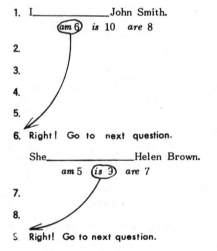

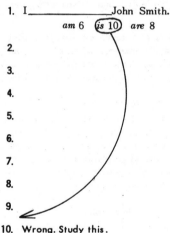

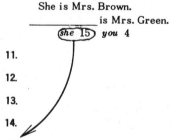

UNIT 1 TELLING ABOUT PAST EXPERIENCES

Write your answers.

1. **Begin here.**

I never imagined that he ____________ there some day.

lives 7 *would live* 3

2. **Wrong. Study these:**

We just avoided hitting your car.
I want to avoid spending time with those people.

I always avoid ____________ food between meals.

being eaten 15 *eating* 11

3. **Right! Go ahead.**

After a while, we ____________ a shady place.

find 13 *found* 9

4. **Wrong. Study these:**

He never used to behave strangely.
We never dreamed that John would become a lawyer.
I can't ever recall the exact circumstances of that accident.
I won't ever forget that experience.

Now do 25 again.

5. **Right! Do this one.**

After a while, he ____________ an apartment.

rents 8 *rented* 9

6. **Wrong. Study these:**

John never learned how to drive a car, did he?
She never realized how hard it is to speak another language, did she?

She ____________ learned how to dance, did she?

ever 20 *never* 14

7. **Wrong. Study these:**
She doesn't realize that we live there now.
He doesn't imagine that you hear him now.

He doesn't know that we ____________ that car last year.
would buy 12 *bought* 10

8. **Wrong. Study these:**
After a while, they bought a new house.
After a while, he can buy a new suit.
After a while, John accepted my advice.
After a while, they can take a trip to Mexico.

Now do 3 again.

9. **Right! Go ahead.**

He just avoided ____________ by that car.
hitting 2 *being hit* 17

10. **Right! Do this one.**

I never imagined that ____________ like to go dancing some night.
you 12 *you would* 3

11. **Right! Do this one.**

She didn't avoid ____________ by the crowd.
being heard 17 *hearing* 15

12. **Wrong. Study these:**
I said that you would visit us some time.
My mother hoped that I would marry some day.
He realized that John went there last night.
She realized that he bought that car last year.

Now do 1 again.

13. **Wrong. Study these:**
After a while, we can find a good place to swim.
After a while, we can buy a new car.

After a while, we ____________ to the store.
can go 5 *go* 8

14. **Right! Do this one.**

Didn't you ____________ want to become a doctor?
ever 25 *never* 20

15. **Wrong. Study these:**
I know that he tried to avoid seeing me.
I always try to avoid speaking English with him.
He avoided being seen there with her.
He jumped back to avoid being hit.

Now do 9 again.

16. **Right! Do this one.**

She doesn't ____________ go shopping.
ever 27 *never* 4

17. **Right! Go ahead.**

Didn't John ____________ learn how to drive a car?
ever 25 *never* 6

18. **Wrong. Study these:**
On the way back home, we can see our friends.
On the way back home, we can go to a restaurant.

On the way back home, we ____________ to have a picnic.
stop 21 *can stop* 24

19 **Wrong. Study these:**

He follows my advice and buys expensive suits.

I eat dinner and then go home.

Tomorrow we ____________ swimming, and then dancing.

are going 23 *went* 26

20. **Wrong. Study these:**

You never went to that restaurant, did you?

Didn't you ever go to that restaurant?

Mary never went to the mountains.

Didn't Mary ever go to the mountains?

Now do 17 again.

21. **Wrong. Study these:**

On the way back home, we had engine trouble.

On the way back home, we can go swimming.

On the way back home, I had a peculiar experience.

On the way back home, we can go by air

Now do 27 again.

22. **Wrong. Study these:**

He never buys inexpensive shirts.

She never has engine trouble with that ca

We ____________ go to that restaurant.

don't never 4 *never* 16

23. **Right! Do this one.**

I wrote a letter and ____________ it in the mail box on the corner.

drop 26 *dropped* 35

24. **Right! Do this one.**

On the way back home, I ____________ a strange story.

hear 21 *heard* 30

25. **Right! Go ahead.**

I don't ____________ like to drive that car.

ever 27 *never* 22

26. **Wrong. Study these:**

I picked up the receiver and dropped a coin in the slot.

He follows my advice and always walks to work.

Every summer they go to the mountains and rent a house.

I went to the corner and crossed the street

Now do 30 again.

27. **Right! Go ahead.**

On the way back home, we ____________ a blowout.

have 18 *had* 30

28. **Wrong. Study these:**

Odd things happen to me.

Strange things often happen to Mary.

____________ happen when I am with you.

Odd things 31 *Something odd* 39

29. **Wrong. Study these:**

He bought a new suit. Did he buy a new suit?

She ate her dinner. Did she eat her dinner?

I wrote a letter to John. Did I write a letter to John?

The car had a flat tire. Did the car have a flat tire?

Now do 42 again.

30. Right! Go ahead.

I crossed the street and ____________ into the store.

go 19 *went* 35

31. Right! Do this one.

Something strange ____________ to him when he goes there.

happen 39 *happens* 37

32. Wrong. Study these:

They heard what I said. Did you hear what I said?

We bought a new car. Did he buy a new car?

We went to the mountains every summer.

____________ to the mountains every summer?

They went 29 *Did they go* 38

33. Wrong. Study these:

They remember the plan. Do you remember the plan?

____________ that story. Don't they know that story?

You don't know 36

Don't you know 41

34. Right! Do this one.

On the subject ____________ trips, did I tell you about Mexico?

of 42 *about* 45

35. Right! Go ahead.

Something amazing ____________ to me whenever I hear that poem.

happen 28 *happens* 37

36. Right! Now do this one.

We have motor trouble. ____________ motor trouble?

You have 41 *Do you have* 43

37. Right! Go ahead.

Speaking ____________ trips, did you know that John went abroad last year?

of 42 *in* 40

38. Right! Do this one.

______ ____ in that restaurant yesterday. Did you eat in that restaurant?

Did we eat 29 *We ate* 44

39. Wrong. Study these:

Peculiar things happen to my stomach when I eat there.

Odd things happen to my head if I drink too much.

Something funny happens whenever I drive that car.

Something interesting happens whenever I go shopping with you.

Now do 35 again.

40. **Wrong. Study these:**
Talking about beautiful places, did I ever tell you about California?
On the subject of poems, do you like the one John wrote?
Speaking of accidents, I had an odd experience last year.

Talking ________ cars, did you see her new one?
about 34 *above* 45

41. **Wrong. Study these:**
You have a headache. Do you have a headache?
I don't look good. Don't I look good?
You live in an apartment. Do you live in an apartment?
That dress is made of silk. Is that dress made of silk?

Now do 44 again.

42. **Right! Go ahead.**

He told you about his experience.

________ you about my experience?
I told 32 *Did I tell* 44

43. **Good! This is the end of Unit 1**

Go on to Unit 2.

44. **Right! Go ahead.**

She recalls the exact circumstances.

________ the exact circumstances?
He recalls 33 *Does he recall* 43

45. **Wrong. Study these:**
Talking about suits, I bought a new one yesterday.
On the subject of airplanes, did I ever tell you about my experience?
Speaking about doctors, did I tell you John is now a doctor?
Speaking about shirts, that store has good ones.

Now do 37 again.

UNIT 2 ASKING ABOUT FURNITURE AND PLACES TO LIVE

Write your answers.

1. **Begin here.**

   The house needs ____________.
   to paint 6   *painting* 4

2. **Right! Do this one.**

   He ____________ a new stove. Now we can cook if we have to.
   turn on 14   *installed* 9

3. **Wrong. Study these:**
   We rented the house instead of buying it
   We'd rather buy furniture than take trips.

   I ________________ by air than by rail.
   would rather go 5   *am going* 10

4. **Right! Go ahead.**

   Mary ____________ the radio at seven o'clock to listen to the news.
   turned on 9   *installed* 7

5. **Right! Do this one.**

   Would you rather go dancing ____________ go swimming?
   instead of 10   *than* 18

6. **Wrong. Study these:**
   I need to paint my house.
   He needs to mail a letter.

   I need ____________ the flower beds.
   weeding 12   *to weed* 8

7. **Wrong. Study these:**
   He installed the washing machine. Now we can wash if we have to.
   Mary turned on the washing machine. She is washing her things.

   We ____________ a new air conditioner. We will be cool when summer comes.
   installed 2   *turn on* 14

8. **Right! Do this one.**

The floor needs ____________.
to wax 12 *waxing* 4

9. **Right! Go ahead.**

We are interested ____________ a house for the summer.
in renting 15 *to rent* 17

10. **Wrong. Study these:**
I would rather give advice than take it.
I give advice instead of taking it.
I would rather read a book than go out tonight.
I am reading a book instead of going out tonight.

Now do 15 again.

11. **Wrong. Study these:**
I am interested in speaking another language.
It is interesting to speak another language.
I am interested in going shopping.
It is interesting to go shopping.

Now do 9 again.

12. **Wrong. Study these:**
The front steps need fixing.
John needs to fix the front steps.
The grass needs cutting.
I have to cut the grass.

Now do 1 again.

13. **Wrong. Study these:**
If he wanted his shoes, he looked down under the bed for them.
If she wanted a trunk, she looked up in the attic for it.

If he ____________ a towel, he looked in the linen closet for it.
wants 25 *wanted* 21

14. **Wrong. Study these:**
She turned on the stove. She is making the meat.
He installed the sink. Now it is ready to use.
He turned on the lamp. He is reading a book.
They installed central heating. The house will be warm next winter.

ow do 4 again.

15. **Right! Go ahead.**

Would you rather rent a house ____________ buy one?
instead of 3 *than* 18

16. **Wrong. Study these:**
I bought a new stove for the kitchen.
She bought a new sofa for the living room.
I have three lamps in the den.

Mary has a new sink and a new refrigerator in her ____________.
kitchen 20 *bedroom* 33

17. **Wrong. Study these:**
It is interesting to take trips.
It isn't interesting to go for a walk here.

________________ to rent a house near the beach.
I am interested 11
It is interesting 19

18. Right! Go ahead.

If you want sheets, you ____________ in the linen closet.

looked 13 *look* 23

19. Right! Do this one.

I am interested ____________ a new car.

to buy 11 *in buying* 15

20. Right! Do this one.

I have a new desk in the ____________.

bathroom 33 *den* 30

21. Right! Do this one.

If you want scissors, you ____________ on the table.

look 23 *looked* 25

22. Wrong. Study these:

I have traditional furniture.
Mrs. Smith has colonial furniture.

____________ modern furniture.

Mary likes 26 *Does Mary like* 38

23. Right! Go ahead.

What kind ____________ would you like?

apartment 28 *of apartment* 27

24. Wrong. Study these:

No, I don't worry as much as you do.
Mrs. Smith worries about everything.

I wish you wouldn't ____________ so mı

worry 29 *worries* 40

25. Wrong. Study these:

If you want a wastebasket, you look beside the desk.
If you want a paper clip, you look inside the drawer of the desk.
If he wanted some shirts, he looked inside his dresser drawer.
If he wanted to make a phone call, he went to the telephone in the hallway.

Now do 18 again.

26. Right! Do this one.

What style furniture

____________________?

does Mrs. Green prefer 36
Mary prefers 38

27. Right! Go ahead.

We've got to get a bed and dresser for

the ____________.

kitchen 16 *bedroom* 30

28. Wrong. Study these:

What style house do you prefer?
What kind of dessert do you want?

What ____________ furniture do you have?

style 32 *kind* 35

29. Right! Do this one.

Do you worry ____________________?

about your appearance 39
your appearance 40

30. Right! Go ahead.

What style furniture ____________?
you have 22 *do you have* 36

31. Wrong. Study these:
Please show your new hat to him.
I'm showing him my new furniture.

I showed the book ____________.
to John 34 *John* 42

32. Right! Do this one.

What kind ____________ did Mrs. Co have?
pie 35 *of pie* 27

33. Wrong. Study these:
I have a new sink, refrigerator, and stove in the kitchen.
I have a new chair and sofa in the living room.
We have a good desk and lamp in the den.
I have a new bed and dresser in my bedroom.

Now do 27 again.

34. Right! Do this one.

I'm showing ____________ my apartment today.
to them 42 *them* 44

35. Wrong. Study these:
What style house is this?
What style sofa do you like?
What kind of room is this?
What kind of restaurant is this?

Now do 23 again.

36. Right! Go ahead.

Do you worry ____________?
about money 39 *money* 24

37. Wrong. Study these:
My father worries about the new dining room set.
My sister doesn't worry about money.

Mrs. Cooper ____________ about me.
worries 43 *does worries* 46

38. Wrong. Study these:
I like traditional furniture.
Does John like period furniture?
I bought colonial style furniture for my bedroom.
Did you buy new furniture for your living room?

Now do 30 again.

39. Right! Go ahead.

Please show ____________ the basement.
to me 31 *me* 44

40. Wrong. Study these:
My uncle worries about me.
Mrs. Green worries about her sister.
I don't worry very much.
I won't worry when you drive your car.

Now do 36 again.

41. **Wrong. Study these:**
I am worrying about everything.
Doesn't Mrs. Green worry a lot?

Is he ____________ about his friend?
worry 46 *worrying* 43

42. **Wrong. Study these:**
I showed him the book.
We showed them some antiques.
Would you show her the stove?
He wouldn't show the stove to her.

Now do 39 again.

43. **Right! Do this one.**

Don't you ____________ about anything?
worry 45 *worries* 46

44. **Right! Go ahead.**

Doesn't he ____________ about the roof?
worrying 41 *worries* 37 *worry* 45

45. **Good! This is the end of Unit 2.**

Go on to Unit 3.

46. **Wrong. Study these:**
I worry about the salesman.
Are they worrying about something?
He worries about the roof.
Mary does worry when you go out.

Now do 44 again.

UNIT 3 TALKING ABOUT THINGS TO WEAR

1. **Begin here.**

You ought ____________ a light jacket.
to wear 4 *wear* 5

2. **Wrong. Study these:**
You should wear a clean shirt.
She had better wear a clean blouse.

John should ____________ clean clothes today.
better wear 19 *wear* 11

3. **Wrong. Study these:**
I have nothing to wear tonight.
Have you nothing to wear tonight?

I ____________ nothing to eat all day.
haven't had 17 *have had* 13

4. **Right! Go ahead.**

This suit doesn't fit him ____________.
any more 7 *no more* 12

5. **Wrong. Study these:**
You must wear a clean shirt today.
John must put on his work clothes now.

Mary ____________ get this coat cleaned.
ought 16 *must* 10

6. **Wrong. Study these:**
She outgrew that dress last year.
They have outgrown all of their clothes.

I guess I ____________ those shoes.
outgrew 20 *outgrown* 25

7. **Right! Go ahead.**

____________ better wear a clean shirt.
You'd 9 *You'll* 2

8. **Right! Do this one.**

She will wear that dress ____________.
any more 18 *no more* 7

9. **Right! Go ahead.**

I don't have ____________ to wear.
anything 15 *nothing* 3

10. **Right! Do this one.**

He ____________ to repair the front steps.
ought 4 *must* 16

11. **Right! Do this one.**

____________ better send some shirts to the laundry today.
He's 19 *He'd* 9

12. **Wrong. Study these:**
That dress doesn't fit any more.
It isn't raining any more.

I ____________ a hat any more.
don't wear 8 *wear* 18

13. **Right! Do this one.**

Don't they have ____________ to do?
nothing 17 *anything* 15

14. **Wrong. Study these:**
She washed a few of my things.
He pressed two coats of hers.
He pressed two of her coats.

She ironed three ____________ dresses.
of hers 30 *of her* 24

15. **Right! Go ahead.**

He ____________ his suit already.
has outgrown 21 *outgrown* 6

16. **Wrong. Study these:**
We ought to go dancing more often.
We must go dancing more often.
John ought to be a better swimmer than he is.
John must be a better swimmer than he seems to be.

Now try 1 again.

17. **Wrong. Study these:**
I didn't want to do anything tonight.
I wanted to do nothing tonight.
Don't they want anything to eat?
They want nothing to eat.

Now try 9 again.

18. **Wrong. Study these:**
I won't wear that shirt any more.
I will wear that shirt no more.
Mary won't go dancing with him any more.
Mary will go dancing with him no more.

Now try 4 again.

19. **Wrong. Study these:**
They'd better not argue so much.
They shouldn't argue so much.
We'd better not go out tonight.
We shouldn't go out tonight.

Now try 7 again.

20. **Right! Do this one.**

Have I ____________ all of my socks?
outgrew 25 *outgrown* 21

21. **Right! Go ahead.**

She washed a few things of ____________.
my 14 *mine* 28

22. **Wrong. Study these:**
I danced as much as Mary did.
He works as much as Mary works.
He works as much as Mary does.

When John and Mary got married, he loved her as much as she ____________ him.
loves 35 *loved* 32

23. **Wrong. Study these:**
This book belongs to my brother.
This book is my brother's .
She is the wife of my brother.
She is my brother's wife.

This shirt belongs to ____________
John's 37 *John* 27

24. **Right! Do this one.**

Mr. Cooper has two books of ____________.
our 30 *ours* 28

25. **Wrong. Study these:**
We have outgrown our clothes.
We outgrew our clothes.
Haven't you outgrown that dress?
Yes, I outgrew that dress.

Now do 15 again.

26. **Wrong. Study these:**
Did you press my dress?
Have you ironed his shirt?

____________ washed the clothes yet?
Has she 31 *Did she* 40

27. **Right! Do this one.**

This one is my ____________ house.
uncle's 36 *uncle* 37

28 **Right! Go ahead.**

Some men keep up with fashions as much as women ____________.
did 22 *do* 33

29. **Wrong. Study these:**
She bought two pairs of shoes.
I need a pair of blue shoes.

He wants ____________ pair of socks to wear tonight.
three 42 *one* 44

30. **Wrong. Study these:**
We have a house of theirs to rent.
She has a hat of yours.
She has your hat.
Did you buy that car of his?

Now try 21 again.

31. **Right! Do this one.**

____________ change his clothes?
Has he 40 *Did he* 38

32. **Right! Do this one.**

Few people want money as much as

he ____________.

does 33 *did* 35

33. **Right! Go ahead.**

I have to buy a new dress for my

____________ wedding.

sister 23 *sisters* 46 *sister's* 36

34. **Wrong. Study these:**

I know what Mrs. Cooper is doing.
What is Mrs. Cooper doing?

________________ Mrs. Smith is ironing for you.

I can guess what 39 *What* 45

35. **Wrong. Study these:**

She wants to go there as much as he does.
She wanted to go there as much as he did.
The waiter likes to give good service as much as we like to get it.
The waiter liked to give good service as much as we liked to get it.

Now try 28 again.

36. **Right! Go ahead.**

________________ the suit yet?

Have you pressed 38
You did press 26

37. **Wrong. Study these:**

I like my sister's husband.
This is the husband of my sister.
Where is the ladies' room?
This cottage belongs to two friends.

Now do 33 again.

38. **Right! Go ahead.**

I need two new ____________ of shoes.

pairs 43 *pair* 29

39. **Right! Do this one.**

What ________________________ tonight when you go out?

will Mary be wearing 41
Mary will be wearing 45

40. **Wrong. Study these:**

Have they fastened their seat belts yet?
Did they fasten their seat belts?
Has he had an accident yet?
Did he have an accident yesterday?

Now do 36 again.

41. **Good! This is the end of Unit 3.**

Go on to Unit 4.

42. **Wrong. Study these:**

I need a new pair of shoes.
Don't you need two pairs of shoes?
I bought a pair of gloves in that store.
Didn't you buy two pairs of gloves there?

Now do 38 again.

43. **Right! Go ahead.**

What ______________________ today?
Mr. Jones is wearing 34
is Mr. Jones wearing 41

44. **Right! Do this one.**

I bought three ____________ of gloves here.
pairs 43 *pair* 42

45. **Wrong. Study these:**
I can only imagine what you are saying.
What are you saying?
I can guess what you are reading.
What are you reading?

Now do 43 again.

46. **Wrong. Study these:**
This is my sisters' house.
My two sisters own this house.
That house belongs to my two sisters.

This apartment belongs to the ____________.
girls 27 *girls'* 37

UNIT 4 DISCUSSING DIFFERENT POINTS OF VIEW

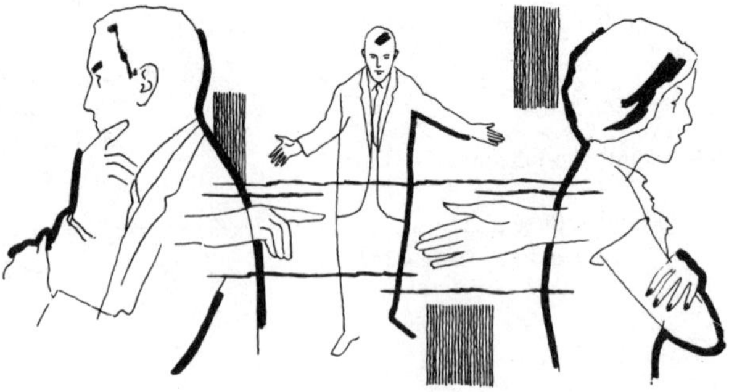

1. **Begin here.**

   ____________ is a new car, isn't it?
   Yours 5   *Your* 6

2. **Right! Do this one.**

   John has his view and I have ____________.
   my 20   *mine* 8

3. **Wrong. Study these:**
   They all have their own opinions.
   The girls have their own ideas about this.

   They want to discuss only ____________ own problems.
   his 25   *their* 7

4. **Wrong. Study these:**
   There is no point in arguing.
   I don't have a point of view to argue.

   Nobody here has a viewpoint ____________
   in arguing 19   *to argue* 12

5. **Right! Go ahead.**

   You have your point of view and they have ____________.
   their 15   *theirs* 8

6. **Wrong. Study these:**
   Our situation is dangerous.
   Ours is a new car.

   This is my sister. ____________ looks good today.
   Mine 14   *She* 11

7. **Right! Do this one.**

   Anyone can discuss ____________ problem with me.
   his 16   *their* 25

8. **Right! Go ahead.**

   I don't see any point ____________ that question.
   in discussing 13   *to discuss* 4

9. Wrong. Study these:

I will become a doctor if I can.
She will speak Spanish if she can.

____________ you give your opinion if you can?

Wouldn't 28 *Won't* 22

10. Wrong. Study these:

They will resolve their differences and become good friends.
She will forgive her and also forget the argument.

I know I will agree with you and

____________ your advice.

taken 26 *take* 17

11. Right! Do this one.

____________ is the liberal viewpoint.

Their 14 *Theirs* 5

12. Right! Do this one.

They don't see the point ____________ this.

in asking 13 *to ask* 19

13. Right! Do this one.

Everyone is entitled to ____________ own opinion.

his 16 *their* 3

14. Wrong. Study these:

His is a good argument.
His argument is good.
Hers is an interesting viewpoint.
Her viewpoint is interesting.

Now do 1 again.

15. Wrong. Study these:

You have your point of view and they have their points of view.
You have your problems and we have our problems.

You like your car better and I like

____________ better.

my car 2 *my* 20

16. Right! Go ahead.

She would start an argument if

she ____________.

can 9 *could* 21

17. Right! Do this one.

She asked peculiar questions and

____________ arguments.

started 27 *starts* 26

18. Right! Do this one.

What point ____________?

you are making 30
are you making 32

19. Wrong. Study these:

There is no point in doing that.
There is some point in resolving our differences now.
I don't have a viewpoint to argue.
We now have the liberal point of view to discuss.

Now do 8 again.

20. **Wrong. Study these:**
You have your choice and she has hers.
You have your choice and she has her choice.
I have my argument and you have yours.
I have my argument and you have your argument.

Now do 5 again.

21. **Right! Go ahead.**

They resolved their differences and

____________ good friends.
become 10 *became* 27

22. **Right! Do this one.**

I ____________ a new car tomorrow if I could.
would buy 21 *am buying* 28

23. **Wrong. Study these:**
He is talking about what alternatives he has.
What alternatives does he have?

They are discussing what arguments

____________.
they have 18 *do they have*

24. **Wrong. Study these:**
There is only one question remaining.
There is only one way to approach the problem.

____________ there another way to do this?
Aren't 35 *Isn't* 29

25. **Wrong. Study these:**
Everyone here has his own car.
All the men have their own cars.
No one here will discuss his problem with me.
They are entitled to have their own opinions.

Now do 13 again.

6. **Wrong. Study these:**
He always argued with me and didn't forgive me for my odd viewpoint.
He always argues with me and doesn't forgive me for my odd viewpoint.
He approached the problem in a different way and resolved it.
He approaches a problem in a different way and tries to resolve it.

w try 21 again.

27. **Right! Go ahead.**

What questions ____________?
you have 23 *do you have* 32

28. **Wrong. Study these:**
I would agree with her if I could.
I will agree with him if I can.
Wouldn't you go abroad if you could?
Won't you go abroad if you can?

Now do 16 again.

29. **Right! Do this one.**

____________ there any houses to rent near the beach?
Aren't 34 *Isn't* 35

30. **Wrong. Study these:**
I know what ideas you have.
What ideas do you have?
I know what questions you will ask.
What questions will you ask?

Now do 27 again.

31. **Wrong. Study these:**
Is that the way to start an argument?
This is a different way to approach the problem.

__________ that an amazing idea?
Aren't 40 *Isn't* 38

32. **Right! Go ahead.**

There __________ always two sides to every argument.
are 34 *is* 24

33. **Wrong. Study these:**
When John had a question, he wanted an answer.
When John has a question, he wants an answer.

When they __________ different opinions the discussion was interesting.
have 45 *had* 37

34. **Right! Go ahead.**

Those were liberal __________.
viewpoints 36 *viewpoint* 31

35. **Wrong. Study these:**
There is a shady spot under the elm.
There are two opposite views on this point.
There is a better way to discuss this problem.
Aren't there some alternatives here?

Now do 32 again.

36. **Right! Go ahead.**

She __________ to start an argument.
meaned 42 *meant* 41

37. **Right! Do this one.**

When he had an idea, he __________ to start a discussion.
tries 45 *tried* 43

38. **Right! Do this one.**

These __________ not good ways to resolve our differences.
were 36 *was* 40

39. **Wrong. Study these:**
I know they didn't mean to start an argument.
I meant to buy you something yesterday, but I forgot.
They've been meaning to resolve their differences.
She means to live near the beach.

Now do 36 again.

40. **Wrong. Study these:**
That is not my viewpoint.
These are a lot of strange ideas you have.
Wasn't this your question?
Weren't those your opinions?

Now do 34 again.

41. **Right! Go ahead.**

When he has an opinion, he ____________ everyone to hear it.
wants 43 *wanted* 33

42. **Wrong. Study these:**
I meant to ask you that question.
She has been meaning to call you.
Do you mean to go there?

She ____________ to go there tomorrow.
means 44 *mean* 39

43. **Good! This is the end of Unit 4.**

Go on to Unit 5.

44. **Right! Do this one.**

I ____________ to phone you yesterday.
meaned 39 *meant* 41

45. **Wrong. Study these:**
When Mary has another choice, she takes it.
When she forgives someone, she also forgets the argument.
When I had an idea, I wanted him to know about it.
When they approached it from different viewpoints, did they resolve their differences?

Now try 41 again.

UNIT 5 THINKING ABOUT POSSIBLE FUTURE ACTIVITIES

1. **Begin here.**

Are you able ________ well at home?
work 4 *to work* 7

2. **Wrong. Study these:**
I go there most weekends, but I do miss a few.
Sometimes I go to the barbershop, but usually I cut my hair myself.

I ________ to the beach some summers, but sometimes I stay home.
went 15 *go* 10

3. **Wrong. Study these:**
I go there every month.
I spent too much money one month.

We have a meeting every ________.
months 19 *month* 8

4. **Wrong. Study these:**
I can work well at home.
She is able to do very good work at home.

________ come to dinner some night?
Can you 9 *Would you be able* 12

5 **Wrong. Study these:**
If you are going to the beach, when will you go?
If they were coming, what time would they arrive?

If he ________ his job, where will he work?
is leaving 18 *were leaving* 16

6. **Wrong. Study these:**
The barber cut my hair yesterday.
I will cut your hair.

The barber cuts my hair ________.
every week 20 *last week* 23

7. Right! Go ahead.

I attended most of the meetings, but I

____________ a few.

miss 2 *missed* 11

8. Right! Do this one.

She buys new shoes for him ____________ months.

every 19 *every three* 13

9. Right! Do this one.

Would you be able ____________ an argument with him?

start 12 *to start* 7

10. Right! Do this one.

I danced with Mr. Cooper a few times, but I

also ____________ with you.

dance 15 *danced* 11

11. Right! Go ahead.

I change jobs every two or three

____________.

month 3 *months* 13

12. Wrong. Study these:

I could have a good discussion with her.
She would be able to have a good discussion with me.
Can you tell me the exact circumstances of the accident?
Are you able to tell me the exact circumstances of the accident?

Now try 1 again.

13. Right! Go ahead.

If you were to attend the wedding, what

____________ you wear?

will 5 *would* 17

14. Wrong. Study these:

As soon as I could, I went home.
As soon as I find it possible, I'll write you.

As soon as I ____________ an opportunity, I danced with you.

had 25 *have* 28

15. Wrong. Study these:

He changes jobs often, but sometimes he stays awhile.
She changed jobs often, but sometimes she stayed awhile.
He likes to go on picnics, but he usually prefers to go swimming.
She liked to go on picnics, but she usually preferred to go swimming.

Now do 7 again.

16. Wrong. Study these:

If you were to follow his plan, when would you start?
If you are following his plan, when will you start?
If you were to plan a picnic, what kind of food would you take?
If you are planning a picnic, what kind of food are you taking?

Now do 13 again.

17. Right! Go ahead.

The barber ____________ my hair too short.

cutted 6 *cut* 22

18. **Right! Do this one.**

If you were to cut my hair, how short

__________ you make it?

would 17 *will* 16

19. **Wrong. Study these:**

We pay the rent once a month.
He needs new shoes every month.
I buy shoes every two or three months.
There is a meeting every six months.

Now do 11 again.

20. **Right! Do this one.**

She __________ his hair last week

cuts 23 *cut* 22

21. **Wrong. Study these:**

Where did you read that story?
Do you know where I can get that book?

__________ where I went?

You can guess 33
Can you guess 26

22. **Right! Go ahead.**

As soon as I can, I __________ home.

went 14 *am going* 30

23. **Wrong. Study these:**

The barber cuts my brother's hair every month.
I just cut my hair yesterday.
The barber cuts my hair very well.
I cut my hair too short last week.

Now do 17 again.

24. **Wrong. Study these:**

What if you can't go? How will you feel?
Let's say you can't hear. What will you do?

Assuming you __________ speak with them, what will you do?

couldn't 35 *can't* 27

25. **Right! Do this one.**

As soon as I am able to, I __________ my job.

am changing 30 *changing* 28

26. **Right! Do this one.**

Did she remember what __________ to her?

did I say 33 *I said* 38

27. **Right! Do this one.**

Supposing you __________ swim, what would you do?

couldn't 40 *can't* 35

28. **Wrong. Study these:**

As soon as I can, I'm going swimming.
As soon as I could, I went swimming.
As soon as I find it possible, I'll buy a new car.
As soon as I found it possible, I bought a new car.

Now try 22 again.

29. **Wrong. Study these:**

There's a chance I won't go to Mexico in December.
I didn't go to Mexico last summer.

__________ went abroad last year.

There's a chance you 31 *You* 36

30. Right! Go ahead.

Do you remember where ____________ the book?

he put 38 *did he put* 21

31. Wrong. Study these:

There's a chance I won't come.
There's a chance she'll visit me.
Is there a chance you'll be off for San Francisco tomorrow?
Isn't there a chance you'll go swimming?

Now try 40 again.

32. Wrong. Study these:

You did see that movie, didn't you?
She doesn't look good today, does she?

We ____________ buy many books, do we?

don't 39 *didn't* 34

33. Wrong. Study these:

Can you remember what books you borrowed?
What books did you borrow?
Do you remember what you did there?
What did you do there?

Now do 30 again.

34. Wrong. Study these:

You don't see them any more, do you?
They've asked you for money, haven't they?
You swim well, don't you?
They wanted to come here, didn't they?

Now try 42 again.

35. Wrong. Study these:

Let's say you could go there again. How would you feel?
Let's say you can go there again. How will you feel?
Assuming you can't go home, what will you do?
Assuming you wouldn't go home, what would you do?

Now do 38 again.

36. Right! Do this one.

Is there a chance you ____________ to San Francisco next week?

went 31 *won't go* 42

37. Wrong. Study these:

When he wanted money, he borrowed it from me.
When she likes something, she wants to buy it.

When he asked me for money, I always

____________ it to him.

gave 43 *give* 45

38. Right! Go ahead.

Suppose you couldn't go. How

____________ you feel?

would 40 *will* 24

39. Right! Do this one.

I didn't ask you before, ____________ I ?

didn't 34 *did* 44

40. **Right! Go ahead.**

There's a chance ____________ home for Christmas.

I'll come 42 *I come* 29

41. **Good! This is the end of Unit 5.**

Go on to Unit 6.

42. **Right! Go ahead.**

I've borrowed money from you before,

____________ I?

didn't 32 *haven't* 44

43. **Right! Do this one.**

When he changes jobs, he always

____________ a better one.

got 45 *gets* 41

44. **Right! Go ahead.**

When she wants something, she

____________ money from me.

borrowed 37 *borrows* 41

45. **Wrong. Study these:**

When she attended your wedding, she looked good.

When she goes to meetings, she gets there on time.

When he cut my hair, he decided to make it very short.

When he plans trips, he likes to go by car.

Now do 44 again.

UNIT 6 TALKING ABOUT PAST POSSIBILITIES

1. **Begin here.**

If you had gotten up earlier, you would

__________ time for breakfast.

have 5 *have had* 3

2. **Wrong. Study these:**

Come to think of it, I wish you wouldn't ask me to go with you.
Come to think of it, I wish you wouldn't ask me to help you.

I wish he wouldn't invite me to go

dancing __________.

last week 19 *all the time* 14

3. **Right! Go ahead.**

I wouldn't have gotten lost if I __________ for directions.

asked 9 *had asked* 6

4. **Wrong. Study these:**

Looking back on it, I'm sorry I went.
Looking back on it, I'm glad I didn't go.

Looking back on it, he __________ you started that discussion.

was glad 15 *wished* 23

5. **Wrong. Study these:**

If you would get up earlier, you would have time for breakfast.
If you would work harder, you would have more money.

If you __________ so many arguments, you would have more friends.

started 11 *wouldn't start* 8

6. **Right! Go ahead.**

Come to think of it, I wish you

__________ me yesterday.

hadn't asked 10 *wouldn't ask* 2

7. **Wrong. Study these:**
I would go except that I have to work.
I would have gone except that I had to work.
We would eat in that restaurant except that it isn't open.
We would have eaten in that restaurant except that it wasn't open.

Now do 12 again.

8. **Right! Do this one.**

If you hadn't fallen down, you wouldn't ____________ your leg.

have broken 3 *break* 11

9. **Wrong. Study these:**
I wouldn't get lost if I asked for directions.
I wouldn't buy that car if I had more money.

I would ____________ dancing if I knew how to dance.

have gone 17 *go* 13

10. **Right! Go ahead.**

Looking back on it, I wish I ____________.

didn't go 4 *hadn't gone* 12

11. **Wrong. Study these:**
If you had started earlier, you wouldn't have been late.
If you would start earlier, you wouldn't be late.
If I hadn't fallen, I wouldn't have broken my arm.
If you would learn how to dance, I would take you dancing.

Now try 1 again.

12. **Right! Go ahead.**

She ____________________ except she didn't have time.

would have gone 16 *would go* 20

13. **Right! Do this one.**

I wouldn't have asked if I ____________ you didn't want to go.

knew 17 *had known* 6

14. **Right! Do this one.**

Come to think of it, I wish you ____________ shopping yesterday.

wouldn't go 19 *hadn't gone* 10

15. **Right! Now do this one.**

Looking back on it, I wish you ____________ me first.

asked 23 *had asked* 12

16. **Right! Go ahead.**

Even if we could have taken him, we might not ____________ to.

want 32 *have wanted* 24

17. **Wrong. Study these:**
I wouldn't have gone if I had known you'd be there.
I wouldn't go if I knew you'd be there.
I would have been hit by a car if I hadn't jumped back in time.
I would go swimming if I knew how to swim.

Now do 3 again.

18. **Right! Do this one.**

He ______________, except he hadn't been invited.

would have come 16 *would come* 7

19. **Wrong. Study these:**

Come to think of it, I wish you hadn't been there last week.

Come to think of it, I wish you wouldn't go there tomorrow.

I wish they hadn't married so young.

I wish they wouldn't marry so young.

Now do 6 again.

20. **Wrong. Study these:**

She would go, except she doesn't have time.

He would buy that car, except he doesn't have enough money.

They would rent that house except it

______________ too expensive.

were 7 *is* 18

21. **Wrong. Study these:**

Had I the time, I would visit you.

Had I the time, I would take you driving.

Had ______________ time, I would go to see that new movie.

I 35 *I had* 26

22. **Wrong. Study these:**

They are waving to me.

The children wave to everyone who passes.

Did they wave back ______________?

to he 39 *to him* 33

23. **Wrong. Study these:**

Looking back on it, I wish you had called me.

Looking back on it, I'm sorry you didn't call me.

Looking back on it, I wish you hadn't called me.

Looking back on it, I'm sorry you called me.

Now try 10 again.

24. **Right! Go ahead.**

Had I had time, I would ______________ you.

call 21 *have called* 28

25. **Wrong. Study these:**

Even if we could get a better apartment, we might not want one.

Even if we could have gotten a better apartment, we might not have wanted one.

Even if she could buy that dress, it might not fit her.

Even if she could have bought that dress, it might not have fitted her.

Now do 16 again.

26. **Wrong. Study these:**

Had she had time, she would have visited you.

Had she time, she would visit you.

Had they had the time, they would have called you.

Had they time, they would call you.

Now try 24 again.

27. Wrong. Study these:

I'm glad you called me back as I asked you to.

She's glad he rented that house as she asked him to.

John ____________ you pressed his suit as he asked you to.

is glad 34 *wish* 41

28. Right! Go ahead.

He's waving ____________.

you 22 *to you* 31

29. Wrong. Study these:

What would you do if you didn't have to work?

What would I wear if I didn't buy a new dress?

What would they ____________ if you didn't agree with them?

do 40 *have done* 43

30. Right! Do this one.

Even if we could have heard better, we might not ____________ to change our seats.

have wanted 24 *want* 25

31. Right! Go ahead.

I wish you ____________ me back as I had asked you to.

had called 37 *called* 27

32. Wrong. Study these:

Even if we could take him, we might not want to.

Even if we could go there, we might not need to.

Even if we could ____________ our differences, we might not do it.

resolve 30 *have resolved* 25

33. Right! Do this one.

Didn't they wave ____________?

them 39 *to them* 31

34. Right! Do this one.

Mary wishes you ____________ her things as she had asked you to.

had washed 37 *washed* 41

35. Right! Do this one.

Had ____________ more money, I would have bought a new coat this winter.

I 26 *I had* 28

36. Wrong. Study these:

I gave in to him.

I gave him his own way.

Do you always give ____________ on everything?

to him 45 *him his way* 38

37. Right! Go ahead.

What would you have done if you ____________ to work yesterday?

didn't 29 *hadn't had* 42

38. Right! Do this one.

Does your mother always give ___________ on things?

you 45 *in to you* 44

39. Wrong. Study these:

They waved to her.
She waved to him.
Didn't you wave to the girls?
Didn't they wave back to you?

Now try 28 again.

40. Right! Do this one.

What would you have said if she

___________?

had asked 42 *asks* 43

41. Wrong. Study these:

I wish you had called as I had wanted you to.
I'm sorry you didn't call as I wanted you to.
I'm glad you called as I wanted you to.
I wish you had asked my advice as I had told you to.

Now try 31 again.

42. Right! Go ahead.

I finally gave ___________ and said "yes."

in to him 44 *him* 36

43. Wrong. Study these:

What would you have done if you hadn't had to study?
What would you do if you didn't have to study?
What would you have worn if you had been invited?
What would you wear if you were invited?

Now try 37 again.

44. Ccod! This is the end of Unit 6.

Go on to Unit 7.

45. Wrong. Study these:

My uncle always gave in to me.
My uncle always gave me my way.
Some people always give in to their children
Some people always give their children the r own way.

w do 42 again.

UNIT 7 ASKING ABOUT LIKES AND DISLIKES

1. **Begin here.**

What ____________ don't like about him?

you 7 *is it you* 3

2. **Wrong. Study these:**
John doesn't like to go to bed early.
Don't you like to go swimming?

We don't ____________ to play bridge any more.

like 13 *like the idea* 22

3. **Right! Go ahead.**

I don't like the taste, ____________ I'll take it anyway.

and 10 *but* 6

4. **Wrong. Study these:**
Why do you hate flying?
Why do you like tennis?

____________ you particularly enjoy winter weather?

What is it 16 *Why do* 8

5. **Wrong. Study these:**
I used to like flying, even though it was expensive.
I used to like winter, even though it was cold.

I ____________ photography, even though it was not a cheap pastime.

like 21 *used to like* 9

6. **Right! Go ahead.**

She doesn't like the idea ____________ to bed early.

of going 11 *to go* 2

7. **Wrong. Study these:**
What don't you like about him?
What do you like about John?

What ____________ they like about winter weather?

is it don't 15 *don't* 12

8. Right! Now do this one.

What is it you don't like ____________?
driving 16 *about driving* 18

9. Right! Do this one.

I like to go driving, even though there

____________ a lot of traffic.
is 25 *was* 21

10. Wrong. Study these:
I don't like the taste, and I don't eat it.
I don't like the color, and I won't buy it

I like everything about it, ____________ I think I'll buy it.
and 14 *but* 19

11. Right! Go ahead.

What is it you hate ____________?
flying 4 *about flying* 18

12. Right! Now do this.

What ____________ doesn't like about the weather in California?
he 15 *is it he* 3

13. Right! Now do this one.

Doesn't she like the idea ____________ bridge tonight?
of playing 11 *to play* 22

14. Right! Do this one.

I don't like all the traffic, ____________ I'll drive there anyway.
and 19 *but* 6

15. Wrong. Study these:
What is it you don't like about golf?
What don't you like about golf?
What is it they don't like about card games?
What don't they like about card games?

Now do 1 again.

16. Wrong. Study these:
What is it you like about summer?
Why do you like summer?
What is it you don't like about this medicine?
Why don't you like this medicine?

Now do 11 again.

17. Wrong. Study these:
The things I don't like about our car are its motor and tires.
The things he likes about it are its motor and tires.

The ____________ he hates about flying are the expense and the long delays.
thing 28 *things* 23

18. Right! Go ahead.

I like to play bridge, even though

____________ a good player.
I wasn't 5 *I'm not* 25

19. **Wrong. Study these:**

He didn't like to play chess, but he played anyway.

I particularly like this dress, and I think I'll buy it.

He hates to dance, but he'll go dancing anyway.

We like everything about this house, and we'll buy it.

Now do 3 again.

20. **Wrong. Study these:**

I like its appearance.

I don't like its taste.

I like milk. It is good for me, too.

I bought it because of ________ color.

its 24 *it's* 26

21. **Wrong. Study these:**

I used to like to play bridge, even though I was a poor player.

I like to play bridge, even though I'm a poor player.

I used to play chess, even though I despised it.

I play chess, even though I despise it.

Now do 18 again.

22. **Wrong. Study these:**

Mary likes to go swimming.

Mary likes the idea of going swimming.

Wouldn't you like to play chess tonight?

Wouldn't you like the idea of playing ch tonight?

Now do 6 again.

23. **Right! Do this one.**

The thing he particularly enjoys about tennis

________ the exercise.

is 30 *are* 28

24. **Right! Do this one.**

Do you want to see that movie because you

think ________ so good?

its 26 *it's* 35

25. **Right! Go ahead.**

The thing I don't like about flying

________ the expense.

is 30 *are* 17

26. **Wrong. Study these:**

It's the best I have.

Do you think it's a good book?

I like its looks.

Did you say its service is fast?

Now do 30 again.

27. **Wrong. Study these:**

I will buy two pairs of shoes, too.

It's too late to go shopping in two stores.

Are these ________ men friends of yours?

too 40 *two* 38

28. Wrong. Study these:

The things I don't like about that towel are its color and size.
The things I like about this bed are its style and quality.
The thing I want to know is its cost.
The thing I like about ice cream is its flavor.

Now do 25 again.

29. Wrong. Study these:

It doesn't matter to him if his shirt is dirty.
Would it matter to her if you were to go?

It won't __________ to her if you don't go.

bother 31 *matter* 33

30. Right! Go ahead.

I like spinach because __________ good for me.

its 20 *it's* 35

31. Wrong. Study these:

It doesn't bother me.
It doesn't matter to me.
Would it bother them?
Would it matter to them?

Now do 37 again.

32. Wrong. Study these:

They went to the beach, too.
They went to the beach too late.

Did they go __________ bed early last night?

too 40 *to* 38

33. Right! Do this one.

Would it bother __________ if I were to invite them?

you 39 *to you* 31

34. Right! Do this one.

Haven't they found __________ with her, too?

faulty 44 *fault* 43

35. Right! Go ahead.

You're being __________ fussy.

to 32 *too* 37 *two* 27

36. Wrong. Study these:

John likes the taste of ice cream.
She despises the taste of spinach.

He likes __________ of any kind of meat.

the taste 41 *taste* 46

37. Right! Go ahead.

It doesn't __________ if his suit isn't pressed.

bother to him 29 *bother him* 39

38. Right! Do this one.

Isn't she __________ particular about her clothes?

two 40 *too* 37

39. Right! Go ahead.

Mary always found ______________ with her friends.

fault 43 *faulted* 42

40. Wrong. Study these:

I bought two pairs of shoes.
He is too fussy about everything.
I'm going to the movies.
He's going, too.

Now do 35 again.

41. Right! Do this one.

Does he have very good taste ______________ shoes?

of 46 *in* 45

42. Wrong. Study these:

She finds fault with no one.
He found fault with everyone.
They have found fault with everything here.

John always finds ______________ with my sister.

faulty 44 *fault* 34

43. Right! Go ahead.

My sister has good taste ______________ clothes.

of 36 *in* 45

44. Wrong. Study these:

Some people find fault with that restaurant.
Do you always find fault with her?
Haven't they always found fault with her?
Weren't they always finding fault with her?

Now do 39 again.

45. Good! This is the end of Unit 7.

Go on to Unit 8.

46. Wrong. Study these:

I like the taste of pie.
She has poor taste in shoes.
Most children like the taste of ice cream.
I wish I had better taste in clothes.

Now do 43 again.

UNIT 8 GIVING ADVICE AND ASKING OPINIONS

1. **Begin here.**

I always tried ____________ interfere in your business.

not 5 *not to* 4

2. **Right! Now do this one.**

Does he ever pay attention ____________ your private affairs?

with 13 *to* 8

3. **Wrong. Study these:**
Let me give advice to someone.
I give a lot of advice to him.

I want to give ____________________.

my opinions to everyone 14
to everyone my opinions 17

4. **Right! Go ahead.**

He never interferes ____________ my affairs.

in 8 *to* 10

5. **Wrong. Study these:**
I decided not to go with you.
She will not go with you.

She ____________ not marry him.

will 7 *decided* 11

6. **Right! Do this one.**

This is my advice: you ____________ that house.

should not buy 15 *aren't buying* 20

Right! Now do this one.

I always tried ____________ be home when he called.

not 11 *not to* 4

8. **Right! Go ahead.**

Let me give ____________ a little simple advice.

to you 3 *you* 12

9. **Wrong. Study these:**
This is my opinion: I think you are working too hard.
This is my advice: you shouldn't work so hard.

This is my ______ ______: I think you aren't working hard enough.
advice 20 *opinion* 6

10. **Wrong. Study these:**
He never pays attention to my work.
He never interferes in my business.

She never interferes ______ my plans.
with 2 *to* 13

11. **Wrong. Study these:**
I decided not to go dancing tonight.
I don't want to go dancing tonight.
They tried not to bother me.
They didn't bother me.

Now do 1 again.

12. **Right! Go ahead.**

This is my advice: you ______ home.
are staying 9 *ought to stay* 15

13. **Wrong. Study these:**
He doesn't pay attention to your problems.
He doesn't interfere in our problems.
He doesn't pay attention to your work.
He doesn't interfere with your work.

Now do 4 again.

14. **Right! Do this one.**

Does anyone ever give ______ an argument?
to them 17 *them* 12

15. **Right! Go ahead.**

This is only a ______.
suggestion 23 *suggest* 19

16. **Right! Do this one.**

If I were a waiter, ______ give fast service.
I'd 26 *I'll* 32

17. **Wrong. Study these:**
I'd give my opinions to anyone.
I'd give anyone my opinions.
Do you give advice to everyone?
Do you give everyone advice?

Now do 8 again.

18. **Wrong. Study these:**
If you take my advice, you will write the letter over again.
If he really is dangerous, we will help you.

If the baby ______ actually a bother, I'll take her home.
were 32 *is* 16

19. **Wrong. Study these:**
I suggest that you follow my advice.
We advise that you follow our suggestion.

I hope you can ______ something for me to wear.
suggestion 29 *suggest* 25

20. Wrong. Study these:

This is my advice: you should work fewer hours a day.
This is my opinion: I feel that you work too many hours a day.
This is my advice: you should learn how to swim.
This is my opinion: I feel that you can't swim.

Now do 12 again.

21. Wrong. Study these:

He took offense at what I did.
Did he take offense at what I said?

John ____________ offense at everything that night.

took 31 *take* 35

22. Wrong. Study these:

What would you prefer wearing tonight?
What would you prefer to wear?

Is there anything you would prefer

____________?

trying on 27 *try on* 38

23. Right! Go ahead.

If I were you, I ____________ begin the letter again.

would 26 *will* 18

24. Wrong. Study these:

I'm accustomed to making up my own mind.
She's old enough to do that now.

We're ____________ to buying our own clothes.

mature enough 41 *accustomed* 36

25. Right! Do this one.

Yours is the best ____________ I've heard.

suggestion 23 *suggest* 29

26. Right! Go ahead.

Please don't ____________ offense at what I say.

took 21 *take* 30

27. Right! Do this one.

Did you say you preferred to ____________ home?

going 38 *go* 34

28. Wrong. Study these:

I'm in the habit of making up my own mind.
She's intelligent enough to make up her own mind.

Isn't he ____________ of driving her car?

in the habit 36 *old enough* 41

29. Wrong. Study these:

I had hoped you would suggest something better.
I hope you will suggest something better.
Is his a better suggestion than yours?
Who had the best suggestion?

Now do 15 again.

30. Right! Go ahead.

You can do what you prefer to

____________.

doing 22 *do* 34

31. Right! Do this one.

Please don't ___________ offense at what he said.

took 35 *take* 30

32. Wrong. Study these:

If you are chilly, I'll get a jacket for you.
If you were chilly, I'd get a jacket for you.
If I am your only friend, I will look after you.
If I were your father, I would look after you.

Now try 23 again.

33. Wrong. Study these:

This is my business, too, and I think you should go.
This is my responsibility, and I want you to try harder.

I have ___________ to do with it, and I think you are wasting money.

anything 44 *something* 42

34. Right! Go ahead.

I'm old enough ___________ up my own mind.

of making 28 *to making* 24
to make 39

35. Wrong. Study these:

He's taking offense at everything I say.
Has he taken offense at what you say, too?
Please don't take offense at what I'm doing.
He took offense at everything that night.

Now do 26 again.

36. Right! Now do this one.

Are you old enough ___________ a car?

of driving 41 *to drive* 39

37. Right! Do this one.

Wouldn't she work in ___________ office?

no 40 *any* 45

38. Wrong. Study these:

How would you prefer to wear your hair?
Wear your hair as you would prefer wearing it.
Where would you prefer going tonight?
Let's go where you would prefer to go tonight.

Now do 30 again.

39. Right! Go ahead.

It's not my affair, ___________ I think you should do more work.

and 33 *but* 43

40. Wrong. Study these:

I won't figure out any problems.
I will figure out no problems.
Can't you drive any car?
You can drive no car.

Now try 43 again.

41. Wrong. Study these:
Mary's accustomed to pressing **her own** clothes.
Mary's in the habit of pressing **her** own clothes.
Mary's old enough to press her own clothes.
Isn't Mary old enough to press her own clothes?

Now try 34 again.

42. Right! Do this one.

It's none of my business, ____________ I think you are just wasting time here.
and 44 *but* 43

43. Right! Go ahead.

She won't pay ____________ attention to you.
any 45 *no* 46

44. Wrong. Study these:
It's none of my business, but I think you'll regret that choice.
It's my business, and I think you'll regret that choice.
It's not my responsibility, but I think you should proceed carefully.
It's my responsibility, and I think you should proceed carefully.

Now do 39 again.

45. Good! This is the end of Unit 8.

Go on to Unit 9.

46. Wrong. Study these:
She will pay no attention to you.
He will ask no questions.

You have ____________ car.
any 40 *no* 37

UNIT 9 ASKING FAVORS OF OTHER PEOPLE

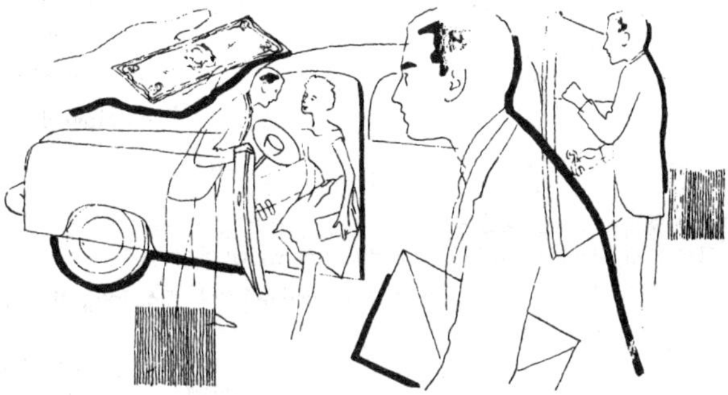

1. **Begin here.**

I wish you __________ help me start my car.

will 8 *would* 5

2. **Right! Do this one.**

I wish that they __________ resolve their differences.

can 15 *could* 7

3. **Wrong. Study these:**

I don't intend to go there any more.
I don't go there any more.
They don't intend to eat at that restaurant any more.
They don't eat at that restaurant any more.

Now do 7 again.

4. **Wrong. Study these:**

Here is a favor you can do for me.
He did it for her.

This is __________ for me.

what you can do 14
how you can repay 18

5. **Right! Go ahead.**

I wish you __________ help me find my wallet.

could 7 *can* 9

6. **Right! Do this one.**

I wish you __________ drive so fast.

won't 13 *wouldn't* 5

7. **Right! Go ahead.**

I didn't intend __________ a discussion with him.

to start 10 *start* 12

. Wrong. Study these:
I hope you will help me start my car.
She is hoping you will go with us.

____________ you will learn how to swim this summer.
I'm hoping 6 *I wish* 13

9. Wrong. Study these:
I hope you can help me find my wallet.
They hope you can rent their cottage next summer.

Doesn't he ____________ you can go abroad with him?
wish 15 *hope* 2

10. Right! Go ahead.

I hope I can repay ____________ sometime for what you've done.
for you 4 *you* 16

11. Wrong. Study these:
This will be the last time I'll see you, won't it?
That was the last time I saw you, wasn't it?

You ____________ married the last time I saw you, were you?
aren't 23 *weren't* 19

12. Wrong. Study these:
I didn't start the argument.
She didn't start that discussion.

Didn't ____________ start the meeting?
they intend 3 *they* 17

13. Wrong. Study these:
I wish you would stay home more often.
I hope you will stay home more often.
They wish you would go to visit them in California.
They hope you will go to visit them in California.

Now do 1 again.

14. Right! Do this one.

I hope I can repay ____________ for your kindness some day.
for you 18 *you* 16

15. Wrong. Study these:
I hope that you can help me.
I wish that you could help me.
My children hope they can go on a picnic.
My children wish they could go on a picnic today.

Now do 5 again.

16. Right! Go ahead.

This is the last time I'll see you,

____________ it?
isn't 21 *won't* 11

17. Right! Do this one.

Doesn't she intend ____________ him?
to marry 10 *marry* 3

18. **Wrong. Study these:**
He did this for me because he likes me.
I don't have to repay him for what he did for me.
I would like to repay her for all of those favors.
Did they do all of those kinds of things for you?

Now do 10 again.

19. **Right! Do this one.**

You danced with me every time,

__________ you?
weren't 23 *didn't* 21

20. **Wrong. Study these:**
I must thank him for what he's done
I am indebted to him for what he's doing

__________ you for all the favors you've done?
Are they indebted 28
Did they thank 32

21. **Right! Go ahead.**

This isn't the letter I wrote,

__________ it?
isn't 25 *is* 24

22. **Wrong. Study these:**
We would be happy to help him in any way we possibly could.
We will be happy to help him in any way we possibly can.
They would be happy to help Mary in any way they could.
They will be happy to help Mary in any way they can.

Now do 30 again.

23. **Wrong. Study these:**
You go swimming once a week, don't you?
You used to drive a car, didn't you?
You were late, weren't you?
You lost your keys, didn't you?

Now do 16 again.

24. **Right! Go ahead.**

I will always be grateful __________ for what you've done.
to you 30 *you* 20

25. **Wrong. Study these:**
That was the last letter I wrote, wasn't it?
This will be the last plane, won't it?

You __________ his wife, aren't you?
are 29 *aren't* 31

26. **Wrong. Study these:**
It was no bother.
Was it no bother at all?

Did you say it __________ no bother?
was 36 *wasn't* 40

27. **Wrong. Study these:**
I wish you would lend me some money.
I wish you would do me a favor.

__________ you would help me with my work.
I wish 43 *I'd appreciate* 45

28. **Wrong. Study these:**

I was obliged to you for opening the door.
Did I thank you for opening the door?
Her mother was grateful to him for asking the girl to dance.
Did her mother thank him for asking the girl to dance?

Now do 24 again.

29. **Right! Do this one.**

He hasn't been here before, ________ he?

hasn't 31 *has* 24

30. **Right! Go ahead.**

I'll be happy to help you in any way

I ________.

can 33 *could* 35

31. **Wrong. Study these:**

This is the first day of your vacation, isn't it?
This isn't the first day of your vacation, is it?
That wasn't your house, was it?
That was your house, wasn't it?

Now do 21 again.

32. **Right! Do this one.**

Was he grateful ________ for finding his wallet?

to the boy 30 *the boy* 28

33. **Right! Go ahead.**

It wasn't ________ bother.

no 26 *any* 38

34. **Right! Do this one.**

He wishes he ________ swim, but he hasn't learned how.

will 44 *could* 42

35. **Wrong. Study these:**

I will be happy to help you in any way I can.
He will be glad to help you in any way he can.

John ________ be happy to help you in any way he possibly can.

will 37 *is* 22

36. **Right! Do this one.**

Mrs. Cooper insisted it isn't ________ bother.

no 40 *any* 38

37. **Right! Do this one.**

Wouldn't he be glad to help you in any way

he ________?

can 22 *could* 33

38. **Right! Go ahead.**

I'd appreciate ________ would lend me ten dollars.

you 27 *it if you* 41

39. **Wrong. Study these:**

I know you will visit me if it is possible.
I wish you could visit me, but it isn't possible.

I wish you would write me a letter, but you

don't ________ to.

know 44 *want* 34

40. **Wrong. Study these:**
Mr. Smith says it isn't any bother.
Mrs. Smith says it is no bother.
Did John say it wasn't any bother?
Did John say it was no bother?

Now do 33 again.

41. **Right! Go ahead.**

I wish you ____________ come here, but it isn't possible.
will 39 *could* 42

42. **Good! This is the end of Unit 9.**

Go on to Unit 10.

43. **Right! Do this one.**

He'd appreciate ____________ would lend him my car.
I 45 *it if I* 41

44. **Wrong. Study these:**
John knows she will dance with him if she wants to.
John wishes she would dance with him, but she doesn't want to.
Mary wishes she could go on a picnic, but she has to work.
Mary can go on a picnic if she doesn't have to work.

Now do 41 again.

45. **Wrong. Study these:**
I wish you would hold the door open for me.
I'd appreciate it if you would hold the door open for me.
He wishes you would help him find his keys.
He'd appreciate it if you would help him find his keys.

Now do 38 again.

UNIT 10 MAKING PREPARATIONS TO TRAVEL

1. **Begin here.**

Does he have anything ____________ for customs?

declare 6   *to declare* 4

2. **Wrong. Study these:**

I should drop by the bank to get some money.
You must drop by tonight to tell us good-bye.

____________ drive me to the airport, or I'll miss my plane.

You've got 22   *You must* 14

3. **Wrong. Study these:**

Don't forget that you must take the dog to the kennels.
Don't forget that you must buy new shoes for her next week.

I had forgotten that ____________ cover up the furniture before I left.

I had to 10   *to* 5

4. **Right! Go ahead.**

You have very little time ____________ your flight.

to make 7   *making* 8

5. **Wrong. Study these:**

Don't forget to have the milk delivery stopped.
Don't forget that you must have the milk delivery stopped.
They didn't forget to have the mail delivery stopped.
They didn't forget that they must have the mail delivery stopped.

Now do 7 again.

6. **Wrong. Study these:**

Does he have anything he must declare for customs?
Does she have something she must not forget to do?

I don't have anything I ____________ him before we begin.

must tell 9   *tell* 13

7. **Right! Go ahead.**

Don't forget __________ the dog to the kennels.

take 3   *to take* 11

8. **Wrong. Study these:**

You have a lot of time left for making your flight.
You have no time left for doing the things you had forgotten to do.

There's enough time left for __________ good-bye to everyone.

to say 18   *saying* 12

9. **Right! Do this one.**

Do you have something else __________ before you leave?

do 13   *to do* 4

10. **Right! Do this one.**

I almost forgot __________ the phone disconnected.

having 5   *to have* 11

11. **Right! Go ahead.**

I've got __________ by the store.

to drop 15   *drop* 2

12. **Right! Do this one.**

I have plenty of money to __________ my ticket.

buy 7   *buying* 18

13. **Wrong. Study these:**

I don't have anything left to do before it's time to leave.
I don't have anything I must do before it's time to leave.
Is there anything you have to do to prepare for winter weather?
Is there anything you must do to prepare for winter weather?

Now do 1 again.

14. **Right! Do this one now.**

You've got __________ yourself a new suit this month.

buy 22   *to buy* 15

15. **Right! Go ahead.**

You had better run, or you __________ left behind.

would be 23   *will be* 21

16. **Wrong. Study these:**

Before I could go, I had to buy a hat.
Before they could leave, they had to say good-bye to everyone.

Before we __________ drive there, we had to fix the car.

could 24   *can* 19

17. **Right! Do this one.**

You had better wash, or you __________ clean for the party.

wouldn't be 28   *won't be* 21

18. **Wrong. Study these:**

You have barely enough time left to catch that train.

You have barely enough time left for catching that train.

She has plenty of money to buy that dress.

She has plenty of money for buying that dress.

Now do 4 again.

19. **Wrong. Study these:**

Before I could go, I had to press my dress.

Before I can go, I have to press my dress.

Before we could go on a picnic, we had to prepare the food.

Before we can go on a picnic, we must prepare the food.

Now do 21 again.

20. **Wrong. Study these:**

Please lend the book to him.

He lent some money to me.

Did she lend ________________?

to you some money 35

some money to you 30

21. **Right! Go ahead.**

Before I can leave, I ____________ some money.

had to get 16 *must get* 26

22. **Wrong. Study these:**

John has got to forget about that girl.

John must forget about that girl.

We must go to that restaurant with you some time.

We've got to go to that restaurant with you some time.

Now do 11 again.

23. **Wrong. Study these:**

You had to run, or you would be left behind.

You had to drive, or you would be home all the time.

You had to work, or you ____________ any money.

won't have 28 *wouldn't have* 17

24. **Right! Do this one now.**

Before I can pay for my ticket, I

____________ go to the bank.

had to 19 *have to* 26

25. **Wrong. Study these:**

She needs a job, and she is looking for one.

He likes a lot of exercise, and he often goes for long walks.

He ____________ card games, but he sometimes plays bridge.

likes 27 *dislikes* 33

26. **Right! Go ahead.**

Would you please lend ____________ that book until tomorrow?

to me 20 *me* 29

27. **Wrong. Study these:**

She wanted to learn how to dance, and she went dancing often.

He wanted to avoid an argument, and he walked off.

She hoped to learn how to swim, but she broke her leg.

He hates to fly, but he took a plane anyway.

Now do 29 again.

28. **Wrong. Study these:**

You had better learn how to swim, or you won't be invited.
You had to learn how to swim, or you wouldn't be invited.
They had better go, or they will be late.
They had to go, or they would be late.

Now do 15 again.

29. **Right! Go ahead.**

They wanted to get here yesterday,

____________ they couldn't.
and 25 *but* 34

30. **Right! Do this one.**

I'm hoping my father can lend ____________ his car tonight.
me 29 *to me* 35

31. **Wrong. Study these:**

He will drive me to the airport.
They will take you to the bus station.

I will ____________ to the train station.
go with you 44 *meet you* 42

32. **Right! Do this one.**

It took much gasoline and time

____________ to the airport.
to driving 37 *to drive* 36

33. **Right! Do this one.**

He wanted to get there early, ____________ he was late.
and 27 *but* 34

34. **Right! Go ahead.**

It will take a lot of money ____________ the ticket.
buying 39 *to buy* 36

35. **Wrong. Study these:**

I've lent you a lot of money already.
I've lent a lot of money to you already.
Did she lend him her car?
Did she lend her car to him?

Now do 26 again.

36. **Right! Go ahead.**

I'll tell you good-bye ____________ the airport.
to 31 *at* 40

37. **Wrong. Study these:**

It takes a long time to learn how to speak another language.
Learning how to speak another language takes a long time.
It took me a long time to read that book.
Reading that book took me a long time.

Now do 34 again.

38. **Wrong. Study these:**
They pushed the car as fast as they could.
We worked on that composition as much as we could.

He ____________ to work as long as he could.
tries 45 *tried* 41

39. **Wrong. Study these:**
Buying the ticket will take a lot of money
Going to the bank wastes a lot of time.

____________ to New York can waste a lot of time if there are long delays.
Flying 32 *Fly* 37

40. **Right! Go ahead.**
I'm pushing this door as hard as

I ____________.
could 38 *can* 43

41. **Right! Do this one.**
Are you driving this car as fast as

you ____________?
can 43 *could* 45

42. **Wrong. Study these:**
I'll take you to the airport.
I'll drive her to the station.
Will you say good-bye to me at the airport?
Will you kiss me good-bye at the station?

Now do 36 again.

43. **Good! This is the end of Book V.**

Go on to Book VI.

44. **Right! Now do this one.**

She'll say good-bye to me ____________ the station.
at 40 *to* 42

45. **Wrong. Study these:**
He argues with her as much as he can.
He argued with her as much as he could.
I went to the airport as fast as I could.
I'm going to the airport as fast as I can.

Now do 40 again.

ENGLISH 900 합본
(원본+주해서+WORKBOOK) 값 9,000원

편저자 정헌진 · 이동호
발행인 김계덕
발행처 계원출판사(자매사 도서출판 문장)
서울특별시 중구 을지로 6가 45-4
전화: 02) 929-9495
팩스: 02) 929-9496
등록번호: 2-204
인 쇄 청림정판
제 책 평범사
공 급 한국출판협동조합
중판발행